The Sovereignty and Goodness of God, by Mary Rowlandson

with Related Documents

SECOND EDITION

Edited with an Introduction by

Neal Salisbury

Smith College

bedford/st.martin's
Macmillan Learning
Boston | New York

For Bedford/St. Martin's

Vice President, Editorial, Macmillan Learning Humanities: Edwin Hill
Program Director for History: Michael Rosenberg
Senior Program Manager for History: William J. Lombardo
History Marketing Manager: Melissa Rodriguez
Director of Content Development: Jane Knetzger
Assistant Editor: Alexandra DeConti
Associate Editor: Mary Posman Starowicz
Content Project Manager: Lidia MacDonald-Carr
Workflow Manager: Lisa McDowell
Production Supervisor: Robert Cherry
Media Project Manager: Michelle Camisa
Manager of Publishing Services: Andrea Cava
Project Management: Lumina Datamatics, Inc.
Composition: Lumina Datamatics, Inc.
Cartographer: Mapping Specialists, Ltd.
Director of Rights and Permissions: Hilary Newman
Permissions Manager: Kalina Ingham
Senior Art Director: Anna Palchik
Cover Design: William Boardman
Cover Photo: Courtesy Dechert Collection, Kislak Center for Special Collections,
    Rare Books and Manuscripts, University of Pennsylvania
Printing and Binding: LSC Communications

Manufactured in the United States of America.

2   1   0   9   8   7
f   e   d   c   b   a

For information, write: Bedford/St. Martin's, 75 Arlington Street, Boston, MA 02116

ISBN 978-1-319-04881-5

Acknowledgments

Acknowledgments and copyrights appear on the same page as the text and art selections they cover; these acknowledgments and copyrights constitute an extension of the copyright page.

At the time of publication all Internet URLs published in this text were found to accurately link to their intended website. If you do find a broken link, please forward the information to history@macmillan.com so that it can be corrected for the next printing.

Foreword

The Bedford Series in History and Culture is designed so that readers can study the past as historians do.

The historian's first task is finding the evidence. Documents, letters, memoirs, interviews, pictures, movies, novels, or poems can provide facts and clues. Then the historian questions and compares the sources. There is more to do than in a courtroom, for hearsay evidence is welcome, and the historian is usually looking for answers beyond act and motive. Different views of an event may be as important as a single verdict. How a story is told may yield as much information as what it says.

Along the way, the historian seeks help from other historians and perhaps from specialists in other disciplines. Finally, it is time to write, to decide on an interpretation and how to arrange the evidence for readers.

Each book in this series contains an important historical document or group of documents, each document a witness from the past and open to interpretation in different ways. The documents are combined with some element of historical narrative—an introduction or a biographical essay, for example—that provides students with an analysis of the primary source material and important background information about the world in which it was produced.

Each book in the series focuses on a specific topic within a specific historical period. Each provides a basis for lively thought and discussion about several aspects of the topic and the historian's role. Each is short enough (and inexpensive enough) to be a reasonable one-week assignment in a college course. Whether as classroom or personal reading, each book in the series provides firsthand experience of the challenge—and fun—of discovering, recreating, and interpreting the past.

Lynn Hunt
David W. Blight
Bonnie G. Smith

Preface

Mary Rowlandson's *The Sovereignty and Goodness of God,* first published in 1682, is an English Puritan woman's account of her captivity among Native Americans during King Philip's, or Metacom's, War (1675–1676) in southeastern New England. Although the war was well documented at the time, most of the primary sources were produced by male English leaders. Their accounts help us understand the chronology of events, and they illustrate what might be called the "official" English viewpoint, along with those of some elite dissenters. But these sources tell us little about the experiences and perspectives of women and nonelite men, and even less about those of Native Americans.

Rowlandson's narrative is quite unlike the other documents. Often termed the first "Indian captivity narrative," *Sovereignty* is far more complex than the kind of formulaic popular literature characterizing most works in that genre. It is a powerful, firsthand rendering of a cross-cultural encounter under the most trying and extreme of circumstances, in which the protagonist/author finds the very boundaries of her identity as an elite English Puritan woman being tested. In this respect, her narrative offers little direct insight into her captors or other Native Americans. Nevertheless, the narrative provides a wealth of concrete evidence on the war as it played out among anti-English Indians. At many points, moreover, a close "reading between the lines" against other evidence reveals more about cultural identities and boundaries in colonial New England than Rowlandson intended or even knew. The fact that *Sovereignty* was also the first North American publication by a living woman makes it still more significant especially because so much of it concerns gender roles and identities in indigenous and settler societies. Finally, because Mary Rowlandson came from one of many English towns located adjacent to a Native American community, her narrative reflects the breakdown of what had formerly been neighborly ties between the two peoples.

This second edition presents Rowlandson's text in relation to her life and to the world she inhabited as a female settler, captive, and published author. The text follows that of the earliest surviving edition, published in Cambridge, Massachusetts, in 1682. Since the fourth edition (London, 1682), most editors have altered Rowlandson's remarkable prose to appeal to their various readers. This edition proceeds on the assumption that the closest possible approximation to Rowlandson's original text will give readers a feeling for the power and rhythm that pervades it and made it so appealing to contemporaries.

In the twenty years since publication of the first edition of this volume, scholars' understandings of issues relating to Rowlandson's captivity and her narrative have been radically transformed. That transformation can be glimpsed in the new Selected Bibliography, in which most titles have been published since the first edition appeared, and it is central to the revised Introduction. Much of the new evidence and thinking has been driven by the remarkable rise of Native American/Indigenous Studies as an academic field that is also influencing scholarship in history, literary studies, anthropology, American Studies, and other fields. In New England, Lisa Brooks's new study situates Rowlandson's captivity in indigenous contexts by re-examining both Native- and English-authored evidence. She and others have dug more deeply into the experiences and writings of Christian Indians, vastly complicating our understanding of their roles and experiences. A second recent development is the outpouring of work on Europeans' enslavement of Native Americans. We now realize that, along with the many more Africans, indigenous captives throughout the Americas were enslaved and sold both to local colonists and to traders who carried them throughout the Atlantic world. New England was no exception, as the work of Margaret Newell and Wendy Warren makes especially apparent. Third, numerous recent works reconsider captivity narratives, including Rowlandson's, from a variety of perspectives. While representations of Indian "savages" as threats to innocent white Anglo-Americans has long been recognized as central to these narratives, some recent studies focus more closely on ways that such representations served colonial and imperial projects, especially in the years leading up to the American Revolution. Others have looked to Latin America and the Muslim world to challenge the assumption that the captivity narrative, beginning with Rowlandson's, is a distinctly American genre. Finally, other new studies have enriched our understanding of the imperial and regional contexts within which New England colonization, King Philip's War, and Rowlandson's captivity transpired. Beyond the works listed in the bibliography, many titles in the citations further extend the new insights that inform this revision.

To introduce readers more fully to Rowlandson's world, her narrative is supplemented by twenty-one related documents, five of which are new to this edition and which are in keeping with new scholarly developments. One is a little-known narrative of Muslim captivity by a Puritan contemporary of Rowlandson's. Two more are visual documents for discussion, dating to the 1770s. Another is a treaty in which the motives of both English and Native American signers can be discussed. The last new document sheds close light on the forced removal of Christian Indians to Deer Island during Metacom's War. Most of the documents concern Native American experiences during the war, and several were written by indigenous authors. The headnotes and footnotes to those documents retained from the first edition have been thoroughly revised in light of recent research and interpretations.

A NOTE ABOUT THE TEXT

Consistent with current practice in Native American Studies and other fields, the volume editor uses the noun and adjective "Native" as a synonym for "Native American," "Indian," and (as adjective only) "indigenous." This usage avoids any confusion with American-born colonists who could rightfully be termed "native" or "native American." The term "Algonquian" applies to speakers of Algonquian languages in New England and elsewhere in the Atlantic Northeast, to the exclusion of Mohawks and other Iroquoian speakers.

Some of the Native Americans who figure in this edition answered to both indigenous and English names. In general, I use the better-known name but alternate between "Philip" and "Metacom" because, in that case, the two names are equally known and that person answered to both. Although Rowlandson herself refers to "king Philip," references to Philip as a "King" only became common after 1716, along with "King Philip's War."

As much as possible, the primary sources appear in their original form, although I have slightly modernized some of the Related Documents in the interest of clarity.

In its dating, this edition follows the modern Gregorian calendar. But Rowlandson's narrative and the other primary sources follow the Julian calendar (used in the British Isles until the mid-eighteenth century), in which each year began on March 25 instead of January 1 and which reckoned dates ten days earlier than the Gregorian calendar. Thus, for example, Mary Rowlandson writes that she was captured on February 10, 1675, which is February 20, 1676, by our calendar.

ACKNOWLEDGMENTS

Like all scholarly undertakings, this revised edition has been a collaborative effort. At Bedford/St. Martin's, Bill Lombardo remained patient, persistent, and supportive for much longer than either of us initially expected. Lexi DeConti displayed the same qualities in so capably seeing through most of the editing, a process that Mary Posman Starowicz brought to a successful conclusion. Hillary Newman relentlessly pursued and obtained permissions to use the illustrations you see, a process far more complicated than one might assume. Thanks are also due to Program Director Michael Rosenberg, History Marketing Manager Melissa Rodriguez, Content Project Manager Lidia MacDonald-Carr, and Cover Designer William Boardman. The Five Colleges Libraries and the William Allan Neilson Library at Smith College, especially Neilson's Interlibrary Loan Service, consistently delivered items that I suddenly realized I needed immediately. Caitlin Jones at the Massachusetts Archives, Andrew Lipman, Robert St. George, and Craig Arthur Williams provided vital assistance at critical moments. Lisa Brooks and Joanne Jahnke Wegner generously shared unpublished writings with me. I am fortunate to live in the region I write about, where descendants of the Native Americans who populate Rowlandson's narrative articulate their histories as ongoing rather than relics of a long-gone past. Their histories were central to my thinking about and preparing this revision, as were my new or continued exchanges with Margaret Bruchac, Christine DeLucia, Rae Gould, Dana Leibsohn, Alice Nash, Barry O'Connell, Robert Paynter, Tom Reney, Dana Salisbury, Pauline Turner Strong, and Kevin Sweeney. Lisa Brooks has been a model colleague and collaborator as we pursued parallel projects relating to Rowlandson. Classroom discussions of the first edition—with my own Smith College students and those in classes taught by Jean Forward and Alice Nash at the University of Massachusetts Amherst—as well as informal conversations with numerous adopters were especially helpful as I revised it for a new generation of readers.

Neal Salisbury

Contents

Maps and Illustrations

PART ONE

Introduction: Mary Rowlandson in a World of Removes

THE SETTING: "KING PHILIP'S WAR" (1675–1676)

In proportion to total population, the bloodiest and most destructive war in American history was neither the Civil War, World War II, nor the Vietnam War. It was, rather, a conflict that later became known as "King Philip's War" (or, recently, "Metacom's War"), named for the Native American misleadingly depicted as its prime instigator. Though confined to a corner of New England and lasting just fifteen months, King Philip's War took the lives of at least five thousand Indians and about two thousand five hundred English colonists, roughly 40 and 5 percent, respectively, of the two peoples' populations. Many more on both sides were left seriously wounded, homeless, impoverished, orphaned, widowed, displaced, and in the case of indigenous peoples, consigned to slavery.[1] The best known of the war's English captives was Mary Rowlandson, seized in February 1676 when anti-English Indians attacked the town of Lancaster, Massachusetts. Rowlandson published an account of her captivity that provides a unique perspective on a war that briefly slowed colonial New England's economic growth and ended the legal and political autonomy of the region's Native peoples.

We tend to think of America's many "Indian wars" as pitting tradition-bound Natives against white "pioneers," newly arrived from some distant eastern locale in search of new lands. In these scenarios, conflict is inevitable because the two peoples are set in their predetermined ways and have no understanding of, or interest in, each other's language and culture. King Philip's War defies that stereotype in several respects. The first settlers had moved westward from England to New England but that was more than thirty years before the war broke out. Those immigrants were now outnumbered by their New England–born children, most of whom lived alongside Native Americans. This was a war waged not by strangers but rather by neighbors. For half a century, Native and English peoples had learned much about each other while trading, working, negotiating, socializing, suing, politically manipulating, fighting, and—in a few cases—attending school and church together and living under the same roof. So strong were these bonds that after the war began, many on each side recognized acquaintances and neighbors on the other. Many Indians fought alongside the English against other Indians, sometimes from the same community or tribe, while other Natives sought to remain neutral.

Why did people so familiar with one another suddenly begin so wantonly destructive a conflict? Part of answer lies in the transformation of New England's physical and political environment (see Map 1). The settler population and its agricultural ways reached a point during the 1660s when continued expansion could come only at the expense of Native Americans who had already suffered considerable losses of population and land. The colonists were pressuring them to give up yet more land as well as sovereign control over their own communities. These pressures drove many Natives to equate settlers' encroachments on their sacred, ancestral homelands with the death of their communities and culture. Other Indians concluded that siding with the English was the only realistic means of ensuring their communities' survival. The war brought to the surface deep-seated resentments by some people on each side toward all those on the other. Many colonists translated their racialized hatred into violence against Christian and other pro-English Indians. As a result, many Native allies of the English died or were persecuted, and others switched to the anti-English side. Growing numbers of Indians concluded that the English were the inveterate enemies of all indigenous people.

We can see how much more deeply rooted the English antagonism toward Native Americans was than the reverse when we look at the ways the two peoples accommodated each other during their period of

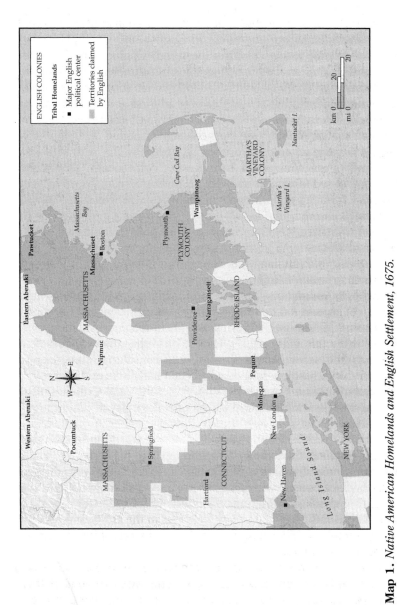

Map 1. *Native American Homelands and English Settlement, 1675.*

By the eve of King Philip's War, English colonies and towns had asserted their authority over vast expanses of indigenous lands and peoples, and were threatening to expand still further.

coexistence. Although the colonists adopted corn cultivation and other indigenous practices to facilitate their settlement in an unfamiliar environment, it was the Indians who did most of the adjusting. Consider the question of languages. Natives and settlers who regularly interacted usually knew a few words in each other's language. Yet while hundreds of Indians became fluent in English and some even read and wrote it, only a few colonists mastered Nipmuc, Narragansett, or one of the other Algonquian languages of southern New England. While many English households used indigenous servants and slaves, there is no evidence that any settler ever labored as a subordinate to a Native person. Between one thousand and two thousand Algonquians converted to Christianity; yet any colonist engaging in indigenous religious practices would have been regarded by the authorities as devil-worshippers who could be punished with death, like many colonists accused of witchcraft. While Native Americans were subject to colonial laws and governments in their dealings with non-Natives, the colonies allowed no English person under any circumstances to be bound over to any Native community for justice. Moreover, while indigenous laborers might live in their English masters' homes, any colonist living with Indians was considered a "renegade" and faced capital punishment if caught.

Underlying the settlers' policies and practices was an ideology that divided human beings into "civilized" and "savage" peoples. European Christians were "civilized" by virtue of their religious, political, and cultural institutions and practices. They stood in sharp contrast to Native Americans and other "savages" who were considered superstitious pagans or devil-worshippers and lacked such hallmarks of "civilization" as the nation-state and land ownership. Protestants and Catholics alike considered it their duty to wage war on enemies of "true" Christianity, be they American "savages," Muslim "infidels," or each other. Many immigrants to New England compared themselves to the Israelites of the Old Testament, guided by God out of Egypt to the "promised land" of Canaan, whose inhabitants they crushed. The settlers were divided among themselves as to whether "savages" could or could not become "civilized" Christians, with many fearing that close and sustained contact between the two peoples would threaten the purity of their own identity. But all colonists agreed on the clear superiority of their own culture to that of indigenous peoples. Whatever their level of tolerance, the English never considered Indians their equals and never relinquished their claims to sovereign authority over Native lands and peoples.

At the human level, then, King Philip's War was a complicated event, characterized at once by the antagonists' familiarity with one another, English assumptions of superiority to Native Americans, and by Native peoples' sense that colonists had betrayed them by violating the alliances that had facilitated coexistence. Such feelings heightened the animosity and cruelty that the two sides visited on one another.

MARY ROWLANDSON AND HER NARRATIVE

Of the several dozen English accounts of King Philip's War, the one exploring the war most deeply as a human experience is Mary Rowlandson's *The Sovereignty and Goodness of God* (1682). Mary White Rowlandson was little known outside the small town of Lancaster, Massachusetts, until the day a party of Native Americans attacked the town, seizing her, her three children, and nineteen of their neighbors. For the next three months, she lived as a captive among Nipmucs, Narragansetts, and Wampanoags as they fought the colonists. She witnessed the violent deaths of her daughter, relatives, neighbors, and other English colonists. In order to survive, she had not simply to live with her Indian captors but to become part of their society. Finally, as the war was winding down in the colonists' favor, she was ransomed and reunited with her family. Six years later, she published an account of her captivity and her understanding of its meaning.

For most readers since it was published more than three centuries ago, the distinctive quality of Rowlandson's narrative lies in the combination of her unique experience and her powerful depiction of that experience. In the book Rowlandson portrays herself as a devout Puritan (as English Protestant followers of the Swiss theologian John Calvin were called), confronting the hellish terror of life among "savages." Stripped of family, home, and all the other forms of comfort and security to which she was accustomed, she wanders frequently to the edge of temptation and despair. But in the end, she always recalls that God, far from abandoning her, is testing her and, through the medium of the destructive war with Indians, her fellow settlers. Her redemption and her return to English society, as well as the colonists' victory in the war, proves that omnipotent God can bestow justice and mercy on both individuals and whole societies. She draws on the Bible to supply not only passages pertaining to particular events but also an overarching meaning to her experience of suffering and redemption.

(Unlike most learned Puritan authors, Rowlandson does not draw on the Greek and Roman classics or any other literature beyond the Bible.) Taken at face value, the narrative vividly dramatizes the Puritans' belief in the inherently sinful nature of human beings, even the relatively few whom God had chosen to save from hell. And more specifically, in her warnings to Puritans about taking God for granted as their lives become more comfortable, the author articulates a theme sounded repeatedly by New England ministers in the late seventeenth century.

Yet the very qualities that have earned Rowlandson a firm place in American literary and cultural history have also raised questions for many readers from her time to ours. In proclaiming the distinctiveness of her experience as a captive, was she also claiming to be elevated spiritually above Puritans who did not share that experience? It would have been troubling for anyone to make such a claim to authority, particularly if that person were not a minister, and above all if that person were female. Rowlandson's gender has raised other questions about the narrative as well. To what extent did she, as opposed to the men who encouraged and sponsored her narrative's publication, shape its contents? Is there within the text a distinctively female voice, independent of other voices, or do Rowlandson's male sponsors speak for her? And what about her relations with her captors? Could any woman in her situation have withstood such an experience with her sexual and spiritual virtues intact? Despite her strident denunciations of the Indians as devilish savages, some scholars have seen her intimate moments with individual Indians and her maneuvering through the Natives' social world as signs that her Anglo-Puritan allegiance weakened during her captivity.

Beyond the meanings of her captivity for Rowlandson and her contemporary readers, the narrative raises questions about the Native Americans who predominate there. Who were these people, and what were they fighting for? And why did they capture people like Mary Rowlandson? Who were the "praying Indians" against whom Rowlandson rails throughout her narrative, and who were the Indians who assisted in obtaining her release? Rowlandson herself provides no direct answers to these questions; indeed, her blatant biases render her suspect as an authority on indigenous people. Nevertheless, the narrative provides valuable insights into the cross-cultural tensions that exploded in war in 1675. In order to appreciate fully her narrative's value in this respect, we must read it as historians read all documents, that is, critically and in conjunction with other available evidence.

Rowlandson divided her narrative into twenty "removes," by which she identified the twenty occasions when she and her captors broke camp and traveled elsewhere. But like most other New England colonists, her entire life was punctuated by removes from one place to another. By examining her life through the places she lived and the removes between them, we can begin to understand why her narrative took the form that it did and how it illuminates the world in which she lived.

FROM ENGLAND TO NEW ENGLAND

Although Mary Rowlandson's narrative is a first-person account, it is not an autobiography that recounts the events of her entire life up to the time of its writing. Rather, it is a memoir that focuses solely on the three months of her captivity and its immediate aftermath, when she was about thirty-nine years of age. We know very little about her life before and after that period. Of Rowlandson's origins, we can be certain only that she was born into a farming family somewhere in Somerset county in the south of England about 1637. Her father, John White, and her mother, Joan West, were married in 1627. Mary was the fifth of eight children born to John and Joan White.[2]

Mary White's personal life in England is largely hidden from us, but we know a great deal about the world into which she was born. England in the early seventeenth century was being swept by economic, social, and religious upheavals. A shift toward specialized, commercial agriculture led many wealthy landowners to "enclose" tracts customarily cultivated by the rural poor, forcing the latter to "remove" from one locale to another in search of work and food. Many "middling" (neither rich nor poor) landowners also tried to profit from raising crops or livestock; while some succeeded, others faltered because their holdings were too small. Like their poorer counterparts, many of the "middling sort" removed within England in hopes of improving their prospects. Against this backdrop, many influential Englishmen envisioned American colonization as a solution to the problems of landlessness and poverty.

England's "middling sort" placed a high premium on achieving and maintaining their personal independence. Perceiving both the rich and the poor as "idle" and, therefore, morally corrupt, many of them were drawn to Puritanism. John Calvin, the Puritans' principal source of inspiration, rejected both the Roman Catholic tenet that God granted salvation to any Catholics who performed "good works" while on earth and the contention of his fellow Protestant, Martin Luther, that "faith alone" would carry believers to heaven. Both were wrong, Calvin insisted, because they maintained that one's fate after death was in her or his hands rather than God's. For Calvin, human beings' sinful nature was rooted in Adam and Eve's tasting the forbidden fruit in the Garden of Eden. Only to demonstrate the power of his grace did God from time to time "elect" a few "saints" for salvation, thereby demonstrating what Calvinists called "divine providence," or destiny. Defying the orthodoxy of the established Church of England (or Anglican Church), which followed Catholic teachings on salvation, many found in Puritanism a measure of assurance that their experience of divine grace *might* mean that they were among the few who would be saved. At the same time, their beliefs provided a code of conduct that enabled them to substitute a stern piety and self-discipline for blind obedience to established authorities. Puritanism enabled them to see themselves as a "godly" people who were morally and politically superior to the ungodly.

Puritanism developed from a set of beliefs into a movement during the late sixteenth and early seventeenth centuries. Charismatic, learned ministers emerged who validated the testimony of followers' conversions, meaning their accounts of having personally experienced God's grace. They established congregations that together formed a powerful movement that addressed economic and political as well as religious issues. Fearful that the Puritans threatened religious and political order, King Charles I supported the Anglican Church's efforts to root out dissenters, especially clergymen, from its ranks. As a result many Puritans developed a heightened alienation toward their homeland. Joan White, Mary's mother, would later tell her congregation in Wenham, Massachusetts, that she "was brought up in a poor, ignorant place."[3] While most Puritans remained in England in hopes of reforming their "elect nation," a sizable minority crossed the Atlantic in what became known as a "Great Migration." Altogether about fourteen thousand English people, mostly Puritans and Puritan sympathizers, migrated to Massachusetts (named for the Native tribe based in what is now greater Boston) and elsewhere in southeastern New England from 1629 until halted by the outbreak of civil war in England in 1642. Joan White would later say that "her heart was drawn to New England because good people [meaning Puritans] came hither."[4]

Arriving in Salem, Massachusetts, in 1639, Mary White and her family found themselves in a society that was young but already heavily populated. By then newcomers to the crowded maritime port and farming community were being granted land far from the town center. As a man of means, John White received a sixty-acre tract located about six miles outside of town. While the tract was more than sufficient to feed his household, White wanted to ensure that his progeny and those who came after would be amply provided for. And, like other relatively affluent colonists, he wanted land that would bring profits to his family's business ventures in both England and New England. Over the ensuing years, White acquired several additional tracts north of Salem, including one that he leased to the operator of a saw and grist mill. By enabling White and his neighbors to obtain necessities such as wood and flour without going to Salem, the mill reinforced their effort to form the separate town of Wenham.[5]

Joan White played an equally critical role in forming the new town by helping establish its church in 1644. When standing before the congregation to give evidence of the workings of God's grace in her, a requirement for membership, she told how she was "for a long space of time living in the far woods" and could not always attend church in Salem or in Ipswich to the north. Like other successful applicants, she cited numerous passages in the Bible that constituted landmarks on her way to the experience of grace, and then answered questions put to her by the minister.[6]

In publicly relating her conversion experience, White acted in a capacity permitted few New England women in the 1640s. Since 1637, when New England's magistrates and ministers had banished a radical "Antinomian" Puritan named Anne Hutchinson, along with her followers, most churches had ceased allowing women to speak publicly in any capacity. Hutchinson had boldly challenged the authority of New England ministers by claiming that all but two of them adhered to a "covenant of works." By this she meant that while pretending to judge the validity of prospective church members' experiences of grace, the ministers were in fact evaluating candidates' outward behavior, thereby following the Catholic doctrine of good works rather than the Puritan insistence on divine grace. Moreover, Hutchinson was a woman who proclaimed her views at meetings that were popular with a large segment of Boston Antinomians, both male and female. While Antinomians flourished among other Puritans in England, they posed a direct challenge to the patriarchal political-clerical elite that was struggling to assert its authority in Massachusetts. Brought to trial before a panel of magistrates led by Governor John Winthrop, Hutchinson successfully repudiated most of the court's objections to her beliefs and activities for several days. But then she declared that she was assured of her own salvation through a direct revelation from God. In other words, an individual was the only one able to judge whether she or he was saved; a sensitive minister could help someone find God's grace within but had no actual authority in the matter. Using this declaration as a pretext, the court rejected what had become a radical woman's challenge to established political as well as religious authorities. After a church trial conducted by ministers excommunicated her and her followers, the magistrates banished them from the colony, with most, including Hutchinson herself, moving to the more tolerant Rhode Island.[7]

By the time the Wenham congregation was convened in 1644, then, it was one of the few in which Joan White and other women still related their conversion experiences in public and spoke regularly in church meetings. White is also noteworthy because her husband, like several other Wenham men, was not a church member.[8] The Whites were not unusual in this respect, for women outnumbered men as members of most New England congregations. Whereas men represented their families regularly in economic and political affairs outside the home, the church was the one public arena in which women had a role, however limited. John White's failure to join did not mean that he was unsympathetic to Puritan views. For example, like all Puritans, he passionately supported the cause of Parliament against the king during England's civil war (1642–1648). While less fervent in his devotion, John apparently respected his wife's capabilities; he not only attended a church in which she enjoyed privileges not available to him but also left her in charge of the household for two years (1648–1650) while he returned to England to settle some financial affairs.[9]

When her father returned from England, Mary White was about thirteen years old. Born in England, she had crossed the Atlantic as a child and grown up in a small, isolated community. Her family's material conditions had steadily improved as a result of hard work and John White's shrewd investments. But as a young girl, and given her father's long absence, she was almost certainly closer to her mother, from whom she was acquiring the combination of boldness, independence, and piety that would one day be revealed in her narrative.

THE ANGLO-INDIAN FRONTIER

In 1653, fourteen years after arriving in Massachusetts, Mary White and her family moved again. Although the Whites had accumulated a considerable amount of land in Wenham, John White wanted to expand his New England holdings still further. Leaving his twenty-year-old son, Thomas, in charge of the Wenham properties, the rest of the family moved fifty miles west to another new town, Lancaster. Lancaster was a study in contrasts to Wenham. Besides being known for its disreputable inhabitants, the town's nearest neighbors were Native Americans.

At the dawn of the seventeenth century, about one hundred thousand Algonquian-speaking people inhabited the area of the present states of Massachusetts and Connecticut east of the Berkshire mountains, and Rhode Island. But visiting colonizers and then settlers brought deadly epidemics of smallpox and other diseases to which Indians had not been previously exposed. Those not mortally stricken by the diseases themselves were malnourished and severely traumatized, especially when settlers rushed in to occupy "abandoned" lands. Hardest hit were coastal communities from Cape Cod northward, where communities formerly numbered in the hundreds or low thousands now held only a few dozen. One Englishman, arriving in 1622, remarked that the "bones and skulls" of the unburied dead "made such a spectacle . . . it seemed to me a new found Golgatha." In 1633, as thousands of settlers were pouring in, a more extensive smallpox epidemic further ravished indigenous communities.[10] Although Mary White probably saw a Native survivor or two from time to time in Salem or Ipswich, she could avoid contact with their diminished communities. Lancaster was another story. The neighboring Nipmuc people of Nashaway had helped the town get started and were contributing to its economic well-being.

The following discussion of the Nipmucs and other Native Americans in southern New England, and of early developments in Lancaster, will provide a background for the rest of Mary Rowlandson's story.

Two Towns Called Nashaway

For thousands of years before there were nations in Europe, Native American communities were rooted in indigenous homelands and linked to one another through ties of exchange and mutual obligation. What we might think of as simply trading for goods or services of practical value—for example, offering corn in exchange for access to the best stones for making an ax—Indians understood as the spiritual exchange of gifts. For northeastern Native Americans, the universe was pervaded by spiritual power—termed *manitou* by Algonquian speakers in New England and *orenda* by Iroquoian speakers to the west. Corn was especially revered but manitou was present even in nonliving stones and the sky. Although individuals certainly traded or shared informally, the most important exchanges occurred in ceremonies involving anywhere from two to several dozen tribal communities, and included "impractical" items such as whelks and quahogs, sea shells from which Indians made sacred wampum beads. They strung the beads into jewelry and massive chains or "belts," and designed symbolic "words" that underscored the sincerity of the presenter's spoken words. They also wore wampum headbands and jewelry on ceremonial occasions. Inter-tribal gatherings often included marriages, which enriched the most deep-seated of all ties—kinship—that bound communities to one another. Gift-giving created obligations on recipients—individuals, families, communities—to return the favor, so that the people were always conscious of their obligations to others. The ideal was to create a balance that was in keeping with the larger balance in a world that did not distinguish between "nature" and human beings.[11]

To be sure, differences between people often reached the point of open hostility. In such cases, *sachems* (political leaders) or other mutually acceptable mediators sought a solution satisfactory to all parties. If violence could not be avoided, two families or communities would make a show of force and try to intimidate each other. In such cases, casualties were few because Native Americans wanted to minimize casualties rather than escalate a cycle of revenge that would undermine the ideal of balance and deplete their populations. One English officer ridiculed an Indian "battle" he witnessed in which the two sides "might fight seven years and not kill seven men" and did so "more for pastime than to conquer and subdue enemies."[12]

When French, Dutch, and English traders began frequenting New England's coast, they sought pelts of beaver and other animals so they could cash in on a European craze for fur hats. Native Americans were just as eager for the manitou of visitors' metal, cloth, and glass wares and the alliances that would result. As a result of this new trade, earlier patterns of exchange shifted so as to favor tribal alliances with the most direct access to European traders, sometimes inducing rivalries over such access. One such conflict fused with English expansionism to produce southern New England's first major war, known as the Pequot War (1637). Other tribes in the region resisted efforts by the powerful Pequots to control trade between themselves and the Dutch on the shores and tributaries of Long Island Sound. Seeking to establish the colony of Connecticut, the English allied with anti-Pequot Mohegan and Narragansett Indians. The coalition's victory was ensured after English troops entered the Pequots' Mystic Fort before dawn and burned it, killing several hundred of those inside, mostly noncombatants. Afterward, the colonies' Narragansett allies complained that English warfare "was too furious and slays too many men."[13] But New England's Native people had now been introduced to a mode of warfare meant "to conquer and subdue enemies."

The Pequot War and the colonization of Connecticut changed the balance of political and economic power in southern New England. The Narragansetts were now the largest and most powerful tribe in the region and, with the support of Rhode Island, the most formidable obstacle to English expansion. In 1643, Massachusetts, Connecticut, and Plymouth established an intercolonial commission, the United Colonies of New England that, as its first act, collaborated with the Mohegans in their assassination of the Narragansett sachem, Miantonomi.[14] Yet the United Colonies and Mohegans were in no position to follow up their provocation by conquering the Narragansetts. Well knowing the colonies' limitations, the Narragansetts drew on a network of alliances that included most Algonquian speakers not connected to the Mohegans as well as the Iroquoian-speaking Mohawks of the powerful Haudenosaunee (or Iroquois Confederacy) farther west.

Like all the major Native American sachemships of the period, the Narragansetts also maintained economic and diplomatic ties with influential English elites, in their case with Roger Williams and other Rhode Island traders. Similarly, the Pocumtucks and their neighbors in western Massachusetts dealt with the Pynchons, a Springfield-based trading family while John Winthrop Jr., in New London, Connecticut, encouraged the Pequots' revival as a distinct people. Williams, the Pynchons, and Winthrop Jr. were closely aligned in promoting Anglo-Indian trade, in wanting to avoid war, and in their hostility to the Mohegans, whose chief English ally was a rival political faction based in Hartford, Connecticut. Although outside the major trade networks, the Wampanoags also established alliances with powerful English interests. Mainland Wampanoags had been tied to Plymouth colony since 1621, and offshore Wampanoags had recently begun a similar relationship with Thomas Mayhew, founder of the multi-island colony of Martha's Vineyard. Like Rhode Island, Martha's Vineyard did not belong to the United Colonies.[15]

By 1643, Showanon, sachem of the Nipmucs of Nashaway, recognized the need for powerful English allies as a survival strategy for his people, who now numbered about two hundred of what had once been several thousand. Accordingly, he reached out to traders and officials in Massachusetts and found that they were equally interested in the Nipmucs. Although the colony's Deputy governor reported in 1631 that the colonists had only heard of the "Nipnett" to the west, a visiting English author met Showanon and Ousamequin, sachem of the Quaboag Nipmucs, just two years later during the smallpox epidemic.[16] In 1641, the

Massachusetts General Court (a legislative-judicial body made up of representatives from each town) authorized a group of investors to seek out potential mines and "to purchase the interest of any Indians in such lands where such mines shall be found." Iron deposits were soon found near Quaboag and Nashaway. Although Quaboag was still far from any English settlements, the Court authorized establishment of an English town at Nashaway. In 1643, several prospective miners, fur traders, and farmers moved to the new town, which they likewise called Nashaway. Showanon welcomed the newcomers as equitable partners of Nipmuc Nashaway and two smaller, affiliated towns. In the following year, Massachusetts signed a formal treaty with the Nashaway and Quaboag Nipmucs along with three other communities that were already allied with the colony and surrounded by settlers (Document 1).[17]

English Nashaway's beginnings were anything but promising. While a network of trails and waterways connected the town to the outside world, it lacked a road over which draft animals could haul English wagons and carts. Newcomers arrived so slowly, complained Governor John Winthrop, "that in two years they had not three built houses there," causing its minister to leave in disgust. For Winthrop, the problem was not simply the town's isolation but also the quality of its settlers, most of whom "were poor men, and some of them corrupt in judgment, and others profane."[18] He was referring to people such as Thomas King, who was charged with "having defiled his wife before their marriage"; Stephen Day, who had been jailed for indebtedness; and Robert Child, a prominent Puritan who challenged Massachusetts' post-Antinomian clampdown on dissenters and publicized its practices in England.[19]

Child, along with most others in Nashaway, soon left the isolated little town. By November 1647, a majority of the town's remaining landowners petitioned the General Court to rescind the grant so they could leave, but the Court refused, saying that it "does not think fit to destroy the said plantation, but rather to encourage it."[20] But in 1650 it was the Court that vainly threatened to force the settlers to withdraw unless they hired a minister to organize a church. During the next year Elizabeth Hall, whose husband was then in England, allegedly greeted a male visitor by stating that all property, including "men's wives," should be owned in common "as in the apostles' time." Although Hall sued her accuser for slander, forcing him to retract, her husband summoned her to England, thereby avoiding further scandal.[21]

The struggle over morality was not confined to English Nashaway, for a parallel conflict was raging among its Nipmuc neighbors. When signing the treaty with Massachusetts in 1644, the sachems had pledged "to be willing from time to time to be instructed in the knowledge and worship of God." This aspect of the agreement opened the way for the colony's effort, led by Puritan minister John Eliot, to convert the colony's eastern Indians to Christianity (Figure 1). But while Eliot organized six Christian Indian "praying towns" among Massachusets and Pawtuckets, he largely ignored the Nipmucs. Nevertheless, the General Court called on Eliot to intervene in Nashaway politics when the Christian sachem Showanon died in 1654. The sachemship among New England Algonquians generally remained within prominent families, but all members of the community met and together decided on a successor. Two of Showanon's relatives were candidates to succeed him: Matthew, a Christian, and Shoshanim, whom the English called a "debauched and drunken fellow." (The English would persist in distinguishing Nashaway's factions as "Christians" and "drunkards" without noting that they had introduced both Christianity and alcohol to the town.) Eliot or another Englishman generously distributed gifts to demonstrate the benefits of electing a Christian. Matthew won and became Nashaway's new sachem.[22]

Although Indian Nashaway's commitment to Christianity was less than unanimous, its loyalty to the colony was never in doubt during the 1640s and 1650s. Its people had welcomed the English not only by selling them part of their land but also by regularly trading them furs for manufactured goods and, most likely, by many other casual acts that went unrecorded. Nashaway's evident security began to attract families who sought the comforts found in older English settlements. Perhaps to make that security even more evident, the inhabitants renamed the town in 1653, first calling it Prescott and then West Towne before finally agreeing on Lancaster, the name of an English county that carried no association with their Indian neighbors. By then the town was also emerging from its isolation by becoming a link on a road connecting eastern Massachusetts to Connecticut.[23]

Lancaster and the Rowlandsons

Arriving in the year of the name change, the Whites were among an influx of new families moving to Lancaster as its prospects seemed to improve. After a decade in which the number of families was never more than about a dozen, it suddenly boasted thirty-five households by 1654. For John White, the motive of acquiring yet more land was once again uppermost; within a year of his arrival, he became the largest landowner in town. How Joan White felt about leaving Wenham is less clear, but she

Figure 1. *Massachusetts Bay Colony Seal*
The seal advertised the colony's missionary ambitions by depicting a Native
American saying "come over and help us."
Courtesy of the American Antiquarian Society, Worcester, Massachusetts.

was probably content in knowing that Lancaster had finally recruited a
minister, Joseph Rowlandson, with whom she had attended church in
Ipswich. As the family's spiritual mentor, Joan most likely helped incline
Mary toward the new clergyman. But John would have encouraged her,
too, for Rowlandson, as the town's minister, was also a large landowner
and the marriage would unite two formidable families. Mary's parents

would undoubtedly have relented had she utterly refused to marry Joseph, but she had little basis for refusing. She may have recalled him as another child in the Ipswich congregation and barely knew him as an adult. She too had much to gain from becoming the wife of the town's minister. Mary and Joseph were married in about 1656.[24]

Like his new wife, Joseph Rowlandson had emigrated from England as a child and settled with his family in Essex County, Massachusetts. But unlike Mary, he was not born wealthy. While the Whites were pillars of the community in Wenham, the Rowlandsons were near the bottom of Ipswich society in wealth, social status, and reputation. Joseph's father appeared frequently in court, most often for failing to pay assessments, and his brother became a target of public ridicule after his wife won a divorce, charging he was impotent.[25] Though studying for the ministry, Joseph had his own brush with the law. In 1651 he posted on the door of the Ipswich meetinghouse—the town's bulletin board—an anonymous broadside denouncing New England as a region where envy had triumphed over truth in the administration of justice. Specific references in the text indicate that he was lashing out at those who had harassed his family by collecting fines and initiating lawsuits. His identity was quickly discovered and Joseph was charged with "scandelous lybell," for which he was fined and forced to make a lengthy apology. Nevertheless, he went on to graduate from Harvard in 1652 and, after waiting more than a year, accepted Lancaster's invitation to become its first minister.[26]

Whereas John White had left a son in Wenham to manage the family's holdings there, Rowlandson brought his destitute parents with him to Lancaster. Whereas all the Whites knew how to read and write, only Joseph among the Rowlandsons could even sign his name.[27] Nevertheless, as a minister, Rowlandson made up for his family's deficiencies not only because he was entitled to a generous allotment of land but also because he had earned the right to be addressed as "Mister" or "Master" (abbreviated as "Mr."). In status-conscious England and its colonies, "Mr." designated men who exercised authority but stood below the ranks of the titled aristocracy and the gentry. Most of those addressed as "Mr." were clergymen, magistrates, military officers, and very wealthy merchants. But mere landowners, even those as affluent as John White, were addressed simply as "goodman." And Joan White was a "goodwife." By marrying Joseph, Mary became "Mistress" (abbreviated as "Mrs.") Rowlandson. Unlike in our society, "Mrs." referred to a woman's rank, not necessarily to her marital status; Mary's daughters would have become "Mrs." upon reaching adulthood whether or not they married. Besides satisfying both families' ambitions, the marriage

Figure 2. *A Minister's House in Seventeenth-Century Massachusetts*
The original structure of this house belonged to a clergyman like Joseph Rowlandson. Ministers' homes were larger than those of most other residents in their towns. Like other wealthy homeowners, they extended their houses to the sides and rear as they became more prosperous.
Courtesy of Historic New England.

of the once penniless and despised "Mr. Rowlandson" to the daughter of the wealthiest "goodman" and "goodwife" created the most powerful family alliance in town.[28]

The White-Rowlandson marriage ought to have brought Lancaster the respectability in the eyes of eastern colonists that kept eluding the town. But the combination of Lancaster and Joseph Rowlandson, with their respective histories of contentiousness, proved too explosive. At around the time the Rowlandsons were married, a female church member, Mary Gates, was charged with "making bold and unbeseeming speeches in the public assembly on the Lord's day" against the minister. While it may be tempting to think of Mary Gates as another Anne Hutchinson, the feud appears to have been a more personal one of the sort that Rowlandson was embroiled in with other Lancaster residents. Many of the disputes arose when townspeople denounced the extent of

Rowlandson's landholdings and challenged the validity of his titles to some of them. In addition, many disliked the minister's threat to accept an offer from a church in another town unless Lancaster enhanced his income. So unpopular was he that only three men had joined the church, not enough to organize an independent town government. To quell the persistent feuding, the General Court appointed a three-man commission to monitor the town. Partial to Rowlandson, the commission in 1657 ordered Lancaster to build a meetinghouse and to further raise Rowlandson's salary and landholdings. It also appointed five selectmen (ordinarily elected at town meetings) to govern the town.[29]

The surviving records are fragmentary, but something of a pattern emerges in these disputes. On one side were the town's early settlers, some of whom traded regularly with the Nipmucs of Nashaway and all of whom chafed under efforts by the General Court in Boston to regulate their affairs. Pitted against them were newer arrivals, especially those like the Rowlandsons and Whites who owned more land than any of the old-timers and who readily looked to the Court for support. Unlike their rivals, the newcomers had no economic stake in relations with Native Americans. Whereas trader Stephen Day could tell the Court he had entertained "both English and Indians at my house from day to day for some years together," Joseph Rowlandson appears to have contributed nothing to the lagging missionary effort at Nashaway beyond taking a Christian Indian boy into his home as a servant.[30] The fault line running through Lancaster had economic and even cultural dimensions.

In the end, however, the fault line proved to be temporary. By the early 1660s, as the townspeople fought yet another battle over Rowlandson's landholdings, relations between Lancaster and Nashaway were beginning to change. While the Nipmucs had once hunted beaver and other fur-bearing animals solely to satisfy their own needs, the relentless English demand for furs led hunters to procure as many pelts as they could in order to retain their trade ties with the colonists. As a result, beaver, otter, marten, mink, and other fur-bearing mammals had become virtually extinct in southern New England. English traders at Lancaster and elsewhere customarily provided their indigenous partners with trade goods in advance of each hunting season, with the understanding that the Natives would satisfy their debt with furs in spring, when the season ended. The abrupt decline in furs left Indians indebted to the traders, who then pressured their clients to satisfy their debts with land. Thus Stephen Day obtained 150 acres of upland from the Nashaway sachem, Matthew, while John Prescott obtained a tract from another Nashaway Christian, James Quanapohit. Other traders, like John Tinker, sold their interest and moved elsewhere. By the end of the 1660s, the end of the fur trade and the transformation of the remaining English traders into major landowners had closed the social and factional divide in Lancaster.[31]

A now-united Lancaster was finally acquiring respectability among the colony's leaders. A sure sign of the change came in 1672 when Joseph Rowlandson, once known for precipitating conflicts, was called to Boston's bitterly divided Third Congregational ("Old South") Church to help resolve one. In 1673, three decades after the establishment of English Nashaway, the General Court's special commission submitted its final report. It found that the people of Lancaster were now living in harmony and capable of handling their own affairs. Accepting this judgment, the Court at long last granted the town full power to govern itself.[32]

Lancaster's new stability came at the expense of its Nashaway Nipmuc neighbors. Indeed, colonization was now undermining the lives of all southern New England Algonquians. While the number of Native Americans continued to decrease from the effects and aftereffects of European-derived diseases, the English population skyrocketed. Not only traders but also the colonial authorities were pressuring Indians to sell land in order to make room for more settlers.[33] Compared to Lancaster with its thirty-five households in 1654, Nashaway numbered only fifteen or sixteen twenty years later. Even on the land remaining, life was becoming more constricted. English livestock invaded Native communities' cornfields and, along with English plows, devoured the grasses that attracted deer and other animals on which the Indians depended for meat.[34] Still further complicating the Algonquians' situation was the collapse of their alliance with the Mohawk Iroquois to the west. Mohawk and Algonquian war parties conducted raids on each other's villages, usually to the Mohawks' advantage. To counter the Mohawks and their alliance with Anglican New York, Puritan Massachusetts supported (ineffectively) Algonquian Christians, but other Algonquians had come to see the settlers' religion as a dangerous kind of manitou.[35] Tensions between Christians and anti-Christians resurfaced in Nashaway after the Christian sachem, Matthew, died and was succeeded by Shoshanim, the "debauched and drunken" anti-Christian who had been passed over in 1658.[36] Comparable religious-political divisions were emerging within Algonquian communities and tribes across New England.

Christianity sharpened these divisions, not simply because its message appealed to some Nipmucs, Massachusets, and Wampanoags, but also because missionaries now had the financial resources to more aggressively recruit prospective Christians. Authorized by the United Colonies, Eliot worked with wealthy contacts in England to establish a lucrative fund-raising operation there that funneled money and English goods to the region. He and other missionaries used this support to foster new praying towns with their own preachers and magistrates, even within communities and tribes whose sachems vehemently opposed the new religion. They also established a separate Indian College at Harvard to expand the Cambridge campus' effort to train Natives in achieving full bilingual literacy, and commissioned the Harvard press, operated by Samuel Green, to publish a bible in Wôpanâak (an Algonquian language spoken by Wampanoags and Massachusets and easily understood by Nipmuc speakers). The key to the publication effort was James (or Wowaus), a Nipmuc hired by the press in 1659, whom Eliot described as the "one man . . . that is able to compose the sheets, and correct the press with understanding." (See Figure 3.) Combining his bilingual literacy with an aptitude for typesetting and printing, James produced numerous missionary tracts publicizing his and other Christian Indians' piety, along with some of the earliest English-language works published in North America. Before long, he was known as James the Printer or simply James Printer.[37]

Of special concern to the English as tensions mounted were Printer's own people, the Nipmucs, whose homeland directly adjoined those of the Wampanoags, Narragansetts, Pocumtucks, and other potential enemies. Anxious to ensure the Nipmucs' loyalty, Daniel Gookin, Massachusetts' Superintendent of Indians, sought in 1674 to reorganize their communities as "praying towns." At Nashaway, he introduced Jethro, a Christian from another town, as its new minister and exhorted Shoshanim and his people to "abstain from drunkenness, whoredom, and powwowing [traditional religious ceremonies and healing practices], and all other evils" in order to be assured of "eternal and temporal happiness." But whereas Gookin's other stops resulted in the establishment of new praying towns, Nashaway did not.[38]

The impact of missionaries and other colonists who were seeking to destabilize indigenous communities and tribes is apparent in Rhode Island governor John Easton's account of his meeting with Philip (also known as Metacom), the Wampanoag sachem of Pokanoket, in June 1675. Philip told Easton how the English had betrayed his father's generosity when welcoming the struggling Plymouth colonists a half-century earlier and thereafter granting them an ever-larger homeland in Wampanoag country. But now the English sought to divide and conquer Wampanoags by pressuring them to turn away from their traditional

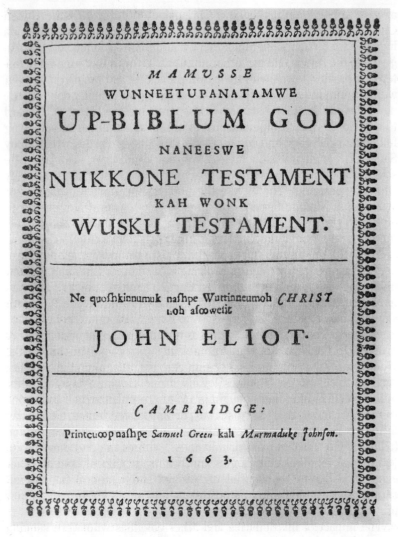

Figure 3. *Algonquian Bible, 1663*

Seeking to reach Native Americans through their own languages, John
Eliot and other missionaries relied on dozens of bilingual, Christian Indian
interpreters, teachers, ministers, and the extraordinary James Printer. Printer
set the type and printed this bible and numerous other Algonquian, English,
and bilingual publications.

religion to Christianity, and to sell still more land and pay tribute directly to the colony instead of to Metacom and other non-Christian sachems. Between Plymouth's efforts to erode Wampanoag political sovereignty and cultural identity altogether, and the clamoring for war by most younger Wampanoags, Metacom was being forced in that direction himself (Document 2).

WORLDS UPENDED

The event that finally triggered open war was the death of another Native person who had played an unusual role in the growing chasm between Indians and English. John Sassamon was a Massachuset orphan who was raised as a Christian in an English household. He served Massachusetts as an interpreter during and after the Pequot War and then worked with John Eliot by translating his sermons and helping him with the preparation of the Algonquian Bible. In 1662 he moved to Pokanoket and became an interpreter, English-language scribe, and counselor for the Pokanoket Wampanoag sachem, Philip. At Eliot's urging, Sassamon initially, but unsuccessfully, tried to interest the powerful sachem in Christianity, but nevertheless remained with him for another decade. By 1673 he had left Philip to become the minister at a Wampanoag praying town. In January 1675, with Anglo-Wampanoag tensions at fever pitch, Sassamon quietly told Governor Josiah Winslow that Metacom was conspiring with other Native Americans to launch all-out war against the English. Sassamon never had a chance to explain his action in public, for a week later he was dead. After several months of investigation by Plymouth, a Christian Wampanoag reported that he had seen three of Philip's associates kill Sassamon and throw his body in a pond. The pond lay on Pokanoket land that some settlers claimed on the basis of deeds written by Sassamon, reinforcing the conviction of many non-Christian Wampanoags that Sassamon had used his literacy to cheat Metacom's Pokanokets out of land. Other doubtful Wampanoags claimed that Sassamon, traveling alone, had fallen through the ice and drowned. Although both the alleged perpetrators and victim were Wampanoags—the kind of case that formerly would have been adjudicated within the tribe—Plymouth asserted its jurisdiction. The colony selected a jury of twelve Englishmen plus six Christian Indians, especially appointed to give the trial an appearance of evenhandedness. The jury found the three guilty and, on June 8, 1675, they were hanged. Recognizing that the trial was a sham and with most Wampanoags and many other Native Americans calling for armed resistance, a previously reluctant Metacom prepared for war. Fighting began later that month after Wampanoags and settlers fired on each other in the Plymouth town of Swansea.[39]

Total War, 1675–1676

The outbreak of full Anglo-Indian war began disastrously for the English. First, English soldiers proved powerless to halt Pokanoket attacks on nearby Plymouth settlements and prevent the Pocasset Wampanoags, led by their *saunkskwa* (female sachem), Weetamoo, from joining forces with Philip's Pokanokets.[40] Then in July, those Nipmucs who had decided to fight the English began attacking towns and troops at will in central Massachusetts. One such attack was staged by Nashaway Nipmucs against their Lancaster neighbors in August 1675. Led by Monoco, known to the English as "One-eyed John," the attack resulted in the deaths of seven settlers. The incident prompted Lancaster to designate several large homes, including the Rowlandsons', as garrison houses, in which all residents gathered to better defend themselves against future attacks.[41] The war spread to western Massachusetts in September when Algonquians in the Connecticut River Valley launched a series of surprise attacks on nearby English towns.[42] Finally, in December 1675, the colonies launched a preventive war against the anti-English but still formally neutral Narragansetts, the most powerful tribal nation in the region. Repeating the tactic that had crushed the Pequots in 1637, an intercolonial force attacked and burned the Narragansetts' massive Great Swamp Fort along with most of the several hundred women and children as well as fighting men who were inside. Although the English devastated the Narragansetts, their own losses were so great that they were unable to seal what might have been a decisive victory. Pursuing troops were utterly unable to locate surviving Narragansetts and Wampanoags who followed others in their tribes who had joined with Nipmucs in forming several encampments in central Massachusetts.[43]

Why did the English, with their far greater numbers, fare so badly? The answer lies partly in the differential effects of Anglo-Indian contact on the two peoples' ways of waging war. Having defeated the Pequots and thinking that other shows of force had intimidated Native Americans, the colonists were confident of their military superiority to "savages." Following European conventions, English troops marched in tight columns, expecting to meet their foes on an open field or to besiege them in a fortress. They modified these practices when fighting "savages" by burning them in their forts. Also following the practices of "civilized" armies, many soldiers still carried a type of musket known as a matchlock, a heavy, cumbersome weapon whose firing mechanism had to be carefully ignited and whose barrel had to be placed on a forked stake known as a "rest" before each shot was fired. Approaching to within fifty yards of their enemies, European armies fired simultaneous volleys straight ahead, relying on the sheer volume of firepower rather than accuracy. Colonists only gradually recognized the disadvantages of matchlocks when engaging with Native Americans, and by 1675 many (but not all) English troops carried flintlocks, far lighter muskets with self-igniting mechanisms. Yet even soldiers with flintlocks still marched in formations and did not try to improve their marksmanship.[44]

Ironically, in turning to flintlocks the colonists followed the example of Native Americans. Upon first encountering armed Europeans, indigenous men recognized that flintlocks would supplement bows in facilitating mobility and long-distance accuracy when hunting or fighting. Despite some early colonial efforts to limit Natives' access to firearms, guns, powder, and ammunition quickly circulated through the exchange networks linking indigenous communities with each other and with English, Dutch, and French suppliers throughout the Northeast. In the years leading up to the war, English attempts to confiscate the guns of Wampanoags and other anti-English Algonquians only heightened the Algonquians' resolve to hold onto them. By 1675 most Native men, regardless of their relations to colonists, carried flintlocks and knew a Native blacksmith who repaired them and molded musket balls. The blacksmiths had acquired their skills when working for colonists. A Narragansett blacksmith's forge was destroyed when the English burned Great Swamp Fort. As war began, Native American fighting men were more effectively prepared and armed than their colonial counterparts.[45]

Also working against the English were many colonists' racialized fear and hatred of all Native Americans. When war first broke out, pro-English, "friend Indians" volunteered their services in all the colonies, where they proved effective as armed warriors, scouts, advisers, and spies, often at great risk to their own lives. But authorities in Massachusetts and Plymouth encountered such formidable popular hostility toward their indigenous allies that they abandoned this most valuable asset to their cause. Unlike in Connecticut and Rhode Island, most "friend Indians" in these two colonies were Christians. The fact that some Christian Nipmucs had joined with kin and community to fight the English only reinforced the popular insistence that all Native Americans were traitors and that "praying" Indians were the most deceitful and treacherous of all. Christian Indians were frequently harassed and, in several notorious instances, killed by English vigilantes. When Eliot, Gookin, and other sympathizers sought to defend and protect Christians, they too were threatened.[46] Indeed the issue of whether to consider pro-English Algonquians friends or foes precipitated a crisis in Massachusetts that threatened to erupt into civil war among colonists, like Bacon's Rebellion, which was then raging in Virginia. In both colonies, some were certain that the two wars represented a single indigenous uprising against all the English while others feared that rebellious Indian-haters in both colonies would join forces against established leaders who did not support genocidal war against all Native Americans.[47] To placate anti-Indian militants within their own colony, Massachusetts authorities rounded up loyal Massachuset and Nipmuc families and moved them to Deer Island in Boston harbor in what today we would call a concentration camp (Document 3). Fearing such incarceration, even more "friend Indians" joined the anti-English cause. While safely separated from hostile colonists and from anti-English Native Americans who might either attack or try to recruit them, the Deer Island prisoners lacked means of obtaining adequate food and shelter for the coming winter. Although some escaped, many more, mostly women and children, perished over the winter. Meanwhile, without Indian assistance, Massachusetts troops proved utterly unable to locate their enemies and prevent the ambushes and surprise attacks that devastated the colony from the fall of 1675 to the following spring.[48]

Meanwhile, the anti-English Wampanoags, Narragansetts, and Nipmucs began removing from their encampments in central Massachusetts. Whereas they customarily broke up into small groups during winter, the Indians waging war in 1675 were amassed in large concentrations. To feed themselves, they pilfered abandoned English towns in their vicinity. At the same time, they sought to broaden their base of Native American support. Early in January Metacom led a delegation west to Schaghticoke, or Hoosic, in upper New York for a large gathering of anti-Mohawk Algonquians from the Hudson Valley, northern New England, and the St. Lawrence Valley in New France. But New York authorities intervened, providing the Mohawks with large numbers of guns and urging them to attack the meeting. Aided by an outbreak of contagious disease among the Algonquians, the Mohawks scattered them and entered the war as a powerful western front in support of the New England colonies.[49]

With the Mohawks attacking from the west while the English still struggled to regroup to the east, the Wampanoag-Narragansett-Nipmuc coalition recognized the need for some decisive blows against the colonists. And with winter having set in, their food shortage was dire. In January 1676 they planned attacks against five exposed frontier towns, beginning with Lancaster. We know about these plans because of the testimony of two Christian Nipmucs, who had been quietly released from Deer Island and who, at extraordinary personal risk, lived among their fellow Nipmucs for a few weeks and pretended to share their hostility to the colonists. One of them, James Quanapohit of Nashaway, who had earlier fought alongside Monoco against the Mohawks, learned from his countryman of the plans to attack Lancaster (Document 4). On January 24, he arrived with the news at Gookin's home in Cambridge after a difficult journey through the snow. But with colonial officials distrusting Quanapohit because he was an Indian, they did not augment the fourteen soldiers already stationed there. Fears and rumors also abounded at Lancaster itself, prompting the town to dispatch several men, including Joseph Rowlandson, to Boston to plead for troops to defend the town. The Lancaster men were still in Boston on the evening of February 9, when the second Nipmuc spy, Job Kattananit, reported to Gookin that an attack on Lancaster was imminent (Document 5). Gookin immediately sent word to troops stationed near Lancaster to fly to the town's rescue. When the first soldiers arrived the next morning, they found the Rowlandsons' garrison house in flames and at least fourteen of the town's inhabitants dead and twenty-three captured.[50]

Although the troops' timely arrival forced the Indians to withdraw, limiting most of the damage and casualties to the Rowlandson garrison, Lancaster was fatally damaged. Even with soldiers guarding the town, the inhabitants remained vulnerable to attack while their food supplies ran dangerously low. A month later, a scouting party reported to the governor that in the woods around Lancaster, they "found several houses deserted, [yet] having corn in them and cattle about them." In a petition sent to the General Court on March 11, the remaining residents asked for carts sufficient to transport them and their possessions to safety, referring to Lancaster as "this prison" (Document 6). By the end of March, all inhabitants of the recently prosperous town had been evacuated.[51]

Joseph Rowlandson had also rushed to Lancaster immediately after the attack, only to find that Mary and sixteen other family members had died or been captured. He quickly returned to Boston to urge that troops pursue the Indians and rescue the captives.[52] Ten days after his family's capture, he invoked divine providence when preaching at the Old South Church. As recorded by one of his listeners, John Hull, Rowlandson reassured worshippers that "God is true to himself and to all that put their trust in him."[53] Clearly, Rowlandson had his family in mind but his hopes were dashed as the war widened far beyond Lancaster. On the morning after he preached, Native Americans based at Menimeset destroyed the English town of Medfield (Document 7), despite the presence within the town of about one hundred soldiers. English reinforcements arrived too late and pursued the attackers only as far as the Baquag River where, within sight of the Indians and their captives, they gave up and turned around. Medfield was twenty miles from Boston itself, and a Native raid two days later struck just ten miles from the capital. Rather than pursuing captors of settlers, colonial authorities now emphasized concentrating colonists in larger coastal towns, with some advocating the fortification of Boston at the expense of all other towns. Meanwhile anti-English Native Americans were scoring similar victories across southern New England. While they had suffered greatly, they maintained their momentum and still held the upper hand.[54]

Captives and Captors

While Increase Mather, in the preface to Mary Rowlandson's narrative, states that the Native Americans who attacked Lancaster were Narragansetts, Rowlandson herself makes clear that Nipmucs and Wampanoags also participated. The Indians were encamped together at the Nipmuc town of Menimeset (which Rowlandson calls "Wenimesset"), about twenty-five miles southwest of Lancaster. It was here that Rowlandson was taken on the day after her capture and, over the next two weeks, transformed from elite settler to indigenous captive. During that time, her daughter Sarah died in her arms; she encountered but could not remain with her two other children, Mary and Joseph Jr.; and her Narragansett captor presented her to his sachem, Quinnapin.

Quinnapin came from a distinguished Narragansett lineage. He was the nephew of a revered sachem, Canonicus, and the nephew of Canonicus's co-sachem, Miantonomi, whom the Mohegans and United Colonies had murdered in 1643. During the 1660s, Quinnapin was at the forefront of those Narragansetts who shifted away from their English ties to connect with their former rivals, the Wampanoags. Quinnapin contributed to the strengthening of that bond in at least two of his three marriages. One of his wives was a sister of Philip's wife, and another was Weetamoo (whom Rowlandson refers to as "Wettimore"), the saunskskwa of the Pocasset Wampanoags. The tribal affiliation of his third wife, Onux, is unknown. His extended household consisted of four wigwams, his own and those belonging to each of his wives.[55]

Weetamoo was even more politically powerful than her husband. Like Quinnapin, she had used marriage to strengthen her Pocasset people in the face of colonization. She first married Wamsutta (later Alexander), son of the sachem of the Pokanoket Wampanoags, and her sister married Wamsutta's younger brother, Metacom (later Philip), thereby solidifying the alliance between the two most powerful Wampanoag sachemships. After Alexander died in 1662 (see Document 2), she appears to have married a Narragansett, a marriage that Philip disapproved of because he did not yet trust that tribe. It is not clear what happened to that husband, before she next married the sachem of a smaller Wampanoag community. That marriage became a casualty of the split within the tribe when her husband cast his lot with Plymouth. Soon thereafter Weetamoo openly allied with the Narragansetts and married Quinnapin.[56] When the Narragansetts and Pocassets entered the war, Weetamoo became, from the English perspective, a formidable foe. An English author at the time wrote that "she is as Potent a Prince as any round about her, and hath as much Corn, Land, and Men [as Philip] at her Command."[57] It was Weetamoo who became Rowlandson's primary "mistress" and her greatest nemesis.

Rowlandson's understanding of her status as a captive was shaped by her English identity, most immediately as Mistress Mary Rowlandson. Mistress Rowlandson was the English wife—the "deputy husband"—of Master Joseph Rowlandson in his patriarchal household, which included their biological children, some of Joseph's relatives, and some servants, at least one of whom was a Christian Nipmuc.[58] In her narrative, Rowlandson refers to Quinnapin as her "master" and to his wives as her "mistresses."

Mary Rowlandson's identity also provided her with resources that helped to sustain her as a captive. While her narrative reflects her thinking when writing several years after her return to English society (to be discussed more fully later), it also points to her experiences at the time. She was deeply traumatized by the shock of the attack and her capture, the death of her child and her separation from the rest of her family, and her entry into a mobile society of Native Americans who, while desperately short of food, continued to wage war against her people. The experience cut Rowlandson off from nearly all the worldly associations that, without her giving it a thought, had constantly reminded her of who she was and where she belonged in the world.

In the face of her trauma, Rowlandson tells how she kept reminding herself that she was a Puritan saint who was utterly dependent on God's grace not only for salvation in the afterlife but for her fate while still on earth. God was testing her and other saints, she believes, when he spared her life and not those of her kin, and when he allowed the escaping Indians to cross the Baquag River and halted the pursuing English troops at its banks. At the same time, it was divine providence that caused an Indian who participated in the attack on Medfield to bring her a bible from the ashes of that town. Divine providence and the bible supplied her with a framework for interpreting her entire experience and the events bearing on it.

Besides being a saint, Rowlandson was a European, a facet of her identity that had assumed special importance after her move to Lancaster, with its proximity to Nashaway. It loomed even larger once she was a captive among her Nashaway neighbors as well as other Native Americans. In Christian European parlance, she belonged to that portion of humanity deemed "civilized," whereas Indians were "savages." In contrast to the virtuous English, she characterizes Indians in her narrative with terms such as "black creatures," "hell-hounds," and "wild beasts of the forest." For Rowlandson, only Europeans—and never Indians—could be Christians.

Alongside the stridently ideological tone of much of Rowlandson's narrative are passages that suggest other perspectives on her experience. Especially as it moves forward in time, the text frequently undermines the impenetrable social and cultural barrier posited in the civilized/savage dichotomy. That Rowlandson communicated with her captors in English, that Native warriors used guns so effectively, that her captors included anti-English Christians, some of whom were literate in English—all testified to the ambiguities that had complicated cultural boundaries at Nashaway, Lancaster, and elsewhere in New England over the preceding half-century. These ambiguities enabled Rowlandson to discover dimensions of her captors' existence that belied the category "savage," as when some of them offered her sustenance and comfort even while others scorned her, when her son's "mistress" quietly took him to visit his mother, and when Quinnapin and Metacom himself treated her with respect and compassion. Even when ascribing such acts to divine providence, Rowlandson undermines her blanket condemnations of Native Americans as inherently "savage," by carefully differentiating among them as individuals. For example, of the many

English accounts of the war, Rowlandson's is the only one, besides that of John Easton (see Document 2), to portray Philip with any degree of humanity. Rowlandson describes how she personally breeched the cultural divide as she maneuvered through the mobile, intertribal society of her captors, exchanging her knitted goods and cultivating the favor of powerful men such as Quinnapin and Philip. Her identification with her new community becomes explicit after she narrates the crossing of the Baquag River. Although she continues using the pronouns "we" and "us" to refer to the captives, she also begins using them to refer to the entire society of captors and captives.

Besides her formal identity and beliefs, what factors in Rowlandson's background shaped her response to captivity? And how did these factors serve her during her ordeal? As a relatively prosperous, married, English Puritan woman, Rowlandson was accustomed to managing a household of a husband and three children, as well as a fluctuating number of servants and visitors. She was intimately familiar with the preparation of food; the sewing and mending of clothing; the bearing, nurturing, and religious education of children; and the many other domestic tasks performed by white New England women. She was also the most prominent member of a community of women that conducted neighborly exchanges of goods and labor, oversaw childbirths, offered charity to the needy, and enforced community mores. In addition, as the minister's wife, she was a leading member of her Lancaster congregation, a role that gave her additional social power.[59] However, except as church members, women in colonial New England derived their identity and whatever formal, public power they exercised from the male head of their household, be he father, husband, or, in the case of servants, master. Thus, while Rowlandson during her captivity considered herself still married to her husband, she represents herself in her narrative as a "servant" in Quinnapin's household.

To Rowlandson, Native women's roles roughly paralleled what she knew in the sense that they too appeared to revolve around marriage, motherhood, and domesticity. But as with other European observers, her biases led her to overlook or misinterpret evidence of women's roles and gender relations in Indian societies as well as the ways that colonization had reshaped or disrupted older practices. Premarital sex was common for indigenous women and men, and they more easily divorced one another than did the English.[60] Unlike their English counterparts, Algonquian women isolated themselves from their families and communities while giving birth and while menstruating. So spiritually powerful was a woman's body when it erupted from within, that she temporarily withdrew so that her community could maintain a stable balance of manitou. Once she returned from giving birth or menstruating, a woman immediately resumed her full range of labors and other social roles. Also unlike the English, women such as Weetamoo often became saunkskwas, who were political leaders of men as well as women.[61]

Native societies were mobile, even in peacetime, and were attached to community homelands rather than to a permanent, year-round structure that could be called a "home" in the English sense. The annual removing of households at seasonal intervals prepared Rowlandson's captors, female as well as male, for their frequent wartime removes. Besides cultivating crops of corn, beans, and squash, indigenous women gathered a wide variety of wild plants, nuts, berries, and shellfish, which they prepared along with the meat and fish brought by the men. (Men did take the lead in clearing fields for planting and in cultivating tobacco.) Although some English men hunted, English women focused on a narrower range of domesticated foods. At the outset of her captivity, Rowlandson was utterly unprepared for finding food or otherwise surviving outside her town, despite having lived most of her life in New England.[62]

One of the most practical aspects of Rowlandson's identity as an English woman was her "pocket" (Figure 4). As Laurel Thatcher Ulrich points out, a New England woman's pocket was not attached to her clothing but rather tied like an apron. In it she carried sewing materials that she could turn to when she had a few minutes of spare time, as well as any number of other objects connected with her various responsibilities. During her captivity, Rowlandson's pocket contained her bible, morsels of food, needles and yarn, and, most likely, other items that she could conceal or suddenly produce as a situation demanded (Figure 5). In this sense her pocket was both a tangible link to her earlier identity as well as a key to her survival and temporary self-fashioning as a captive.[63]

Rowlandson's adoption of the terminology of English servitude— "master," "mistress," "servant"—to describe her position in Quinnapin's household is also instructive because she had experience with the institution as a mistress in Lancaster. Yet in defying Weetamoo and in speaking alone and casually with Philip, Rowlandson broke the rules of her own society whereby servants obeyed their masters and mistresses and deferred to all others of superior status. But Rowlandson had no intention of remaining a lowly servant, much less a "slave," to "savages." During the twelfth remove, after she complained about the weight of her load and Weetamoo slapped her, Rowlandson remarks on her captors'

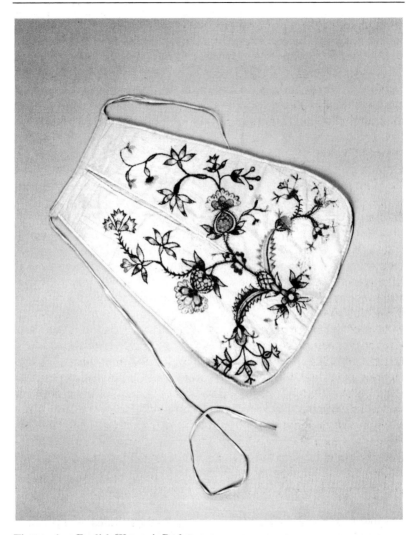

Figure 4.   *English Woman's Pocket*
This handmade pocket is the kind that Mary Rowlandson wore. During her captivity, it enabled Rowlandson to carry and conceal personal possessions.
Courtesy of Strawberry Banke, Portsmouth, New Hampshire.

"insolency," as if they were defying her authority rather than the other way around. Indeed, it is the Indians' treatment of the English more than the customs they observe themselves that Rowlandson finds especially repulsive. For example, she notes straightforwardly that Quinnapin had

Figure 5. *Puritan Minister with Pocket Bible*

Besides large family bibles, many Puritan men and women had small bibles that fit in their pockets. Mary Rowlandson obtained one during her captivity that was a source of emotional and religious sustenance. The minister in this print is Richard Mather, father of Increase.

AC6.Ad198.Zz683t no.5, Houghton Library, Harvard University.

three wives, and even describes two ceremonial dances in a tone that is more condescending than contemptuous. For Rowlandson, it was the fact of her captivity and subordination rather than indigenous culture as such that inverted the proper order of things.

In actuality Rowlandson was not a servant in the English sense but was instead an adopted member of Quinnapin's household with a highly ambiguous status. Well before Europeans arrived, Native Americans in northeastern North America were forcibly seizing captives from one another for a variety of reasons. How such captives were treated depended on several factors: their usefulness, their comportment, and their captors' needs and dispositions. They faced a variety of possible outcomes. Captives might become full, beloved members of their adopted families, remain in subservient positions, be given or traded to other households, be held as hostages to be ransomed or exchanged for opponents' captives or gifts from opponents, be killed instantly, or—in relatively rare instances—be tortured and executed.[64] These traditional practices had been modified as the scale and political complexity of warfare escalated in the face of colonization.

Rowlandson's narrative indicates that the Native Americans who captured English settlers during King Philip's War tried to keep most of them alive, slaying only those whose condition impeded their movements or who tried to escape. Quinnapin's and Metacom's kind treatment of Rowlandson undoubtedly arose in part from a recognition of her status among colonists and her value—political more than economic—as a hostage. For her part Rowlandson shrewdly seized on her status and reputation among the English to enhance her position in her new community.

Rowlandson's consciousness of status and rank comes through most vividly in her depiction of Weetamoo. In her resentment of this "mistress," we can sense "Mistress Rowlandson," the woman accustomed to deference from all the goodwives and other women of Lancaster. In her description, Rowlandson makes no allusion to Weetamoo's position as a political leader. In the nineteenth remove, Rowlandson describes a "severe and proud" Weetamoo whose attention to her personal appearance is vain and obsessive rather than the concern of one whose ceremonial dress and body decoration mark her political position. Rowlandson further attempts to diminish Weetamoo's stature by stating that, after all her preparation, the Pocasset saunkskwa went to "work," making "girdles of wampum and beads," as though Weetamoo herself were little more than a servant. But the actual labor of drilling the wampum shells had already been performed by Indians near the shores where the shells were found in abundance. (Weetamoo is undoubtedly making the belts she will wear in the ceremony described in the twentieth remove.) In her evident contempt, Rowlandson betrays her rivalry with the most prominent woman in her new community.

During her captivity, then, Rowlandson was neither the entirely unreconstructed English Puritan nor the "white Indian" who, like some later captives, completely forsook her original identity.[65] Not only did she learn how to function in her captors' society, but she also learned to live as they did, subsisting on minuscule portions of ground nuts, horses' hooves, and other food that she would formerly have found inedible. (She acknowledges only indirectly that her captors were also starving under such extraordinary circumstances.) Yet however much she might have lived like an Indian, Rowlandson's sense of her own identity was either too secure or too rigid to permit her to become one. It is noteworthy that when her sense of who she was momentarily weakened,

Figure 6:   *Wampum Headband or "Crown"*
A contemporary wampum belt woven of whelk and quahog shell beads
by Wampanoag artist Elizabeth James-Perry. The belt is based on
seventeenth-century headbands worn by Wampanoags and Narragansetts.
Photo: Elizabeth James-Perry.

she became less like an actual Native than like the "savages" that she and other colonial authors constructed in their writings. Rowlandson's most remarkable lapse from "civilization" occurs during the eighteenth remove when, ravenous after eating her own measly portion of horse feet, she grabs another from the mouth of a starving child—not a Native but an English child—and quickly devours it. More generally, Rowlandson depicts herself with none of the generosity she frequently ascribes to individual Native Americans.

Redemption

The severe shortage of food described by Rowlandson had prompted Native Americans' attacks on Lancaster and other towns in late winter 1676. The success of these attacks momentarily masked the forces threatening her captors. Having driven Philip's party from Schaghticoke in January, the Mohawks were now a serious military threat from the west. Moreover, the Indians' triumphant destruction of Sudbury came with unusually heavy casualties at the hands of English troops aided, for the first time, by friendly Indian fighters. It was then that the Natives also learned that English troops to the south had captured and executed an inspirational Narragansett sachem and warrior, Canonchet.[66] In this situation, Rowlandson's captors realized that they had one of two choices if they hoped to survive. They could remain north of the Baquag River, try to find enough arable land and seed corn to grow crops sufficient to sustain their large numbers, and hope that English troops would continue to regard the Baquag as a boundary they would not cross. Or they could return south, resume attacking English settlements for enough food until they could once again plant in their own fields and gather for spring fish runs. Choosing the latter course, the Nipmucs, Narragansetts, and Wampanoags headed toward their respective homelands. In early April, Rowlandson and a party of Nipmucs crossed back over the Baquag River, first to Menimeset and then to Mt. Wachusett, near the abandoned towns of Nashaway and Lancaster. There Shoshanim and other sachems prepared to begin negotiations with Massachusetts officials for a peace that would include the release of Rowlandson and other English captives.

On the colonists' side, it had become clear that pro-English Native Americans would be the key to securing the release of the captives. But even after the anti-English Indians had recrossed the Baquag, most potential go-betweens were still struggling to survive on Deer Island as prisoners of their supposed Christian allies. On one occasion after

Rowlandson's capture, Daniel Gookin had gone to the island at Joseph Rowlandson's behest to seek volunteers willing to carry a message to the captors of his family and others from Lancaster. It is hardly surprising that, given the colonists' treatment of them and the prospect of death or enslavement should they be seized while serving the English, none of the imprisoned Native Americans immediately stepped forward. But in late March, Gookin heard that a Deer Island prisoner, Tom Dublet (or Nepanet) "had some inclination to run that adventure" to Mt. Wachusett. Dublet carried the letter that opened negotiations between Massachusetts and the anti-English Nipmucs (Document 8).[67]

While the anti-English Nipmuc sachems could not write their own letters, there were men in their ranks who could write for them. These scribes had become literate in English while attending Christian Indian schools. While embracing much in the religion and culture of the English, they joined the anti-English cause either when the war broke out or as an alternative to confinement at Deer Island. One of these scribes was Peter Jethro, whose father Gookin had unsuccessfully urged Nashaway to accept as its Christian minister two years earlier. Another was James Printer, one of the most extraordinary presences among the anti-English Indians. At the outbreak of war, Printer had left the press in Cambridge for his home and family in the Nipmuc praying town of Hassanamesit. Falsely accused along with ten other Christian Nipmucs of participating in the earlier (August 1675) raid on Lancaster, he narrowly escaped death at the hands of an English lynch mob. Three months later, anti-English Indians attacked Hassanamesit and gave the outnumbered Christian Indians the choice of accompanying them to their encampment or remaining and having their corn stores burned. Knowing that if they left their village in search of food, they would almost certainly be seized by the English and sent to Deer Island or worse, Printer and the other Hassanamesit Nipmucs accompanied their captors.[68]

Despite the Nipmucs' participation, negotiations proceeded slowly at first. In the sachems' first reply to the English, they and Peter Jethro reminded the English of their many losses and the fact that the colonists now "on your backside stand" (Document 9). In responding to this message, the English focused on redeeming Mary Rowlandson. At this point the Indians turned to Rowlandson and insisted that she set her own price. After some hesitation, she suggested twenty pounds. Writing for the sachems, James Printer demanded not only the ransom but also that Joseph Rowlandson come personally for his wife (Document 10). The English instead dispatched John Hoar, a lawyer and prominent advocate and protector of Christian Indians, whom they probably trusted to be a more effective, less emotionally invested negotiator. The sachems were satisfied to deal with someone who was so highly regarded by their Christian counterparts (Document 11). Nevertheless, it took three agonizing days, until May 2, 1676, for Rowlandson to be released from captivity in Hoar's care.[69]

A freed Mary Rowlandson spent her first night near abandoned Lancaster and on the following day was reunited with her husband. As she relates, they spent eleven weeks in the home of another minister and his family in Charlestown. They then moved to a house in Boston, the rent for which was paid by a local congregation. By late June, their two surviving children, as well as most of the other captives, had also been freed.

War's Terrifying End

Instead of the peace that Native Americans hoped for once the captives were released, they confronted a vengeful English determination to crush all vestiges of indigenous resistance to colonization. After returning to the vicinity of Pokanoket, Metacom was shot and killed by Alderman, a former Pocasset follower of Weetamoo. Alderman was one of Wampanoags who had been recruited by Benjamin Church, one of New England's most effective military officers, to fight against their own people. Church authorized his English and Indian fighters to decapitate, draw, and quarter Metacom's body. After presenting Alderman with one of his hands, Church's men carried the sachem's head to the colony capital. Five days later, Plymouth held a day of thanksgiving in front of Metacom's head, which remained posted for several decades.[70] Weetamoo likewise returned to the Plymouth area. While most authors ever since have stated that English soldiers found her drowned body in a river, Lisa Brooks draws on overlooked evidence to argue that such accounts may well conceal a different scenario, one in which English troops captured, perhaps raped, and killed Weetamoo. To the distress of other Indian prisoners, her body was decapitated and displayed without the head in nearby Taunton.[71] Quinnapin was captured and tried by a Rhode Island court that sentenced him to death. One of his judges was John Easton, who had listened to Philip's grievances little more than a year before (see Document 2).[72]

The Nipmucs who returned the English captives as part of making peace, suddenly found that Massachusetts was equally intent on punishing them and other formerly hostile Native Americans in the colony. Even Christian Indians who had returned peacefully to the colony were executed upon the word of anyone who impugned their loyalty. One of the most contested cases centered on Captain Tom, or Wuttasacomponom, a Christian Nipmuc whom some English soldiers claimed they recognized among the Indians at the battle of Sudbury. Although leading Christian Indian allies of the colony as well as John Eliot defended him, Captain Tom was executed (Documents 12 and 13).[73] Meanwhile other Nipmucs, in a desperate quest for food, scattered to their planting fields and fishing grounds. Once dispersed, they were more vulnerable to English attacks than when they had been at Mt. Wachusett and other mass encampments. Colonial troops and their Native allies set about attacking Nipmuc camps and villages, killing or enslaving whomever they could. Most Nipmucs and many other former anti-English Indians wanted peace with the English but feared that if they surrendered the English would execute or enslave them. Women and children, even of peacefully inclined sachems, were especially vulnerable to capture. In this context, Shoshanim and three other Nipmuc sachems petitioned Massachusetts' governor and council, pleading for the release of one sachem's wife and reiterating their earlier offers of peace (Document 14). Their pleas were in vain; colonial troops seized most of the sachems and other prominent Nipmucs—Shoshanim, Monoco, Peter Jethro, and even the latter's father, Jethro, designated by Gookin two years earlier to be Nashaway's preacher—who were quickly found guilty and hanged to great public fanfare.[74]

James Printer, however, was spared. He had left the Nipmuc sachems before they were captured and then took advantage of the Council's limited opening to any Native Americans who were not accused of murdering settlers and who could demonstrate their loyalty to the English (see the final paragraph of Document 13). On July 2, he arrived at Cambridge with about a dozen relatives and the heads of two Indians. The colony then allowed him to go out and retrieve more Christian Indians who sought English protection but feared being killed or enslaved.[75] Within weeks, Printer returned to his employer and resumed printing books and tracts for the New England reading public.

Most indigenous male captives who were not killed, along with the wives and children of both executed and enslaved men, were sold to slave traders who carried them to the West Indies, Bermuda, Virginia, Spain, Portugal, North Africa and, most likely, other destinations that were never documented. Many were Christian men, women, and children who had never resisted the colonists.[76] Most captives taken to the English colonies of Barbados and Jamaica, where thousands of enslaved Africans already labored on prosperous sugar plantations under brutal conditions. Africans on Barbados had recently attempted to overthrow their masters, who brutally suppressed the uprising. As the colony's assembly, dominated by wealthy planters, tightened legal controls over Africans in 1676, it simultaneously passed a law to prohibit the importation of enslaved Indians from New England and calling for the expulsion of those who had already arrived. The legislators feared that the combination of rebellious Algonquians and rebellious Africans would lead to the overthrow of English rule. Jamaica's assembly passed a similar law in December 1676, though without mandating the return of those Algonquians already there.[77] Despite the laws, most Indians in Barbados were not returned to New England, where they remained unwelcome. Instead they were probably shipped elsewhere or remained in Barbados without being noticed.

The forced removal of indigenous captives to the Caribbean enhanced New England's participation in the transatlantic slave trade and brought it, among other profits, increased numbers of enslaved Africans. Through a variety of means, hundreds of Native men, women, and children who remained in the colonies became servants or slaves under English masters (Documents 15 and 16).[78]

REORDERING AND REMEMBERING

The Rowlandsons finally ended their dependence on the charity of other colonists in the spring of 1677 when Joseph accepted an offer to become the minister at Wethersfield, Connecticut. Capitalizing on Mary's fame, he was able to command a starting annual salary of one hundred pounds with annual twenty-pound increments over the ensuing five years, making him one of the highest paid clergymen in New England. When he died a year and a half later, his library of books—all of which he had acquired after the destruction of his home in Lancaster—was worth eighty-two pounds.[79]

Postwar Diasporas

Like the Rowlandsons, most other characters, both Native American and English, who figured in the events surrounding Mary's captivity did not return to their prewar homes. But unlike the Rowlandsons, they found few comforts. Those who survived dispersed in many directions, often far from southern New England.

Many Algonquians, particularly those who had fought against the English, removed themselves from the southern colonies to avoid being killed or enslaved. From a distance, they continued what became an expansion of King Philip's War. Some moved to eastern New York, where the colony tried, with little success, to prevent them from taking up arms against the New Englanders. Far more Nipmucs, Narragansetts, Pocumtucks, and others joined Abenaki communities, both in upper New England and at Catholic praying towns established by French missionaries in Canada. While attempting to cultivate friendship with both imperial powers, most Abenakis leaned toward the French who likewise sought to roll back New England's northward expansion.[80]

Native Americans who remained in southern New England and avoided slavery or indentured servitude were nevertheless subordinated to colonists and vulnerable to abuse. Most Native men worked either as day laborers for colonists or as scouts for English troops fighting Indians in the north (including recently departed people from their own region). Their closely monitored communities in Massachusetts lay on English-owned land or in Natick, Wamesit, Punkapoag, and Hassanamesit, the only praying towns of the earlier fourteen to be reopened (Document 17). When Massachusetts failed to honor terms of its postwar treaty with the Iroquois, Mohawks resumed their attacks on Algonquians the colony had sworn to protect.[81] In the face of such challenges, indigenous communities sought to retain or, if displaced, regain control over homelands through lawsuits or simple reoccupation. In this way, the Nipmucs maintained a presence in eastern and central Massachusetts that persists to this day despite repeated claims that they have "disappeared."[82]

Whereas the Rowlandsons cut their ties to Lancaster and moved to Wethersfield, most of their former neighbors lacked the options Joseph's occupation provided. Only in 1680 did Massachusetts authorities allow some to resettle their lands in Lancaster. Thereafter the returnees struggled with poverty while the threat of Indian attacks led them, once again, to gather in garrisoned houses. During the international Nine Years' War (1689–1697) and the War of the Spanish Succession (1702–1713), French-allied Indians attacked Lancaster five times, taking yet more captives. But Lancaster was better prepared than in King Philip's War to withstand these attacks. The Glorious Revolution in England (1688–1689) had reorganized the empire and effectively subordinated Puritan Massachusetts. Subordination to London brought effective military support for the larger-scale wars Lancaster and other towns now faced. When fighting ended in 1711, the town was stronger and more prosperous than at the beginning of King Philip's War. It numbered 458 residents, compared to about 325 in 1675, and had grown to 150 square miles of what had been Nipmuc land.[83] Nashaway was not reoccupied; the nearest Nipmucs were now about twenty miles away at the praying town of Hassanamesit.

Interpreting War and Captivity

The postwar order taking shape in New England, then, was one in which the disparities in numbers and power between Native Americans and English settlers were even greater than before. It was in this setting that colonists engaged in a struggle among themselves over how they would publicly remember and interpret the recent war. By the end of 1677—little more than a year after the war ended in southern New England—more than a dozen accounts and explanations of the conflict had been published in Massachusetts and England, and more were in preparation. To a great extent this outpouring can be ascribed to authors' efforts to cash in on the tastes of a lucrative literary market. But for some writers, the war raised issues that went directly to the heart of New England's collective identity. For Increase Mather, the most powerful and prolific clergyman at the time, the devastation inflicted by Native Americans demonstrated God's anger with the colonists for abandoning the spiritual rigor and piety of New England's founding generation and lapsing into the pursuit of personal, material gratification. Only a thoroughgoing spiritual reformation in which the colonists collectively begged God for forgiveness and changed their ways would lift the threat of Indian attacks.

Another minister, William Hubbard, countered Mather by asserting that the war was caused not by God but by Satan, who unleashed the barbaric "savages" resisting the expansion of "civilization" into the "wilderness." What New England needed, he believed, was not a search for collective sin but unity in the face of a threat by alien others to destroy a vibrant, godly society. Both men were responding to the region's growing absorption into a transatlantic commercial economy and the resulting influx of material goods and of non-Puritan colonists and ideas that did not fit comfortably within the Calvinist vision of the founders. Whereas Mather viewed these developments as frightening, Hubbard welcomed them.[84]

Meanwhile Daniel Gookin, the Massachusetts Superintendent of Indians, had written a very different kind of history. Rather than presenting a comprehensive overview of the war, Gookin set out explicitly to vindicate the praying Indians' loyalty and conduct during the war and to demonstrate the extent to which these pious Christians had been persecuted because of an unyielding hatred of all Native Americans on the part of many colonists. Gookin knew that he would have a hard time finding a publisher and readers in New England's hostile environment, so he sent it in 1677 to the mission's supporters in London in hopes of having it published there. His hopes were not realized; the manuscript remained unpublished until 1836.[85] In their different interpretations of the war, Mather, Hubbard, and Gookin were attempting not simply to inform their readers but to influence current debates among the colonists over what kind of society New England was and should be, who was part of it and who was not, and—by implication—to suggest where the locus of political and moral authority should lie.

As these debates unfolded, Mary Rowlandson was preparing her own interpretation of the war and its meanings. Although the circumstances under which Rowlandson began composing her narrative are not made explicit in any surviving evidence, she probably began working on it soon after she returned to English society. If we look to the narrative itself for clues, we find that Rowlandson refers to her family's stay in Boston in the past tense, suggesting that it was written after about May 1677. And the narrative implies that Joseph Rowlandson was still living, which would place its composition before November 1678. While such implicit dating could well be an artifice deliberately constructed to make it appear that the narrative was authored at this time, the emotional and sensory power of her writing—unmatched by Mather or any other author of the time—suggests that her experiences were still fresh in her mind when she wrote them down. Indeed several scholars have argued that Rowlandson penned her narrative soon after her release for therapeutic reasons, in order to gain the distance she needed to recover from, and reframe, her trauma.[86] Increase Mather reinforces this contention in his preface to the published narrative, characterizing it as a "memorandum of Gods dealing with her, that she might never forget, but remember the same . . . all the days of her life."

Rowlandson's manuscript initially circulated for several years among private hands at a time when Mather was soliciting accounts of the workings of divine providence in shaping human lives and events. As early as 1670, he had begun collecting examples to present in his sermons. At the same time, he led the way among New England ministers in using the press to publish his sermons and other writings, thereby spreading his fame and his ideas far beyond those who heard him in person. In 1674 Mather engineered the establishment of the first printing house in Boston, breaking the long monopoly held by Cambridge (where the publications in Algonquian and English had originated) across the Charles River.[87] He probably heard about Rowlandson's narrative through her husband, Joseph, and recognized its potential appeal to readers.[88]

Despite the preface's protests on behalf of Rowlandson's modesty, the narrative itself makes clear that she intended to participate in the debates among those who were interpreting the war's history in print. In understanding the war and her captivity as manifestations of divine providence, Rowlandson aligned herself with Mather's viewpoint as opposed to Hubbard's. In doing so, she not only derives numerous spiritual lessons for herself, she asserts that the English cause itself was dependent on God's favor. Thus of the five "remarkable passages of providence" she enumerates during the final remove, three were military failures by the English army. Rowlandson also cites divine providence to explain the humanity showed her by individual Indians, while at the same time embracing Hubbard's racialized contempt for Native Americans in general.

Rowlandson parted company with Mather and Hubbard on one critical point: the treatment of Christian Native Americans. Both men noted praying Indians' loyalty and contributions to the English cause, and Mather included mistreatment of them as one of New England's sins. Rowlandson, on the other hand, reserves her greatest contempt for Christian Indians. For this reason it would seem that, of all contemporary authors, her primary target was Gookin. Rowlandson counters Gookin with examples of praying Indians mocking, fighting against, and killing colonists—and in some cases going unpunished. She saw one of her tormentors, she writes, "walking up and down Boston, under the appearance of a Friend-Indian, and several others of the like cut." Moreover, she uncritically repeats fraudulent accounts of praying Indian behavior. At the end of the first remove, for example, she blames Printer and the other Christian Nipmucs accused in the earlier attack on Lancaster, ignoring the fact that they were exonerated in court.[89] Yet as in her other statements about Indians, she speaks in strikingly different tones when referring to individual Christians whose actions benefited her. "Though they were Indians," she writes when Tom Dublet and Peter Conway arrived to effect her release, "I got them by the hand, and burst out into tears; my heart was so full I could not [at first] speak to them."

There are suggestions in her narrative and elsewhere that Rowlandson also wrote to clear her name with respect to rumors and innuendoes circulating among colonists. Shortly after her capture, Nathaniel Saltonstall, a prolific chronicler of the war, took pains in one of his reports to dispel a rumor that Rowlandson had been forced to marry Monoco, the Nashaway Nipmuc known to the English as One-eyed John.[90] In his preface to the narrative, Mather implicitly repudiates any suggestion that Rowlandson's virtue had been violated, noting the "coy phantasies" that some may entertain wrongly about her captivity, and the "anxieties and perplexities" attending her experience. Rowlandson herself remarks, during the ninth remove, that no Indian offered her "the least imaginable miscarriage," and notes, during the twentieth, that on the one occasion she saw an Indian drunk, it was her master, Quinnapin, who treated her properly even while chasing two of his wives. Although never expressed directly, some colonists apparently accused Rowlandson of glorying too much in her victimhood, for near the conclusion of the narrative, she notes that "some are ready to say, I speak it [her experience] for my own credit; but I speak it in the presence of God, and to His glory." There may also have been resentment over Rowlandson being elevated publicly above the other captives, especially near the end when she was the focus of English efforts at redemption and was in fact the first to be freed.

Rowlandson was not the only New England colonist writing a captivity narrative. Although she and most other New England captives had been held by Native Americans, some had been captured by other non-European Christians — Muslims from the North African regencies of the Ottoman (Turkish) empire and the independent kingdom of Morocco. One of these was Joshua Gee, a Boston seaman who recorded his experiences while a captive of various Muslim "masters" between 1680 and 1687. Gee's captivity grew out of a longstanding maritime rivalry in which Christians and Muslims, sailing on the Mediterranean Sea, attacked and (when successful) seized one another's ships, crews, and cargo. Sailors on each side who were captured alive were generally put to work as laborers aboard ships or on land. Muslim captivity narratives written by Englishmen had begun appearing in the 1560s. These narratives differed from Rowlandson's in part because they grew out of an ongoing religious-imperial conflict rather than a sudden war with familiar enemies. Even more important, most captives and captors in Muslim narratives were men; Muslim women figured only in a few narratives. Nevertheless most Muslim narratives paralleled Rowlandson's in condemning their captors' religion and culture while crediting divine providence for their own survival. New England readers were familiar with Muslim narratives, and they helped to shape how Mather, and probably Rowlandson, interpreted captivity. At least several dozen New England mariners had been captured over the preceding half-century, but Gee was the first to write a narrative. However, his account departs from all the others in not condemning all his captors on the basis of their religion or ancestry; instead he distinguishes among them by the extent to which they, as individuals, display humanity and tolerance (Document 18). In this respect, Gee exemplifies a tradition of Puritan tolerance that was always contending with the clerical establishment in Massachusetts. Gee was initially acclaimed upon his return to Boston, but once his manuscript began to circulate, it was ignored by most influential colonists. As with Gookin and unlike with Rowlandson, no one encouraged Gee to publish his narrative.[91]

Publicizing Captivity

By the time Rowlandson's narrative was published, she was no longer "Mary Rowlandson." Her life had taken another abrupt, shocking turn when, in November 1678, her husband, Joseph, died suddenly at the age of forty-seven. Soon thereafter the Wethersfield town meeting voted that she should receive Joseph's current compensation of 120 pounds for the rest of that year and thereafter a stipend of 30 pounds annually "so long as she shall remain a widow among us."[92] Like most other widows in the English colonies, she did not remain one for long. Nine months later she married Samuel Talcott, also of Wethersfield, whose own wife had recently died. Talcott was a wealthy, Harvard-educated landowner who represented Wethersfield in Connecticut's General Court and, during King Philip's War, sat on the colony's war council. Like Joseph Rowlandson, Samuel Talcott was addressed as "Mister."[93] Thus Mistress Mary Rowlandson was now Mistress Mary Talcott. But her fame derived entirely from her earlier name, so she retained it as what we would call a "pen name" for her published narrative.

Increase Mather was instrumental in moving Rowlandson's narrative toward publication. In 1681, Samuel Green Jr., a Boston printer, published an edition of English author John Bunyan's *The Pilgrim's Progress*, a fictionalized account of one Puritan's spiritual journey to redemption that had many thematic parallels with Rowlandson's account. On the last page, Green advertised two forthcoming publications, including a pair of sermons, one of which was by Mather, and Mary Rowlandson's narrative.[94]

Green's advertisement implied that Rowlandson's tract would appear by itself, but it actually arrived as part of a larger package. The packaging offers some important clues about the anxieties surrounding the publishing of a female author in colonial New England. It had been only four years since the first woman author, poet Anne Bradstreet, had been published in New England—forty years after she began writing and twenty years after some of her work was published in London.[95] In Rowlandson's case, her tract was bound with the final sermon preached by her previous husband, Joseph Rowlandson, before his death in 1678 (Figure 7). To be sure, Joseph's sermon was entirely compatible with Mary's narrative. Entitled *The Possibility of God's Forsaking a People that have been Visibly Near and Dear to him, together with the Misery of a People thus Forsaken*, the sermon was a standard jeremiad[96] in which Rowlandson cited the Old Testament to show precedents for God's being angry with his chosen people. Like the ancient Israelites, he maintained, New Englanders were guilty of pride, ingratitude toward God, and a litany of other sins betraying their spiritual complacency. His final words echoed a theme that his wife's experience may have driven home with particular intensity: "Forsake your sins whereby you have forsaken him. . . . If there be any, Son or Daughter, that will not leave their sins for God, God will leave such."[97] In general, the sermon is a long theological footnote to the narrative that is in no way distinctive in either its ideas or its prose. Still, it reinforced Mather's war with those who opposed his insistence on spiritual reformation. But while final sermons by well-known New England ministers were often published posthumously, Joseph Rowlandson's fame derived from that of his remarried widow, and his sermon was hardly the main attraction in this package. Not only did Green not mention the sermon in his advance advertising, he placed it *after* the narrative in the bound volume. There is little reason to suppose that anyone would have bothered to publish Joseph's sermon were it not for his wife and her narrative (Figure 8).

But if Joseph Rowlandson could not appear in print without Mary, neither could she stand alone without him and without Increase Mather's preface. The preface begins by situating the attack on Lancaster in the context of the war's military history and goes on to mention Joseph Rowlandson before referring in any way to Mary. And when Mary finally does become the center of discussion, the preface never directly names her but refers to her sometimes as Joseph's "precious yokefellow" and

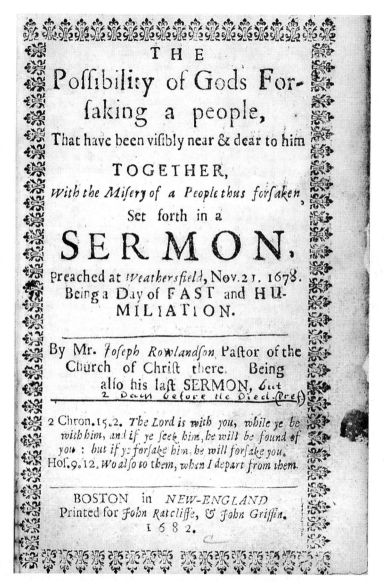

THE
Poſſibility of Gods For-
ſaking a people,
That have been viſibly near & dear to him

TOGETHER,
With the Miſery of a People thus forſaken,
Set forth in a
SERMON.
Preached at *Weathersfield*, Nov. 21. 1678.
Being a Day of FAST and HU-
MILIATION.

By Mr. *Joſeph Rowlandſon* Paſtor of the
Church of Chriſt there.   Being
alſo his laſt SERMON, *but*
2 Days before he Died. (Pref)

2 Chron. 15. 2. *The Lord is with you, while ye be*
with him, and if ye ſeek him, he will be found of
you : but if ye forſake him, he will forſake you.
Hoſ. 9. 12. *Wo alſo to them, when I depart from them.*

BOSTON in *NEW-ENGLAND*
Printed for *John Ratcliffe*, & *John Griffin*.
1 6 8 2.

Figure 7.   *Title page, Joseph Rowlandson's Final Sermon, 1682*
The sermon was published as an appendix to Mary Rowlandson's captivity
narrative. It appeared five years after his death and three years after Mary had
married Samuel Talcott. As with the narrative, it was set and printed by James
Printer.

A
NARRATIVE
OF THE

CAPTIVITY, SUFFERINGS AND REMOVES

O F

Mrs. *Mary Rowlandson,*

‘Who was taken Prifoner by the INDIANS with feveral others, and treated in the moft barbarous and cruel Manner by thofe vile Savages : With many other remarkable Events during her TRAVELS.

Written by her own Hand, for her private Ufe, and now made public at the earneft Defire of fome Friends, and for the Benefit of the afflicted.

B O S T O N :

Printed and Sold at JOHN BOYLE's Printing-Office, next Door to the *Three Doves* in Marlborough Street.

Figure 8. *Title page, 1773 Edition of Rowlandson's Narrative*

This image, like those in Document 20 and other editions published during the 1770s, depicts an armed Rowlandson resisting British and Native American forces.

Courtesy of the American Antiquarian Society, Worcester, Massachusetts.

"dear consort," but mostly as "Gentlewoman." Mather seems to have hoped that an emphasis on Rowlandson's marital status and social rank and an avoidance of her individuality would in some measure obviate the fact of her gender. At the same time, Mather is at pains to assure readers that the "Narrative was penned by the Gentlewoman herself" and published in spite of her "modesty." In this way, he strives to overcome the doubts of those who believed a woman incapable of writing on her own, who feared that the act of writing would somehow detract from a woman's femininity, or who assumed that a woman could not have survived captivity without compromising her marital fidelity or her cultural identity. (While most colonists feared otherwise, there is no evidence anywhere in eastern North America of sexual violence against captives by Native Americans.) Mather expresses the hope that "none will cast any reflection upon this Gentlewoman, on the score of this publication of her affliction and deliverance." She has a "dispensation of public note, and universal concernment," he says, which is the stronger for her being married to a minister. She is fulfilling a vow to praise God publicly: "Excuse her, then, if she comes thus into public, to pay those vows, Come and hear what she has to say."

Mather's preface is an elaborate effort to legitimize Rowlandson's appearance not simply as a female author but also as a woman offering her direct, unique perspectives on the experience of God's grace in her own life. In a society that had not, after nearly half a century, forgotten the threat posed by Anne Hutchinson's claims to spiritual authority independent of the clergy, Mather understood the need to frame Rowlandson's narrative by emphasizing that its author was a woman whose orthodoxy could not be challenged. Popular expectations surrounding her narrative, anticipated in Green's advertisement, made clear that Rowlandson was going to have a following no matter what form her narrative took. The goal of the preface was simultaneously to emphasize the narrative's theological significance and to reassure advocates of reform that Rowlandson was in agreement with them. The presence of Joseph Rowlandson's sermon—whether or not anyone read it—was a further attempt to signal that Mary's act of writing and publishing took place within and not outside conventional boundaries of theology and gender as established in the United Colonies of New England.

Rowlandson herself provides ample guidance for gleaning her narrative's theological message. The most obvious way she does this is through frequent citations of biblical passages as demonstrating the meaning of her experience or state of mind on a given occasion. Some commentators have pointed to such references as evidence that Mather was the narrative's actual author and that he merely used Rowlandson to advance his own agenda. There is no reason to doubt that Mather and others read the manuscript and made suggestions that its author incorporated, as is the case with most published works. But as the daughter of a woman who converted to Puritanism independently of her husband and as the wife of a minister, Rowlandson was sufficiently steeped in the Bible and in Puritan interpretations of it to draw such conclusions on her own.

In fact Rowlandson does more than cite scripture to establish herself as an authority on spiritual matters. The entire narrative serves to remind her readers that, as indicated in Mather's preface, she has experienced the extremes of terror and redemption as few other mortals have. She summarizes this experience and its meaning in an eloquent passage near the end of the narrative, after she and her family have found refuge and security in the Boston home of James Whitcomb:

> *I can remember the time, when I used to sleep quietly without workings in my thoughts, whole nights together, but now it is other wayes with me.* When all are fast about me, and no eye open, but his who ever waketh, my thoughts are upon things past, upon the awful dispensation of the Lord towards us; upon his wonderful power and might, in carrying of us through so many difficulties, in returning us to safety, and suffering none to hurt us.

And further on:

> *Before I knew what affliction meant, I was ready sometimes to wish for it.* . . . . But now I see the Lord had his time to scourge and chasten me. . . . Affliction I wanted, and affliction I had, full measure; . . . yet I see, when God calls a person to any thing, and through never so many difficulties, yet he is fully able to carry them through and make them see, and say they have been gainers thereby.

In such passages, Rowlandson crosses the line from saying that she experienced God's grace through divine providence to suggesting that God spoke directly to her, without the mediation of a male minister. While a man's testimony of such an experience might have escaped notice, a woman's was highly problematic. Recall that Rowlandson's mother, forty years earlier, was an exception among women who could voice such experiences, and then only within the confines of her congregation. All that stands between Rowlandson and the direct revelation from God that sealed Anne Hutchinson's fate is the mantle of clerical authority provided by her husband's sermon and Mather's preface.[98]

Protected by that authority, Rowlandson goes beyond strictly reporting her private, spiritual experience and enters the all-male realm of public discourse. She joins Mather, Joseph Rowlandson, and other jeremiad preachers by castigating those who concern themselves with worldly goods and pleasures at the expense of concern over their own and New England's spiritual fate. Rowlandson goes still further when she criticizes Massachusetts's conduct of the war. Although ascribing to God's providence such failures as the army's refusal to pursue her captors across the Baquag River, her very mention of these failures is a thinly veiled criticism of the army. It also indicts Massachusetts political officials whose priorities, she suggests, placed settlers (like her and her Lancaster neighbors) in harm's way.

Even more bold is Rowlandson's condemnation of Christian Indians. Here she takes on the entire missionary enterprise in New England and in so doing defies virtually the entire clerical and political elite in New England, including Mather. In a radical departure from Puritan orthodoxy, she says in effect that some groups of people have no potential for being saved because their lack of humanity means they have no souls. In so suggesting, Rowlandson contributes to a growing shift in the way Anglo-Americans distinguished Europeans from alien "others," from a basis in religion and culture to one that is biological and would, in the nineteenth century, be called "race." In short, Rowlandson uses her position as a clerically approved author to pronounce judgments on some fundamental political and intellectual questions, ranging well beyond where any other female writer in the seventeenth-century colonies was permitted to go.

Although Rowlandson was the first woman to publish such views, militant, Indian-hating white women were already becoming a political force in New England. In October 1675, Mary Pray of Providence warned a Massachusetts officer that Christian Indian allies were openly betraying the English. Repeating rumors deliberately planted by the Narragansetts to demoralize colonists, she claimed that "they never shoot at the other Indians, but up into the tops of trees or into the ground." She went on to claim that Daniel Gookin "helps them to powder, and they sell it to those that are employed by Philip to buy it for him."[99] Pray contributed importantly to the hysteria that soon led Massachusetts to intern Christian Indians at Deer Island.

Other women went beyond writing to action. As the war continued north of the major Massachusetts settlements in 1677 (and as Rowlandson was beginning to write), anti-English Native Americans were seizing English fishing boats and their crewmen, based at the town of Marblehead. After some fishermen overcame and killed most of their captors, they carried two surviving Indians to Marblehead, intending to turn them over to the authorities. But a crowd of English women seized the prisoners and, according to one of the fishermen, "with stones, billets of wood, and what else they might, they made an end of these Indians." Later, he continued, "we found them with their heads off and gone, and their flesh in a manner pulled from their bones."[100] A subdued Increase Mather worried only that such treatment might lead the Natives to treat their English captives in similar fashion.[101]

Rowlandson goes beyond these women and others in more broadly proclaiming herself an authority on public matters. Yet in asserting her authority so boldly, Rowlandson seems to be trying to quash any lingering doubts among her readers—and perhaps in herself—that she had ever been attracted in any way to life among her captors. While a claim to authority, her nighttime thoughts "upon things past" also suggest a persistent discomfort, as if what Rowlandson knew, what haunted her in the stillness of night, was the realization that her experience among Native Americans—and Native people themselves—could not be fully contained by her narrative, by Puritan theology, even by the Bible. Perhaps her experience had touched her in ways she herself could not fully fathom.

However her readers understood such passages, Rowlandson's published narrative proved to be an instant success. The first edition sold out so quickly that the printer, Samuel Green Jr., already working on several other projects, was unable to answer the demand. He therefore referred the narrative to his father, Samuel Green Sr., a Cambridge printer, who published not only a second but also a third edition in 1682.[102] An authoritative study of American bestsellers, written before evidence of the first Boston edition was discovered, calculates that the second and third editions alone sold more than one thousand copies, meaning that more than 1 percent of the New England population purchased the book. It is clear, not only from the evidence of sales but also from what is known about colonial New England readers, that many people read, or heard read aloud, each copy and that Rowlandson's audience included large numbers of ordinary colonists as well as ministers and other members of the region's elite.[103]

An irony connected with the second and third editions is that Green Sr. had rehired James Printer as his typesetter and printer. Thus the text that made the strongest and most virulent case for Christian Indian disloyalty was literally put together by someone whose own life directly defied the blanket categorization that divided New Englanders into "savage" Indians and "civilized" English. Printer illustrates how, even after King Philip's War, the colonists still depended, in certain crucial ways, on Native Americans who embodied the cultural and political ambiguities prompting Rowlandson's hatred of Christian Natives. Moreover, since all but four pages from one copy of the Boston edition have disappeared, Printer's edition (including Joseph's sermon) is the earliest one we have and, therefore, the one closest to Rowlandson's own writing. Some scholars have maintained that the second edition's unusually large number of spelling "errors" is evidence that its compositor was not fully literate in English. This despite John Eliot's praise of his abilities as early as 1659 (quoted above, p. 21). Also, spelling in seventeenth-century New England was anything but standardized, as can be seen, for example, in the other documents included in this volume. Finally, as literary scholar Billy Stratton has observed, it is absurd to think that Green would have published the narrative without noticing the spelling at least on the cover page, with the first word of the title, *Soveraignty*, and the label "second Addition."[104] Such renderings often appeared because of shortages of type and other limitations and were usually corrected if a revised edition were published. This was the case with the third (second Cambridge) edition that Printer produced a few months later.

Later in 1682, a fourth edition was published in London, but with a different title. The New England editions, aimed at Puritan readers and intended to reinforce calls for spiritual reformation, appeared as *The Soveraignty* (and subsequently *Sovereignty*) *and Goodness of God*. For England's more religiously diverse reading public, it appeared as *A True History of the Captivity and Restoration of Mrs. Mary Rowlandson*. In New England, where Rowlandson's sponsors sought in every way to downplay her personal role as both author and actor and were narrowly concerned with their own region, the subject was God; in England, where readers' interests were more secular and cosmopolitan, the title foregrounded Rowlandson and suggested a more sensationalist and exotic adventure.[105]

Mary Rowlandson's Legacies

Fifteen years after *The Sovereignty and Goodness of God* was published, another English woman captured by Native Americans gained fame that rivaled Rowlandson's. Near the end of the Nine Years War, a party of French-allied Abenakis attacked the Massachusetts town of Haverhill and captured about forty inhabitants. The fleeing Indians then broke up into several smaller bands, one of which held an English woman named Hannah Dustin, her newborn child's nurse, and six other children, including a twelve-year-old boy. Unlike Rowlandson, Dustin concocted a plan to escape. One night she, the boy, and the nurse arose, quietly and methodically killed and scalped ten of their captors' party (a woman and a small child escaped), and led the captives to safety. A few weeks later, a scalp-bearing Dustin entered Boston to great acclaim and successfully petitioned the General Court for scalp bounties for herself, her nurse, and the boy. She received not only her allocation, but many gifts as well as literary immortality when Cotton Mather, son of Increase and by now a prominent minister and author in his own right, recorded her story (Document 19). Like the women at Marblehead, Dustin distinguished herself by killing, rather than merely condemning, Native captors. Mather depicted Dustin's triumph as a Puritan victory even though, in contrast to Rowlandson, Dustin was not a Puritan, for she repeatedly declined to acknowledge God's grace and join a church.[106]

Dustin also visited another prominent Bostonian, Judge Samuel Sewall, who, in recording their meeting in his diary, noted a connection between New England's two best-known captives. Dustin told him that "her Master, whom she killed, did formerly live with Mr. Rowlandson at Lancaster." In this brief statement lies the only explicit evidence of contact between Rowlandson and Native Americans before her capture. Sewall's entry goes on to say that her unnamed captor told Dustin "that when he prayed the English way, he thought that was good; but now he found the French way was better."[107] Apparently the Rowlandsons, like many English families during the seventeenth century, had taken a Christian Indian as a servant into their home, thereby gaining some labor while promoting Christianity and "civilization." The servant was most likely a Nipmuc from nearby Nashaway. Whether or not he fought against the English in King Philip's War—and perhaps in the attack on Lancaster—thereby reinforcing Rowlandson's hostility toward Christian Indians, is not clear. In any case, he was one of many Natives from the southern colonies who had joined with Abenakis to continue their struggle against the English.

Although "Mary Rowlandson," the Lancaster captive, remained widely known in New England, she was actually Mary Talcott, quietly living out her days in Wethersfield, Connecticut, as Samuel Talcott's wife and, after he died in 1691, as his widow. Her one appearance in the historical record as Mary Talcott came late in her life and constituted a strange postscript to her captivity. In 1707 she posted bond following the arrest of her son, Joseph Rowlandson Jr., the pious boy of the narrative who was now a prosperous Wethersfield landowner and merchant. A man claiming to be the long-vanished brother of Rowlandson Jr.'s wife suddenly appeared and charged that, five years earlier, Rowlandson and another brother-in-law had gotten him drunk and sold him as an indentured servant to a shipowner bound for Virginia. The court, perhaps fearing to alienate the Talcott/Rowlandson family, postponed making its decision for thirteen years before finally ruling in favor of Rowlandson's accuser. By then the verdict was moot, for Rowlandson Jr. and his accuser had both died. But the incident brought the theme of forced captivity back into the life of Mary Rowlandson when, as the widow Talcott, her former good name could not dispel the allegations about her son. She too was spared further ignominy, having died in January 1711 at about seventy-three years of age.[108]

Five years after Rowlandson's death, there appeared a new edition of a memoir by Benjamin Church, the Plymouth soldier who had led the crushing of Wampanoag resistance in 1676. As with earlier editions, it was actually written by Church's son, Thomas, who, on this occasion, called the war "King Philip's War," the name that has stuck ever since.[109] The publication aroused interest in the war among a new generation of colonists, an interest that led to publication of a fifth edition of Rowlandson's narrative in 1720.[110]

Rowlandson and King Philip's War became even more popular during the decade preceding the American Revolution. As Britain attempted to subordinate its American colonies to imperial rule, many white colonists idealized past experiences of Indian war and captivity as moments of settler resistance to combined indigenous and British aggression.[111] During the decade before 1776, New England publishers produced eleven Indian captivity narratives. Most were re-issues of earlier editions, including five by Rowlandson. The new editions dropped the original title, with its emphasis on God's providence, and shifted to a secularized and racialized one: *A Narrative of the Captivity, Sufferings, and Removes of Mrs. Mary Rowlandson, Who Was Taken Prisoner By the Indians with Several Others, and Treated in the Most Barbarous and Cruel Manner By these Vile Savages.*[112] At the same time, other publishers put out new editions of Benjamin Church's and William Hubbard's histories of King Philip's War.[113] Some of the Rowlandson editions included illustrations that depict her with a gun, which neither she nor even the Marblehead women and Hannah Dustin had ever used (Document 20). A new edition of Church's narrative featured an engraving of "King Philip," likewise holding a gun (Document 21).

Taken together, the two portraits symbolize the struggle by "patriots," as they called themselves, to establish a new nation with a distinctively white identity.

Rowlandson's narrative has remained almost continually in print in the United States since it gained independence.[114] Well into the twentieth century, it was read primarily by those seeking religious or moral edification or simply a good adventure story. The fact that Rowlandson was a woman enabled readers to see either her vulnerability or her empowerment, or both. The narrative began to draw sustained academic and critical attention in the late twentieth century.

Rowlandson's influence extends beyond the popularity of her own narrative. While narratives of captivity were common before she published, it was she who invented the Anglo-American formula for narrating Indian captivity. Her account gave rise to hundreds of imitators, first from New England, then from other colonial regions and, finally, from throughout the independent American republic. The earliest narratives followed Rowlandson by opening with a dramatic, surprise attack by Native Americans and ending with her or his release. In between, they recounted the captive's travels and experiences, usually stressing the religious and moral meanings of captivity and reinforcing constructions of the sharp divide separating "civilized" from "savage" peoples. Variations on Rowlandson's formula soon developed. New England captives taken northward often interwove captivity among both Native Americans and French Catholics. There were third-person accounts, narrated by someone other than the captive, such as Cotton Mather's account of Hannah Dustin (see Document 19). Others ostensibly conveyed the captive's voice but betrayed the heavy hands of white editors. Narratives often told of captives who, instead of returning home at the end, chose (or had no choice) to remain with and join their captors' societies. Some (mostly men) escaped, and went on to either fight their former captors or serve as bilingual interpreters and negotiators. Some men and women returned but remained openly sympathetic to their former captors and their suffering in the face of Anglo-American expansion. Many narratives introduced elements of fiction or were entirely fictional, heightening the commercial appeal to readers seeking a taste of terror or exoticism. Over time, the captivity theme spread to novels for both adults and children, live theater, and movies.[115] It also spread beyond captivity by Native Americans to include fictional and actual accounts of other kinds of captives such as prisoners of war and hostages held by kidnappers or terrorists, in which captivity has struck closer to home for so many.[116]

Although Rowlandson invented one variation of the captivity narrative, other Europeans and their colonial offspring had established the form and earlier variations well before she wrote. These narratives drew on accounts in English, Spanish, and other languages of Muslim captivity. The first English-language narrative of Native American captivity was John Smith's fictitious tale of his being captured by Powhatans in Virginia in 1609 and saved from execution by the chief's besmitten daughter, Pocahontas. In fact, it was Pocahontas herself who was later captured and taken to England.[117] Before Smith, dozens of narratives set elsewhere in the Americas had been published. One of the earliest was set within the present boundaries of the United States and written by a shipwrecked Spanish explorer, Álvar Núñez Cabeza de Vaca, who published it in 1542.[118] As Lisa Voigt has demonstrated, these narratives—like Rowlandson's—asserted that their authors' experiences inside indigenous communities made them especially authoritative when it came to defining the boundaries of European Christian identities in the "New World." [119]

No matter how sympathetic toward their captors, most captivity narratives written by Europeans are one-sided in juxtaposing Euro-American suffering to Native American aggression, subtly inverting the colonial dispossession of indigenous peoples that was the actual context for captivity. In New England and throughout the Western Hemisphere, European captives were vastly outnumbered by the indigenous captives of Europeans, millions of whom remained enslaved for life.[120] Nabil Matar has discussed and translated Arab-language narratives written by Muslim captives of Europeans, and Catherine M. Cameron has recently surveyed captivity and its significance throughout history and around the world.[121] Nevertheless, the many voices of Native Americans articulating their own captivity experiences remain largely ignored. Even when noticed, the stories of the James Quanapohits, James Printers, and Weetamoos throughout American history are never thought of as "captivity narratives."[122] Yet New England Indians had experienced European captivity throughout the sixteenth century before some English captors began documenting their captivities after 1600.[123] The best known was Tisquantum, or Squanto, a Wampanoag captive of English, Spanish, and, upon returning home, his fellow Wampanoags. Although the Wampanoags released him to the new Plymouth colony in 1621, he quickly regained their distrust, sparking Anglo-Wampanoag tensions that were not resolved until after he died the next year. Well before any colonists had been captured, the captivity and enslavement of Indians were central to the founding of "New England." [124]

Contemporary Native American authors have been the most forceful in repudiating Mary Rowlandson's continued grip on the imaginings of Euro-American readers. They recognize her legacy as an ideological component of the continuing colonization of indigenous people.[125] Spokane–Coeur d'Alene writer Sherman Alexie is perhaps the most direct, linking Rowlandson's righteous victimhood to the captives who live on Indian reservations more than three centuries later. From this vantage point, his counter-narrative dismisses Rowlandson once and for all: "Mary Rowlandson, the water is gone and my cousins are eating Lysol sandwiches. They don't need you, will never search in the ash after your house has burned to the ground one more time. It's over. That's all you can depend on."[126] Alexie challenges us to rethink what Rowlandson and her captivity can mean in the twenty-first century.

NOTES

[1] Sherburne F. Cook, "Interracial Warfare and Population Decline among the New England Indians," *Ethnohistory* 20 (1973): 1–24; U.S. Department of Commerce, Bureau of the Census, *Historical Statistics of the United States, Colonial Times to 1970*, 2 vols. (Washington, D.C.: U.S. Government Printing Office, 1975), 2:1168 (Series Z 1–19); James D. Drake, *King Philip's War: Civil War in New England, 1675–1676* (Amherst: University of Massachusetts Press, 1999), 168–69; Margaret Ellen Newell, *Brethren by Nature: New England Indians, Colonists, and the Origins of American Slavery* (Ithaca, N.Y.: Cornell University Press, 2015), 131–88.

[2] Almira Larkin White, *Genealogy of the Descendants of John White of Wenham and Lancaster, Massachusetts, 1638–1900*, 4 vols. (Haverhill, Mass.: Chase Brothers, 1900–1909), 1:11, 13; 4:11; David L. Greene, "New Light on Mary Rowlandson," *Early American Literature* 20 (1985): 24; Kathryn Zabelle Derounian, "A Note on Mary (White) Rowlandson's English Origins," *Early American Literature* 24 (1989): 70–73; Kathryn Zabelle Derounian and David L. Greene, "Additions and Corrections to 'A Note on Mary (White) Rowlandson's English Origins'," *Early American Literature* 25 (1990): 305–6.

[3] Robert G. Pope, ed., *The Notebook of the Reverend John Fiske, 1644–1675*, Publications of the Colonial Society of Massachusetts, 47 (1974): 30.

[4] Ibid.

[5] White, *Genealogy*, 1:9–10; 4:11.

[6] Pope, *Notebook*, 30–31; Mary Maples Dunn, "Saints and Sisters: Congregational and Quaker Women in the Early Colonial Period," *American Quarterly* 30 (1978): 589.

[7] Mary Beth Norton, *Founding Mothers and Fathers: Gendered Power and the Forming of American Society* (New York: Alfred A. Knopf, 1996), 359–99, esp. 374–88.

[8] Pope, *Notebook*, 13–20 passim.

[9] White, *Genealogy*, 4:11–13, 15–21.

[10] Neal Salisbury, *Manitou and Providence: Indians, Europeans, and the Making of New England, 1500–1643* (New York: Oxford University Press, 1982), 22–30, 101–6, 190–92; David S. Jones, "Virgin Soils Revisited," *William and Mary Quarterly* 60 (2003):

703–42. Quotes from Thomas Morton, *New English Canaan*, ed. Charles Francis Adams (Boston: Prince Society, 1883), 132–33. Golgotha, or Calvary, was the place where Jesus, and many others convicted by Roman authorities, was crucified.

[11] Salisbury, *Manitou and Providence*, 48–49; Lisa Brooks, *The Common Pot: The Recovery of Native Space in the Northeast* (Minneapolis: University of Minnesota Press, 2008), 9–10.

[12] John Underhill, *Newes from America; or, A New and Experimentall Discoverie of New England* (London: Peter Cole, 1638), 26; Patrick M. Malone, *Technology and Tactics among the New England Indians* (Baltimore, Johns Hopkins University Press, 1993), 29–31.

[13] Salisbury, *Manitou and Providence*, 203–25; Underhill, *Newes from America*, 27.

[14] Salisbury, *Manitou and Providence*, 228–35; Eric S. Johnson, "Uncas and the Politics of Contact," in Robert S. Grumet, ed., *Northeastern Indian Lives, 1632–1816* (Amherst: University of Massachusetts Press, 1996), 35–37.

[15] Neal Salisbury, "Toward the Covenant Chain: Iroquois and Southern New England Algonquians, 1637–1684," in Daniel K. Richter and James H. Merrell, eds., *Beyond the Covenant Chain: The Iroquois and Their Neighbors in Indian North America, 1600–1800* (Syracuse, N.Y.: Syracuse University Press, 1987), 62–65; Paul A. Robinson, "Lost Opportunities: Miantonomi and the English in Seventeenth-Century Narragansett Country," in Grumet, ed., *Northeastern Indian Lives*, 23–28; Johnson, "Uncas and the Politics of Conquest, 39–44; Kevin A. McBride, "The Legacy of Robin Cassacinamon: Mashantucket Pequot Leadership in the Historic Period," in Grumet, ed., *Northeastern Indian Lives*, 78–86; Drake, *King Philip's War*, 44–54; David J. Silverman, *Faith and Boundaries: Colonists, Christianity, and Community among the Wampanoag Indians of Martha's Vineyard, 1600–1871* (Cambridge: Cambridge University Press, 2005), 17.

[16] Everett Emerson, ed., *Letters from New England: The Massachusetts Bay Colony, 1629–1639* (Amherst: University of Massachusetts Press, 1976), 68; William Wood, *New England's Prospect* (1634), ed. Alden T. Vaughan (Amherst: University of Massachusetts Press, 1976), 123.

[17] *Mass. Recs.*, 1:327, 2:11; David Jaffe, *People of the Wachusett: Greater New England in History and Memory, 1630–1860* (Ithaca, N.Y.: Cornell University Press, 1999), 34–35.

[18] Henry S. Nourse, ed., *Early Records of Lancaster, Massachusetts, 1643–1725* (Lancaster, 1884), 12–15; Richard S. Dunn, et al, eds., *The Journal of John Winthrop, 1630–1649* (Cambridge, Mass.: Harvard University Press), 504.

[19] *Mass. Recs.*, 2:16; Nourse, *Early Records of Lancaster*, 308–9; Samuel Eliot Morison, "The Plantation of Nashaway—An Industrial Experiment," *Publications of the Colonial Society of Massachusetts* 27 (1932): 209–10, 213; Jaffe, *People of the Wachusett*, 43–44; Philip F. Gura, *A Glimpse of Sion's Glory: Puritan Radicalism in New England, 1620–1660* (Middletown, Conn.: Wesleyan University Press, 1984), 196–204.

[20] *Mass. Recs.*, 2:212.

[21] Nourse, *Early Records of Lancaster*, 17–19; Jaffe, *People of the Wachusett*, 47.

[22] *Mass. Recs.*, 3:365–66.

[23] Ibid., 3:302–4; Nourse, *Early Records of Lancaster*, 22–23; Dunn, ed., *Winthrop Journal*, 710; Jaffe, *People of the Wachusett*, 47–51.

[24] D. Greene, "New Light on Mary Rowlandson," *Early American Literature* 20 (1985): 24.

[25] Thomas Franklin Waters, *Ipswich in the Massachusetts Bay Colony* (Ipswich, Mass.: Ipswich Historical Society, 1899), 1:493; George A. Schofield, ed., *Ancient Records of Ipswich* (Ipswich, Mass.: G.A. Schofield, 1899), vol. 1 entries for 1646–1650, passim;

George Francis Dow, ed., *Records and Files of the Quarterly Courts of Essex County, Massachusetts*, 4 vols. (Salem, Mass.: Essex Institute 1911–1975), 1:37, 109, 112, 142, 143, 147, 168, 221, 233, 261, 275–76, 277, 385, 387.

[26] John L. Sibley, *Biographical Sketches of Graduates of Harvard University*, 3 vols. (Cambridge, Mass.: Charles William Sever, 1873), 1:311–16.

[27] Nourse, *Early Records of Lancaster*, 62.

[28] Ibid., 41; Norton, *Founding Mothers and Fathers*, 18–19.

[29] Nourse, *Early Records of Lancaster*, 41, 46–51 passim, 55–56, 64, 76–77; *Mass. Recs.*, 3:428; Jaffee, *People of the Wachusett*, 52.

[30] Nourse, *Early Records of Lancaster*, 309; Samuel Sewall, *The Diary of Samuel Sewall, 1674–1729*, ed. M. Halsey Thomas, 2 vols. (New York: Farrar, Straus and Giroux, 1973), 1:372–73.

[31] *Mass. Recs.*, 4(2):340; Henry S. Nourse, ed., *Lancastriana*, vol. 1: *A Supplement to the Early Records and Military Annals of Lancaster, Massachusetts* (Lancaster: W.J. Coulter, 1900–1901), 7; Jaffee, *People of the Wachusett*, 54–57.

[32] Robert K. Diebold, "Joseph Rowlandson," in James A. Lavernier and Douglas A. Wilms, eds., *American Writers before 1800*, 3 vols. (Westport, Conn.: Greenwood Press, 1983), 3:1244; *Mass. Recs.*, 4 (2): 556–57.

[33] William Cronon, *Changes in the Land: Indians, Colonists, and the Ecology of New England* (New York: Hill and Wang, 1983), 88–89; Salisbury, "Indians and Colonists after the Pequot War," 91–92; John J. McCusker and Russell R. Menard, *The Economy of British America, 1607–1789* (Chapel Hill, N.C., 1985), 104; Nourse, *Early Records of Lancaster*, 41; Daniel Gookin, "An Historical Account of the Doings and Sufferings of the Christian Indians in New England," *Transactions and Collections of the American Antiquarian Society* 2 (1836): 85.

[34] Cronon, *Changes in the Land*, 128–37; Virginia DeJohn Anderson, *Creatures of Empire: How Domestic Animals Transformed Early America* (New York: Oxford University Press, 2004).

[35] Salisbury, "Toward the Covenant Chain," 65–70; Jaffee, *People of the Wachusett*, 58–59; Drake, *King Philip's War*, 54–56.

[36] Daniel Gookin, *Historical Collections of the Indians in New England*, ed. Jeffrey Fiske (n.p.: Towtaid), 1970, 85.

[37] Jill Lepore, *The Name of War: King Philip's War and the Origins of American Identity* (New York, Alfred A. Knopf, 1998), 34–37 (quote at 34); Lisa Brooks, *Our Beloved Kin: A New History of "King Philip's War"* (New Haven: Yale University Press, 2018), chap. 2.

[38] Jaffee, *People of the Wachusett*, 63–64; Gookin, *Historical Collections*, 85–86.

[39] Drake, *King Philip's War*, 68–74; Lepore, *Name of War*, 21–34, 38–44; Brooks, *Our Beloved Kin*, chap. 3.

[40] Drake, *King Philip's War*, 83–84.

[41] Ibid. 84–85; Nourse, *Early Records of Lancaster*, 352.

[42] Drake, *King Philip's War*, 85–87.

[43] Ibid. 109, 119–20; Brooks, *Our Beloved Kin*, chaps. 4–6 passim.

[44] Malone, *Skulking Way of War*, 29–31, 39–42, 67–77.

[45] Silverman, *Thundersticks*, 96–106; Glenn W. LaFantasie, ed., *The Correspondence of Roger Williams*, 2 vols. (Hanover, N.H.: University Press of New England, 1988), 2:727 n.25.

[46] Gookin, "Historical Account," 433–534; Jenny Hale Pulsipher, *Subjects unto the Same King: Indians, English, and the Contest for Authority in Colonial New England* Philadelphia: University of Pennsylvania Press, 2005), 135–59.

[47] James D. Rice, *Tales from a Revolution: Bacon's Rebellion and the Transformation of Early America* (New York: Oxford University Press, (2012), esp. 36; April L. Hatfield, *Atlantic Virginia: Intercolonial Relations in the Seventeenth Century* (Philadelphia: University of Pennsylvania Press, 2004), 183–84.

[48] Drake, *King Philip's War*, 87–88; Malone, *Skulking Way of War*, 110–12.

[49] Salisbury, "Toward the Covenant Chain," 70–71; Jon Parmenter, *The Edge of the Woods: Iroquoia, 1534-1701* East Lansing: Michigan State University Press, 2010), 149–50.

[50] Gookin, "Historical Account," 488–90; Nourse, *Early Records of Lancaster*, 103–6.

[51] Nourse, *Early Records of Lancaster,* 107, 109.

[52] Sibley, *Biographical Sketches*, 1:319.

[53] Quoted in Edmund S. Morgan, "Light on the Puritans from John Hull's Notebooks," *New England Quarterly* 15 (1942): 96–98.

[54] Gookin, "Historical Account," 492-95; Drake, *King Philip's War*, 123–24.

[55] Ebenezer W. Peirce, *Indian History, Biography, and Genealogy: Pertaining to the Good Sachem Massasoit of the Wampanoag Tribe, and His Descendants* (North Abington, Mass.: Zerviah Gould Mitchell, 1878), 210; Howard Chapin, *Sachems of the Narragansetts* (Providence: Rhode Island Historical Society, 1931), 88.

[56] Peirce, *Indian History, Biography, and Genealogy*, 210.

[57] N[athaniel] S[altonstall], "Present State of New-England," in Charles H. Lincoln, ed., *Narratives of the Indian Wars, 1675–1699* (1913; reprinted New York: Barnes and Noble, 1966), 25.

[58] Laurel Thatcher Ulrich, *Good Wives: Image and Reality in the Lives of Women in Northern New England, 1650–1750* (New York: Alfred A. Knopf, 1982), 36, 232–33; Thomas, ed., *Diary of Samuel Sewall*, 1:372–73.

[59] Ulrich, *Good Wives*.

[60] Ann Marie Plane, *Colonial Intimacies: Indian Marriages in Early New England* (Ithaca, N.Y.: Cornell University Press, 2000), 1–13, 41–105; Kathleen J. Bragdon, *Native People of Southern New England, 1500–1650* (Norman: University of Oklahoma Press, 1996), 175–83; Kathleen J. Bragdon, *Native People of Southern New England, 1650–1775* (Norman: University of Oklahoma Press, 2009), 99–114.

[61] Bragdon, *Native People, 1650–1775*, 177, 196–97.

[62] Ibid,, 107–23.

[63] Ulrich, *Good Wives,* 34.

[64] Pauline Turner Strong, "Transforming Outsiders: Captivity, Adoption, and Slavery Reconsidered." In *A Companion to American Indian History*, ed. Philip J. Deloria and Neal Salisbury, 339–56 (Malden, Mass.: Blackwell, 2002), 343–46.

[65] James Axtell, "The White Indians of Colonial America," *William and Mary Quarterly* 32 (1975): 55–88; Kathryn Zabelle Derounian-Stodola and James Arthur Levernier, *The Indian Captivity Narrative, 1550–1900* (New York: Twayne, 1993), 5–8; Strong, "Transforming Outsiders," 340–43.

[66] Drake, *King Philip's War*, 131–32.

[67] Gookin, "Historical Account," 507.

[68] Ibid., 507–8.

[69] Gookin, "Historical Account," 475–76; Lepore, *Name of War*, 137–38.

[70] Cf. Ibid., 173–75.

[71] Cf. Ibid, 55, and Brooks, Our Beloved Kin, pp. 319–22.

[72] Ibid., 143–45, 155, 304 n. 21.

[73] Ibid, 143–45.

[74] Ibid., 143–45; 155–57; Linford D. Fisher, "'Why shall wee have peace to be made slaves': Indian Surrenderers during and after King Philip's War," Ethnohistory 64 (2017): 91–114; Lepore, *Name of War*, 155–57; Jaffe, *People of the Wachusett*, 68.

[75] Lepore, *Name of War*, 126.

[76] Newell, *Brethren by Nature*, esp. 174–88.

[77] Linford D. Fisher, "'Dangerous Designs': The 1676 Barbados Act to Prohibit New England Indian Slave Importation," *William and Mary Quarterly* 71 (2014), 99–124.

[78] Wendy Warren, *New England Bound: Slavery and Colonization in Early America* (New York: Liveright, 2016), 11–12; Newell, Brethren by Nature, 139–88.

[79] Robert Kent Diebold, "A Critical Edition of Mrs. Mary Rowlandson's Captivity Narrative" (Ph.D. diss., Yale University, 1972), xcv–xcvii.

[80] Salisbury, "Toward the Covenant Chain," 71; Evan Haefli and Kevin Sweeney, "Revisiting *The Redeemed Captive*: New Perspectives on the 1704 Attack on Deerfield," *William and Mary Quarterly*, 3d ser., 52 (1995): 9–26, 45; Brooks, *Common Pot*, 25–28.

[81] Daniel K. Richter, *Facing East from Indian Country: A Native History of Early America* (Cambridge, Mass.: Harvard University Press, 2001), 140–49 passim.

[82] Donna Keith Baron et al., "They Were Here All Along: The Native American Presence in Lower Central New England in the Eighteenth and Nineteenth Centuries," *William and Mary Quarterly*, 3d ser., 53 (1996): 561–86; Thomas L. Doughton, "Unseen Neighbors: Native Americans of Central Massachusetts, A People Who Had 'Vanished'," in Colin G. Calloway, ed., *After King Philip's War: Presence and Persistence in Indian New England* (Hanover, N.H.: University Press of New England, 1997), 207–30; Rae Gould, "The Nipmuc Nation, Federal Acknowledgment, and a Case of Mistaken Identity," in Amy E. Den Ouden and Jean M. O'Brien, eds., *Recognition, Sovereignty Struggles, and Indigenous Rights in the United States: A Sourcebook* (Chapel Hill: University of North Carolina Press, 2013), 213–33; "Nipmuc," in Siobhan Senier, ed., *Dawnland Voices: An Anthology of Indigenous Writing from New England* (Lincoln: University of Nebraska Press, 2014), 371–426.

[83] Jaffee, *People of the Wachusett*, 74–88.

[84] The principal texts are Increase Mather, *A Brief History of the War with the Indians in New-England* (London, 1676); Mather, *Newes from New-England* (London, 1676); Mather, A Relation of the Troubles which have hapned in New-England, By Reason of the Indians there (Boston, 1677); Hubbard, *A Narrative of the Troubles with the Indians in New-England* (Boston, 1677). On the rivalry between the two authors, see Anne Kusener Nelsen, "King Philip's War and the Hubbard-Mather Rivalry," *William and Mary Quarterly*, 3d ser., 27 (1970): 615–29; Michael G. Hall, *The Last American Puritan: The Life of Increase Mather, 1639–1723* (Middletown, Conn.: Wesleyan University Press, 1988), 112–26; Billy J. Stratton, *Buried in Shades of Night: Contested Voices, Indian Captivity, and the Legacy of King Philip's War* (Tucson: University of Arizona Press, 2013), 102–5.

[85] Gookin, "Historical Account"; Louise A. Breen, *Transgressing the Bounds: Subversive Enterprises among the Puritan Elite in Massachusetts, 1630–1692* (New York: Oxford University Press, 2001), 174–96.

[86] See especially Kathryn Zabelle Derounian, "Puritan Orthodoxy and the 'Survivor Syndrome' in Mary Rowlandson's Indian Captivity Narrative," *Early American Literature* 22 (1987): 82–93; Mitchell Robert Breitwieser, *American Puritanism and the Defense of Mourning: Religion, Grief, and Ethnology in Mary White Rowlandson's Captivity Narrative* (Madison: University of Wisconsin Press, 1990).

[87] Hall, *Last American Puritan*, 131–40; Kathryn Zabelle Derounian, "The Publication, Promotion, and Distribution of Mary Rowlandson's Indian Captivity Narrative in the Seventeenth Century," *Early American Literature* 23 (1988), 242.

[88] Derounian, "Publication, Promotion, and Distribution," 240–43.

[89] Gookin, "Historical Account," 456–61.

[90] N[athaniel] S[altonstall], "A New and Further Narrative of the State of New England" (1676), in Lincoln (ed.), *Narratives*, 83.

[91] For a lucid, richly contextualized discussion, see Paul Baepler, "The Barbary Captivity Narrative in Early America," *Early American Literature* 30 (1995): 97–118.

[92] Nourse, ed., *Lancastriana,* 1:20; Greene, "New Light on Mary Rowlandson," 25, 27.

[93] Greene, "New Light on Mary Rowlandson," 28–30.

[94] Derounian, "Publication, Promotion, and Distribution," 242–44.

[95] Robert Daly, "Anne Bradstreet," in Susan Ware (gen. ed.), *American National Bibliography Online* (Oxford University Press), http://www.anb.org.libproxy.smith.edu:2048/articles/16/16-00169.html?a=1&n=bradstreet&d=10&ss=0&q=3. Accessed 01/10/2017.

[96] A type of sermon named for the Old Testament prophet Jeremiah, a jeremiad warned God's people of impending doom if they did not soon mend their ways. As such, it was widely used by Increase Mather and other New England ministers advocating spiritual reform, especially during the late seventeenth century.

[97] Nourse, *Narrative of the Captivity*, 145.

[98] Cf. John D. Seelye, *Prophetic Waters: The River in Early American Life and Literature* (New York: Oxford University Press, 1977), 289–91.

[99] *Winthrop Papers*, Mass. Hist. Soc. Colls, 5 ser. 1 (1871), 106.

[100] James Axtell, "The Venegeful Women of Marblehead: Robert Roules's Deposition of 1677," *William and Mary Quarterly* 31 (1974), 647–52. Quotes at 652.

[101] Ibid., 648.

[102] Derounian, "Publication, Promotion, and Distribution," 244–45.

[103] Ibid., 255–56, 257.

[104] Stratton, *Buried in the Shades of Night*, 108–11.

[105] Derounian, "Publication, Promotion, and Distribution," 250.

[106] Ulrich, *Good Wives*, 167–70, 171, 205.

[107] Sewall, *Diary*, 1:372–73.

[108] Greene, "New Light on Mary Rowlandson," 31–35.

[109] As Jenny Hale Pulsipher notes, the name "King Philip's War" may have originated before 1716. Pulsipher, *Subjects unto the Same King*, 128, 302 n. 44. But the Church edition that year popularized it.

[110] Pauline Turner Strong, *Captive Selves, Captivating Others: The Politics and Poetics of Colonial American Captivity Narratives* (Boulder, Colo.: Westview Press, 1999), 213.

[111] Samuel Fisher, "Fit Instruments in a Howling Wilderness: Colonists, Indians, and the Origins of the American Revolution," *William and Mary Quarterly*, 73 (2016), 647–80 passim.

[112] Strong, *Captive Selves, Captivating Others*, 216–17.

[113] Ibid., 216–17; Lepore, *Name of War*, 186–90; Fisher, "Fit Instruments," 671–72.

[114] R. W. G. Vail, *The Voice of the Old Frontier* (Philadelphia: University of Pennsylvania Press, 1949), 366, 397–98, 407, 418–19, 456–59.

[115] Derounian-Stodola and Levernier, *Indian Captivity Narrative*, 112–191.

[116] Stratton, *Buried in the Shades of Night*, 141–43.

[117] Camilla Townsend, *Pocahontas and the Powhatan Dilemma* (New York: Hill and Wang, 2004).

[118] Lisa Voigt, *Writing Captivity in the Early Modern Atlantic: Circulations of Knowledge and Authority in the Iberian and English Imperial Worlds* (Chapel Hill: University of North Carolina Press, 2009), 41–207.

[119] Ibid. See also Ralph Bauer, "Creole Identities in Colonial Space: The Narratives of Mary White Rowlandson and Francisco Núñez de Pineda y Bascuñán," *American Literature* 69, 4 (1997): 665–95.

[120] Arne Bialuschewski and Linford D. Fisher, "Guest Editor's Introduction: New Directions in the History of Native American Slavery Studies," *Ethnohistory* 64 (2017): 2.

[121] Nabil Matar, *Europe through Arab Eyes, 1578–1727* (New York: Columbia University Press, 1999); Catherine M. Cameron, *Captives: How Stolen People Changed the World* (Lincoln: University of Nebraska Press, 2016).

[122] Joyce E. Chaplin, "Enslavement of Indians in Early America: Captivity without the Narrative," in Elizabeth Mancke and Carole Shammas, eds., *The Creation of the British Atlantic World* (Baltimore: Johns Hopkins University Press, 2005), 45–70. A recent and important exception for New England is Brooks, *Our Beloved Kin*.

[123] Salisbury, *Manitou and Providence*, 90–96.

[124] Salisbury, "Squanto: Last of the Patuxets," in David Sweet and Gary B. Nash, eds., *Survival and Struggle in Colonial America* (Berkeley: University of California Press, 1981), 228–46; Salisbury, *Manitou and Providence*, 106–8, 114–17, 122–23.

[125] Stratton, *Buried in the Shades of Night*, 138–39.

[126] Alexie, "Captivity," in *First Indian on the Moon*, 100–101. Both Alexie and Louise Erdrich (Turtle Mountain Chippewa), in a poem, "Captivity," begin their powerful pieces with a quote they attribute to Rowlandson but which actually appears in a later narrative by John Gyles, who was captured by Abenakis in Maine in 1689. Alexie, "Captivity," 98; Erdrich, "Captivity" [1984], in *Original Fire: Selected and New Poems* (New York: HarperCollins, 2003), 9–11; John Gyles, "Memoirs of Odd Adventures, Strange Deliverances, etc.," [1736], in Alden T. Vaughan and Edward W. Clark, eds., *Puritans among the Indians: Accounts of Captivity and Redemption, 1676–1724* (Cambridge, Mass.: Harvard University Press, 1981), 99.

PART TWO

The Document

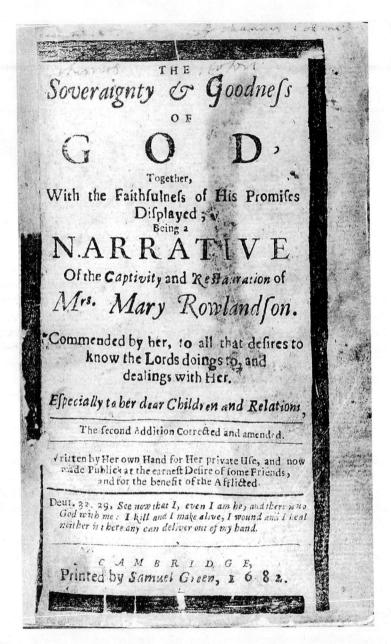

THE
Soveraignty & Goodness
OF
G O D,
Together,
With the Faithfulness of His Promises
Displayed ;
Being a
NARRATIVE
Of the *Captivity* and *Restauration* of
Mrs. Mary Rowlandson.

Commended by her, to all that desires to
know the Lords doings to, and
dealings with Her.

Especially to her dear Children and Relations,

The second Addition Corrected and amended.

Written by Her own Hand for Her private Use, and now
made Publick at the earnest Desire of some Friends,
and for the benefit of the Afflicted.

Deut. 32. 39, See now that I, even I am he, and there is no
God with me: I kill and I make alive, I wound and I heal,
neither is there any can deliver out of my hand.

CAMBRIDGE,
Printed by *Samuel Green*, 1 6 8 2.

Figure 9. *Title page, First Complete Edition of Mary Rowlandson's Narrative, 1682.*
Courtesy of the Trustees of the Boston Public Library, Boston.

The Sovereignty and Goodness of God
By Mary Rowlandson

The Preface to the Reader

It was on Tuesday, Feb. 1, 1675,[1] in the afternoon, when the *Narrhagansets* quarters (in or toward the *Nipmug* Country, whither they are now retyred for fear of the *English* Army lying in their own Country) were the second time beaten up by the Forces of the united Colonies,[2] who thereupon soon betook themselves to flight, and were all the next day pursued by the *English*, some overtaken and destroyed. But on *Thursday*, Feb. 3d, the *English* having now been six dayes on their march, from their head quarters, at *Wickford*, in the *Narrhaganset* Country, toward, and after the Enemy, and provision grown exceeding short, insomuch that they were fain to kill some Horses for the supply, especially of their *Indian* friends, they were necessitated to consider what was best to be done: And about noon (having hitherto followed the chase as hard as they might) a Councill was called, and though some few were of another mind, yet it was concluded by far the greater part of the Councill of War, that the Army should desist the pursuit, and retire: the Forces of *Plimoth* and the *Bay*[3] to the next Town of the *Bay*, and *Connecticut* Forces to their own next Towns; which determination was immediately put in execution. The consequent whereof, as it was not difficult to be foreseen by those that knew the causless enmity of these *Barbarians*, against the *English*, and the malicious and revengefull spirit of these Heathen: so it soon proved dismall.

The *Narrhagansets* were now driven quite from their own Country, and all their provisions there hoarded up, to which they durst not at

---

[1] By the modern Gregorian calendar (already used everywhere in Europe outside of the British Isles), the date was February 11, 1676. Until the mid-eighteenth century, England observed the Julian calendar, in which the year began on March 25 instead of January 1 and which reckoned dates ten days earlier than the Gregorian calendar.

[2] The United Colonies of New England was a loose confederation consisting of the Puritan-dominated colonies of Massachusetts Bay, Connecticut, and Plymouth. It pointedly excluded religiously tolerant Rhode Island.

[3] The colony of Massachusetts Bay.

present return, and being so numerous as they were, soon devoured those to whom they went,[4] whereby both the one and other were now reduced to extream straits, and so necessitated to take the first and best opportunity for supply, and very glad, no doubt of such an opportunity as this, to provide for themselves, and make spoil of the *English* at once; and seeing themselves thus discharged of their pursuers, and a little refreshed after their flight, the very next week upon *Thurseday*, Feb. 10, they fell with mighty force and fury upon *Lancaster*: which small Town, remote from aid of others, and not being Gerisoned as it might, the Army being now come in, and as the time indeed required (the design of the *Indians* against that place being known to the *English* some time before),[5] was not able to make effectual resistance: but notwithstanding utmost endeavor of the Inhabitants, most of the buildings were turned into ashes; many People (Men, Women and Children) slain, and others captivated. The most solemn and remarkable part of this Trajedy, may that justly be reputed, which fell upon the Family of that reverend Servant of God, Mr. *Joseph Rolandson*, the faithfull Pastor of Christ in that place, who being gone down to the Councill of the *Massachusets* to seek aid for the defence of the place, at his return found the Town in flames, or smoke, his own house being set on fire by the Enemy, through the disadvantage of a defective Fortification, and all in it consumed: his precious yokefellow, and dear Children, wounded and captivated (as the issue evidenced, and following Narrative declares) by these cruel and barbarous Salvages. A sad Catestrophe! Thus all things come alike to all: None knows either love or hatred by all that is before him. It is no new thing for Gods precious ones to drink as deep as others, of the Cup of common Calamity: Take just Lot (yet captivated) for instance beside others.[6] But it is not my business to dilate on these things, but only in few words introductively to preface to the following script, which is a Narrative of the wonderfully awfull, wise, holy, powerfull, and gracious providence of God, towards that worthy and precious Gentlewoman, the dear Consort of the said Reverend Mr. *Rowlandson*, and her Children with her, as in casting of her into such a waterless pit, so in preserving, supporting, and carrying through so many such extream hazards, unspeakable difficulties and disconsolateness, and at last delivering

---

[4] Meaning that the Narragansett refugees quickly depleted their Nipmuc hosts' food supply.

[5] This is a reference to the report by James Quanapohit (Document 4).

[6] See Genesis 14, esp. 12–16.

her out of them all, and her Surviving Children also. It was a strange and amazing dispensation, that the Lord should so afflict his precious Servant, and Hand maid. It was a strange, if not more, that he should so bear up the spirits of his Servant under such bereavements and of his handmaid under such captivity, travels and hardships (much too hard for flesh and blood) as he did, and at length deliver and restore. But he was their Saviour, who hath said, *When thou passest through the Waters, I will be with thee, and through the Rivers, they shall not overflow thee: When thou walkest through the fire thou shalt not be burnt, nor shall the flame kindle upon thee,* Isa. 43, ver. 2, and again, *He woundeth and his hands make whole. He shall deliver thee in six troubles, yea in seven there shall no evil touch thee. In Famine he shall redeem thee from Death, and in War from the power of the sword.* Job 5.18, 19, 20. Methinks this dispensation doth bear some resemblance to those of *Joseph, David* and *Daniel*; yea, and of the three Children too,[7] the Stories whereof do represent us with the excellent textures of divine providence, curious pieces of divine work: and truly so doth this, and therefore not to be forgotten, but worthy to be exhibited to, and viewed, and pondered by all, that disdain not to consider the operation of his hands.

The works of the Lord (not only of Creation, but of Providence also, especially those that do more peculiarly concern his dear ones, that are as the Apple of his Eye, as the Signet upon His Hand, the Delight of his Eyes, and the Object of his tenderest Care) are great, sought out of all those that have pleasure therein. And of these verily this is none of the least.

This Narrative was penned by the Gentlewoman her self, to be to her a memorandum of Gods dealing with her, that she might never forget, but remember the same, and the severall circumstances thereof, all the dayes of her life. A pious scope which deserves both commendation and imitation: Some friends having obtained a sight of it, could not but be so much affected with the many passages of working providence discovered therein as to judge it worthy of publick view, and altogether unmeet that such works of God should be hid from present and future Generations: And therefore though this Gentlewomans modesty would not thrust it into the Press, yet her gratitude unto God made her not hardly perswadable to let it pass, that God might have his due glory and others benefit by it as well as herself. I hope by this time none

---

[7] See Daniel 3.

will cast any reflection upon this Gentlewoman, on the score of this publication of her affliction and deliverance. If any should, doubtless they may be reckoned with the nine lepers, of whom it is said, *Were there not ten cleansed, where are the nine? but one returning to give God thanks.*[8] Let such further know that this was a dispensation of publick note, and of universall concernment, and so much the more, by how much the nearer this Gentlewoman stood related to that faithfull Servant of God, whose capacity and employment was publick in the house of God, and his name on that account of a very sweet savour in the Churches of Christ. Who is there of a true Christian spirit, that did not look upon himself much concerned in this bereavement, this Captivity in the time thereof, and in this deliverance when it came, yea more than in many others; and how many are there, to whom so concerned, it will doubtless be a very acceptable thing to see the way of God with this Gentlewoman in the aforesaid dispensation, thus laid out and portrayed before their eyes.

To conclude, whatever any coy phantasies may deem, yet it highly concerns those that have so deeply tasted, how good the Lord is, to enquire with *David, What shall I render to the Lord for all his benefits to me? Psal.* 116. 12. He thinks nothing too great; yea, being sensible of his own disproportion to the due praises of God he calls in help. *Oh, magnifie the Lord with me, let us exalt his Name together,* Psal. 34. 3. And it is but reason, that our praises should hold proportion with our prayers: and that as many hath helped together by prayer for the obtaining of this Mercy, so praises should be returned by many on this behalf; And forasmuch as not the generall but particular knowledge of things make deepest impression upon the affections, this Narrative particularizing the several passages of this providence will not a little conduce thereunto. And therefore holy *David* in order to the attainment of that end, accounts himself concerned to declare what God has done for his soul, *Psal.* 66.16. *Come and hear, all ye that fear God, and I will declare what God hath done for my soul,* i.e. *for his life,* see v. 9, 10. *He holdeth our soul in life, and suffers not our feet to be moved, for thou our God hast proved us, thou hast tried us, as silver is tried.* Life-mercies, are heart-affecting mercies, of great impression and force, to enlarge pious hearts in the praises of God, so that such know not how but to talk of Gods acts, and to speak of and publish his wonderfull works. Deep troubles, when the waters come in unto thy soul, are wont to produce vowes: vowes must

[8]See Luke 17:18–19.

be paid. *It is better not vow, than vow and not to pay.*[9] I may say, that as none knows what it is to fight and pursue such an enemy as this, but they that have fought and pursued them: so none can imagine what it is to be captivated, and enslaved to such atheistical, proud, wild, cruel, barbarous, brutish (in one word) diabolicall creatures as these, the worst of the heathen; nor what difficulties, hardships, hazards, sorrows, anxieties and perplexities do unavoidably wait upon such a condition, but those that have tryed it. No serious spirit then (especially knowing anything of this Gentlewomans piety) can imagine but that the vows of God are upon her. Excuse her then if she come thus into publick, to pay those vows. Come and hear what she hath to say.

I am confident that no Friend of divine Providence will ever repent his time and pains spent in reading over these sheets, but will judg them worth perusing again and again.

Here *Reader*, you may see an instance of the Soveraignty of God, who doth what he will with his own as well as others; and who may say to him, *What dost Thou?*[10] Here you may see an instance of the faith and patience of the Saints, under the most heart-sinking tryals; here you may see, the promises are breasts full of consolation, when all the world besides is empty, and gives nothing but sorrow. That God is indeed the supream Lord of the world, ruling the most unruly, weakening the most cruel and salvage, granting his People mercy in the sight of the unmercifull, curbing the lusts of the most filthy, holding the hands of the violent, delivering the prey from the mighty, *and gathering together the out casts of* Israel. Once and again you have heard, but here you may see, *that power belongeth unto God*; that our God is the God of Salvation, and to him belong the issues from Death. That our God is in the Heavens, and doth whatever pleases him. Here you have *Sampsons* Riddle exemplified, and that great promise, *Rom.* 8. 28. verified, *Out of the Eater comes forth meat, and sweetness out of the strong*;[11] The worst of evils working together for the best good. How evident is it that the Lord hath made this Gentlewoman a gainer by all this affliction, that she can say, *'tis good for her, yea better that she hath been, than that she should not have been thus afflicted.*

Oh how doth God shine forth in such things as these!

---

[9] See Ecclesiastes 5:5.

[10] Job 9:12.

[11] Although Romans 8:28 refers to a promise by God, Samson's riddle and the passage quoted are found in Judges 14:14.

Reader, if thou gettest no good by such a Declaration as this, the fault must needs be thine own. Read therefore, Peruse, Ponder, and from hence lay up something from the experience of another, against thine own turn comes, that so thou also through patience and consolation of the Scripture mayest have hope.

TER AMICAM[12]

A Narrative of the Captivity and Restauration of Mrs. Mary Rowlandson

On the tenth of February 1675,[13] Came the *Indians* with great numbers upon *Lancaster*: Their first coming was about Sun-rising; hearing the noise of some Guns, we looked out; several Houses were burning, and the Smoke ascending to Heaven. There were five persons taken in one house, the Father, and the Mother and a sucking Child, they knockt on the head; the other two they took and carried away alive. There were two others, who being out of their Garison upon some occasion were set upon; one was knockt on the head, the other escaped: Another there was who running along was shot and wounded, and fell down; he begged of them his life, promising them Money (as they told me) but they would not hearken to him but knockt him in head, and stript him naked, and split open his Bowels. Another seeing many of the *Indians* about his Barn, ventured and went out, but was quickly shot down. There were three others belonging to the same Garison who were killed; the *Indians* getting up upon the roof of the Barn, had advantage to shoot down upon them over their Fortification. Thus these murtherous wretches went on, burning, and destroying before them.

At length they came and beset our own house, and quickly it was the dolefullest day that ever mine eyes saw. The House stood upon the edge of a hill; some of the *Indians* got behind the hill, others into the Barn, and others behind any thing that could shelter them; from all which places they shot against the House, so that the Bullets seemed to fly like hail; and quickly they wounded one man among us, then another, and then

---

[12] This phrase does not make grammatical sense in Latin. It was corrected in the next (third) edition to read "Per Amicam," meaning "for my (female) friend." Thanks to Craig Arthur Williams for clarifying this matter. The correction was one of many made in the third edition.

[13] By our calendar, February 20, 1676. See note 1.

a third. About two hours (according to my observation, in that amazing time) they had been about the house before they prevailed to fire it (which they did with Flax and Hemp, which they brought out of the Barn, and there being no defence about the House, only two Flankers[14] at two opposite corners, and one of them not finished) they fired it once and one ventured out and quenched it, but they quickly fired again, and that took. Now is that dreadfull hour come, that I have often heard of (in time of War, as it was the case of others) but now mine eyes see it. Some in our house were fighting for their lives, others wallowing in their blood, the House on fire over our heads, and the bloody Heathen ready to knock us on the head, if we stirred out. Now might we hear Mothers & Children crying out for themselves, and one another, *Lord, What shall we do?* Then I took my Children[15] (and one of my sisters,[16] hers) to go forth and leave the house: but as soon as we came to the door and appeared, the *Indians* shot so thick that the bullets rattled against the House, as if one had taken an handfull of stones and threw them, so that we were fain to give back. We had six stout Dogs belonging to our Garrison, but none of them wou'd stir, though another time, if any *Indian* had come to the door, they were ready to fly upon him and tear him down. The Lord hereby would make us the more to acknowledge his hand, and to see that our help is alwayes in him. But out we must go, the fire increasing, and coming along behind us, roaring, and the Indians gaping before us with their Guns, Spears and Hatchets to devour us. No sooner were we out of the House, but my Brother in Law (being before wounded, in defending the house, in or near the throat) fell down dead, whereat the *Indians* scornfully shouted, and hallowed, and were presently upon him, stripping off his cloaths, the bulletts flying thick, one went through my side, and the same (as would seem) through the bowels and hand of my dear Child in my arms.[17] One of my elder Sisters Children, named *William*, had then his Leg broken, which the *Indians* perceiving, they knockt him on head. Thus were we butchered by those merciless Heathen, standing amazed, with the blood running down to our heels. My eldest Sister being yet in the House, and seeing those wofull sights, the Infidels haling Mothers one way, and Children another, and some wallowing in their blood: and her elder Son telling

---

[14] Projecting fortifications.

[15] Rowlandson had three children, Joseph, Jr. (b. 1661), Mary (b. 1665), and Sarah (b. 1669).

[16] Two of Rowlandson's sisters and their families were among the thirty-seven persons housed in the Rowlandson garrison.

[17] Her youngest child, Sarah.

her that her Son *William* was dead, and my self was wounded, she said, And, *Lord, let me dy with them*; which was no sooner said, but she was struck with a Bullet, and fell down dead over the threshold. I hope she is reaping the fruit of her good labours, being faithfull to the service of God in her place. In her younger years she lay under much trouble upon spiritual accounts, till it pleased God to make that precious scripture take hold of her heart, 2 *Cor*. 12. 9. *And he said unto me, my grace is sufficient for thee*. More than twenty years after I have heard her tell how sweet and comfortable that place was to her. But to return: the *Indians* laid hold of us, pulling me one way, and the Children another, and said, *Come go along with us*; I told them they would kill me: they answered, *If I were willing to go along with them, they would not hurt me*.

Oh the dolefull sight that now was to behold at this House! *Come, behold the works of the Lord, what desolations he has made in the Earth*.[18] Of thirty seven persons who were in this one House, none escaped either present death, or a bitter captivity, save only one, who might say as he, *Job* 1. 15. *And I only am escaped alone to tell the News*. There were twelve killed, some shot, some stab'd with their Spears, some knock'd down with their Hatchets. When we are in prosperity, Oh the little that we think of such dreadfull sights, and to see our dear Friends, and Relations ly bleeding out their heart-blood upon the ground. There was one who was chopt into the head with a Hatchet, and stripped naked, and yet was crawling up and down. It is a solemn sight to see so many Christians lying in their blood, some here, and some there, like a company of Sheep torn by Wolves. All of them stript naked by a company of hell-hounds, roaring, singing, ranting and insulting, as if they would have torn our very hearts out; yet the Lord by his Almighty power preserved a number of us from death, for there were twenty-four of us taken alive and carried captive.

I had often before this said, that if the *Indians* should come, I should chuse rather to be killed by them than be taken alive, but when it came to the tryal my mind changed; their glittering weapons so daunted my spirit, that I chose rather to go along with those (as I may say) ravenous Beasts, than that moment to end my dayes; and that I may the better declare what happened to me during that grievous Captivity, I shall particularly speak of the severall Removes we had up and down the Wilderness.

---

[18] Psalm 46:8.

THE FIRST REMOVE[19]

Now away we must go with those Barbarous Creatures, with our bodies wounded and bleeding, and our hearts no less than our bodies. About a mile we went that night, up upon a hill within sight of the Town, where they intended to lodge. There was hard by a vacant house (deserted by the English before, for fear of the *Indians*). I asked them whither I might not lodge in the house that night to which they answered, what will you love *English men* still? This was the dolefullest night that ever my eyes saw. Oh the roaring, and singing and danceing, and yelling of those black creatures in the night, which made the place a lively resemblance of hell. And as miserable was the waste that was there made, of Horses, Cattle, Sheep, Swine, Calves, Lambs, Roasting Pigs, and Fowls (which they had plundered in the Town) some roasting, some lying and burning, and some boyling to feed our merciless Enemies; who were joyfull enough though we were disconsolate. To add to the dolefulness of the former day, and the dismalness of the present night: my thoughts ran upon my losses and sad bereaved condition. All was gone, my Husband gone (at least separated from me, he being in the Bay;[20] and to add to my grief, the *Indians* told me they would kill him as he came homeward) my Children gone, my Relations and Friends gone, our House and home and all our comforts within door, and without, all was gone, (except my life) and I knew not but the next moment that might go too. There remained nothing to me but one poor wounded Babe, and it seemed at present worse than death that it was in such a pitiful condition, bespeaking Compassion, and I had no refreshing for it, nor suitable things to revive it.[21] Little do many think what is the savageness and brutishness of this barbarous Enemy, aye even those that seem to profess more than others among them,[22] when the *English* have fallen into their hands.

Those seven that were killed at *Lancaster* the summer before upon a Sabbath day, and the one that was afterward killed upon a week day, were slain and mangled in a barbarous manner, by One-ey'd *John*, and *Marlborough's* Praying *Indians*, which Capt. *Mosely* brought to *Boston*, as the *Indians* told me.[23]

---

[19] For Rowlandson's "removes" during her captivity, see Map 2 (p. 79).

[20] In the eastern part of the colony, near the bay known as Massachusetts Bay.

[21] Seventeenth-century English people referred to small children by the gender-neutral pronoun "it," rather than "he" or "she."

[22] Meaning those Indians who profess Christianity.

[23] Rowlandson refers here to the earlier attack on Lancaster of August 7, 1675, led by Nipmuc sachem Monoco ("One-eyed John"). Captain Samuel Moseley's attempt to implicate the Christian Indians of Marlborough in the attack proved unsuccessful in court.

THE SECOND REMOVE

But now, the next morning, I must turn my back upon the Town, and travel with them into the vast and desolate Wilderness, I knew not whither. It is not my tongue, or pen can express the sorrows of my heart, and bitterness of my spirit, that I had at this departure: but God was with me, in a wonderfull manner, carrying me along, and bearing up my spirit, that it did not quite fail. One of the *Indians* carried my poor wounded Babe upon a horse, it went moaning all along, I shall dy, I shall dy. I went on foot after it, with sorrow that cannot be exprest. At length I took it off the horse, and carried it in my arms till my strength failed, and I fell down with it: Then they set me upon a horse with my wounded Child in my lap, and there being no furniture[24] upon the horse back, as we were going down a steep hill, we both fell over the horses head, at which they like inhumane creatures laught, and rejoyced to see it, though I thought we should there have ended our dayes, as overcome with so many difficulties. But the Lord renewed my strength still, and carried me along, that I might see more of his Power; yea, so much that I could never have thought of, had I not experienced it.

After this it quickly began to snow, and when night came on, they stopt: and now down I must sit in the snow, by a little fire, and a few boughs behind me, with my sick Child in my lap; and calling much for water, being now (through the wound) fallen into a violent Fever. My own wound also growing so stiff, that I could scarce sit down or rise up; yet so it must be, that I must sit all this cold winter night upon the cold snowy ground, with my sick Child in my armes, looking that every hour would be the last of its life; and having no Christian friend near me, either to comfort or help me. Oh, I may see the wonderfull power of God, that my Spirit did not utterly sink under my affliction: still the Lord upheld me with his gracious and mercifull Spirit, and we were both alive to see the light of the next morning.

THE THIRD REMOVE

The morning being come, they prepared to go on their way: One of the Indians *got up upon a horse, and they set me up behind him, with my poor sick Babe in my lap.* A very wearisome and tedious day I had of it; what

---

[24] Saddle, stirrups, bridle, reins, and so forth.

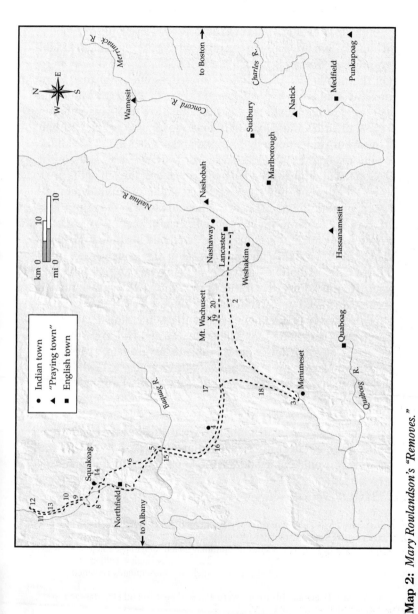

Map 2: *Mary Rowlandson's "Removes."*
During her three months as a captive, Rowlandson traveled over Nipmuck, Pocumtuck, and Western Abenaki homelands.

with my own wound, and my Childs being so exceeding sick, and in a lamentable condition with her wound. It may be easily judged what a poor feeble condition we were in, there being not the least crumb of refreshing that came within either of our mouths, from *Wednesday* night to *Saturday* night, except only a little cold water.[25] This day in the afternoon, about an hour by Sun, we came to the place where they intended, *viz.* an Indian town called *Wenimesset*, northward of *Quabaug*.[26] When we were come, Oh the number of Pagans (now merciless enemies) that there came about me, that I may say as *David*, Psal 27. 13, *I had fainted, unless I had believed, &c.* The next day was the Sabbath: I then remembered how careless I had been of Gods holy time: how many Sabbaths I had lost and misspent, and how evilly I had walked in Gods sight; which lay so close unto my spirit, that it was easie for me to see how righteous it was with God to cut off the thread of my life, and cast me out of his presence forever. Yet the Lord still shewed mercy to me, and upheld me; and as he wounded me with one hand, so he healed me with the other. This day there came to me one *Robert Pepper* (a man belonging to *Roxbury*) who was taken in Captain *Beers* his fight,[27] and had been now a considerable time with the *Indians*; and up with them almost as far as *Albany* to see king *Philip*, as he told me, and was now very lately come into these parts. Hearing, I say, that I was in this *Indian* Town, he obtained leave to come and see me. He told me, he himself was wounded in the leg at Captain *Beers* his Fight; and was not able some time to go, but as they carried him, and as he took Oaken leaves and laid to his wound, and through the blessing of God he was able to travel again. Then I took Oaken leaves and laid to my side, and with the blessing of God it cured me also; yet before the cure was wrought, I may say, as it is in *Psal.* 38. 5, 6. *My wounds stink and are corrupt, I am troubled, I am bowed down greatly, I go mourning all the day long.* I sat much alone with a poor wounded Child in my lap, which moaned night and day, having nothing to revive the body, or cheer the spirits of her, but in stead of that, sometimes one *Indian* would come and tell me in one hour, that your *Master*

---

[25] But they were given at least one small piece of food, which neither of them ate during this period, as Rowlandson later reveals (p. 99).

[26] Wenimesset was a Nipmuc town more commonly called Menameset. Like Nashaway, Quabaug was the name both of a Nipmuc town and of a nearby English settlement. Rowlandson is most likely referring to the latter, which was subsequently renamed Brookfield.

[27] Captain Richard Beers and his troops were attacked near Northfield, Massachusetts, in September 1675.

will knock your Child in the head, and then a second, and then a third, your *Master* will quickly knock your Child in the head.

This was the comfort I had from them, miserable comforters are ye all,[28] *as he said.* Thus nine days I sat upon my knees, with my Babe in my lap, till my flesh was raw again; my Child being even ready to depart this sorrowful world, they bade me carry it out to another Wigwam (I suppose because they would not be troubled with such spectacles) Whither I went with a very heavy heart, and down I sat with the picture of death in my lap. About two houres in the night, my sweet Babe, like a lamb departed this life, on *Feb. 18. 1675,* It being about six *yeares,* and *five months* old. It was *nine dayes* from the first wounding, in this miserable condition, without any refreshing of one nature or other, except a little cold water. I cannot but take notice, how at another time I could not bear to be in the room where any dead person was, but now the case is changed; I must and could ly down by my dead Babe, side by side all the night after. I have thought since of the wonderfull goodness of God to me, in preserving me in the use of my reason and senses, in that distressed time, that I did not use wicked and violent means to end my own miserable life. In the morning, when they understood that my child was dead they sent for me home to my Masters Wigwam: (by my Master in this writing, must be understood *Quanopin,* who was a *Saggamore,*[29] and married King *Philips* wives Sister; not that he first took me, but I was sold to him by another *Narhaganset Indian,* who took me when first I came out of the Garison). I went to take up my dead child in my arms to carry it with me, but they bid me let it alone: there was no resisting, but goe I must and leave it. When I had been at my masters *wigwam,* I took the first opportunity I could get, to go look after my dead child: when I came I askt them what they had done with it? then they told me it was upon the hill: then they went and shewed me where it was, where I saw the ground was newly digged, and there they told me they had buried it: *There I left that Child in the Wilderness, and must commit it, and my self also in this Wilderness-condition, to him who is above all.* God having taken away this dear Child, I went to see my daughter *Mary,* who was at this same *Indian Town,* at a *Wigwam* not very far off, though we had little liberty or opportunity to see one another: she was about ten years old, & taken from the door at first

---

[28] Job 16:2.
[29] On Quinnapin, see the Introduction, esp. pp. 28–29. A sagamore was a sachem, or political leader.

by a *Praying Indian* & afterward sold for a gun. When I came in sight, she would fall a weeping; at which they were provoked, and would not let me come near her, but bade me be gone; which was a heart-cutting word to me. I had one Child dead, another in the Wilderness, I knew not where, the third they would not let me come near to: *Me* (as he said) *have ye bereaved of my children,* Joseph *is not, and* Simeon *is not, and ye will take* Benjamin *also, all these things are against me.*[30] I could not sit still in this condition, but kept, walking from *one* place to another. And as I was going along, my heart was even overwhelm'd with the thoughts of my condition, and that I should have Children, *and a Nation which I knew not ruled over them.* Whereupon I earnestly entreated the Lord, that he would consider my low estate, and shew me a token for good, and if it were his blessed will, some sign and hope of some relief. And indeed quickly the Lord answered, in some measure, my poor prayers: for as I was going up and down mourning and lamenting my condition, my Son came to me, and asked me how I did; I had not seen him before, since the destruction of the Town, and I knew not where he was, till I was informed by himself, that he was amongst a smaller parcel of *Indians*, whose place was about six miles off; with tears in his eyes, he asked me whether his sister *Sarah* was dead; and told me he had seen his sister *Mary*; and prayed me, that I would not be troubled in reference to himself. The occasion of his coming to see me at this time, was this: There was, as I said, about six miles from us, a smal Plantation of *Indians*, where it seems he had been during his Captivity: and at this time, there were some Forces of the *Indians* gathered out of our company, and some also from them (among whom was my Sons master) to go to assault and burn *Medfield*: In this time of the absence of his master, his dame brought him to see me. I took this to be some gracious answer to my earnest and unfeigned desire. The next day, *viz.* to this, the *Indians* returned from *Medfield*, all the company, for those that belonged to the other smal company, came through the Town that now we were at. But before they came to us, Oh! the outragious roaring and hooping that there was: They began their din about a mile before they came to us. By their noise and hooping they signified how many they had destroyed (which was at that time twenty three). Those that were with us at home, were gathered together as soon as they heard the hooping, and every time that the other went over their number, these at home gave a shout, that the very Earth

[30] Genesis 42:36.

rung again: And thus they continued till those that had been upon the expedition were come up to the *Sagamores Wigwam*; and then, Oh, the hideous insulting and triumphing that there was over some *English-mens* scalps that they had taken (as their manner) and brought with them. I cannot but take notice of the wonderfull mercy of God to me in those afflictions, in sending me a Bible. One of the *Indians* that came from *Medfield* fight, had brought some plunder, came to me, and asked me, if I wou'd have a Bible, he had got one in his basket. I was glad of it, and asked him, whether he thought the *Indians* would let me read? He answered, yes: So I took the Bible, and in that melancholy time, it came into my mind to read first the 28. *Chap*. of *Deut*. which I did, and when I had read it, my dark heart wrought on this manner, *That there was no mercy for me, that the blessings were gone, and the curses come in their room, and that I had lost my opportunity.* But the Lord helped me still to go on reading till I came to *Chap*. 30 the seven first verses, where I found, *There was mercy promised again, if we would return to him by repentance; and though we were scattered from one end of the Earth to the other, yet the Lord would gather us together, and turn all those curses upon our Enemies.* I do not desire to live to forget this Scripture, and what comfort it was to me.

Now the *Indians* began to talk of removing from this place, some one way, and some another. There were now besides my self nine *English* Captives in this place (all of them Children, except one Woman). I got an opportunity to go and take my leave of them; they being to go one way, and I another, *I asked them whether they were earnest with God for deliverance*; they told me, they did as they were able, and it was some comfort to me, that the Lord stirred up *Children to look to him.* The Woman *viz.* Goodwife *Joslin*[31] told me, she should never see me again, and that she could find in her heart to run away; I wisht her not to run away by any means, for we were near *thirty miles* from any *English Town*, and she very big with Child, and had but one week to reckon; and another Child in her Arms, two years old, and bad Rivers there were to go over, and we were feeble, with our poor and coarse entertainment. I had my Bible with me, I pulled it out, and asked her whether she would read; we opened the Bible and lighted on *Psal*. 27. in which Psalm we especially took notice of that, *ver. ult.,*[32] *Wait on the Lord, Be of good courage, and he shall strengthen thine heart, wait I say on the Lord.*

---

[31] Ann Joslin, also captured in the Rowlandson garrison.
[32] Last verse.

THE FOURTH REMOVE

And now I must part with that little company I had. Here I parted from
my daughter *Mary*, (whom I never saw again till I saw her in *Dorchester*,
returned from Captivity), and from four little Cousins and Neighbours,
some of which I never saw afterward: the Lord only knows the end of
them. Amongst them also was that poor Woman before mentioned, who
came to a sad end, as some of the company told me in my travel: She
having much grief upon her Spirit, about her miserable condition, being
so near her time, she would be often asking the Indians to let her go
home; they not being willing to that, and yet vexed with her importu-
nity, gathered a great company together about her, and stript her naked,
and set her in the midst of them; and when they had sung and danced
about her (in their hellish manner) as long as they pleased, they knockt
her on head, and the child in her arms with her: when they had done
that, they made a fire and put them both into it, and told the other Children that were with them, that if they attempted to go home, they would
serve them in like manner: The Children said, she did not shed one tear,
but prayed all the while. But to return to my own Journey; we travelled
about half a day or little more, and came to a desolate place in the
Wilderness, where there were no *Wigwams* or *Inhabitants* before; we
came about the middle of the afternoon to this place; cold and wet, and
snowy, and hungry, and weary, and no refreshing, for man, but the cold
ground to sit on, and our poor *Indian cheer.*

Heart-aking thoughts here I had about my poor Children, who were
scattered up and down among the wild beasts of the forrest: My head
was light and dizzy (either through hunger or hard lodging, or trouble
or all together) my knees feeble, my body raw by sitting double night
and day, that I cannot express to man the affliction that lay upon my
Spirit, but the Lord helped me at that time to express it to himself.
I opened my Bible to read, and the Lord brought that precious scripture
to me, *Jer.* 31. 16. *Thus saith the Lord, refrain thy voice from weeping, and
thine eyes from tears, for thy work shall be rewarded, and they shall come
again from the land of the Enemy.* This was a sweet Cordial to me, when
I was ready to faint, many and many a time have I sat down, and wept
sweetly over this Scripture. At this place we continued about four dayes.

THE FIFTH REMOVE

The occasion (as I thought) of their moving at this time, was, the English
Army, it being near and following them: For they went, as if they had

gone for their lives, for some considerable way, and then they made a stop, and chose some of their stoutest men, and sent them back to hold the *English* army in play whilst the rest escaped: And then, *like Jehu, they marched on furiously,*[33] with their old, and with their young: some carried their old decrepit mothers, some carried one, and some another. Four of them carried a great *Indian* upon a Bier;[34] but going through a thick Wood with him, they were hindered, and could make no haste; whereupon they took him upon their backs, and carried him, one at a time, till they came to *Bacquaug* River.[35] Upon a *Friday*, a little after noon we came to this River. When all the company was come up, and were gathered together, I thought to count the number of them, but they were so many, and being somewhat in motion, it was beyond my skil. In this travel, because of my wound, I was somewhat favored in my load; I carried only my knitting work and two quarts of parched meal: Being very faint I asked my mistriss[36] to give me one spoonfull of the meal, but she would not give me a taste. They quickly fell to cutting dry trees, to make Rafts to carry them over the river: and soon my turn came to go over: By the advantage of some brush which they had laid upon the Raft to sit upon, I did not wet my foot (which many of themselves at the other end were mid-leg deep) which cannot but be acknowledged as a favour of God to my weakened body, it being a very cold time. I was not before acquainted with such kind of doings or dangers. *When thou passeth through the waters I will be with thee, and through the rivers they shall not overflow thee*, Isai. 43. 2. A certain number of us got over the River that night, but it was the night after the Sabbath before all the company was got over. On the *Saturday* they boyled an old Horses leg which they had got, and so we drank of the broth, as soon as they thought it was ready, and when it was almost all gone, they filled it up again.

The first week of my being among them, I hardly ate any thing; the second week, I found my stomach grow very faint for want of something; and yet it was very hard to get down their filthy trash: but the third week, though I could think how formerly my stomach would turn against this or that, and I could starve and die before I could eat such things, yet they were sweet and savory to my taste. I was at this time knitting a pair of white cotton stockins for my mistriss: and had not yet

---

[33] See II Kings 9:20.

[34] A bier is a framework for carrying either a corpse or an exalted person. This is a rare reference to a New England sachem being carried this way. The practice was far more common among Native Americans in the Southeast.

[35] Now known as Miller's River.

[36] Weetamoo, whom Rowlandson will later refer to as Wettimore.

wrought upon a Sabbath day; when the Sabbath came they bade me go to work; I told them it was the Sabbath-day, and desired them to let me rest, and told them I would do as much more tomorrow; to which they answered me, they would break my face. And here I cannot but take notice of the strange providence of God in preserving the heathen: They were many hundreds, old and young, some sick, and some lame, many had *Papooses* at their backs, the greatest number at this time with us, were *Squaws*, and they travelled with all they had, bag and baggage, and yet they got over this River aforesaid; and on *Munday* they set their *Wigwams* on fire, and away they went: On that very day came the *English* Army after them to this River, and saw the smoak of their *Wigwams*, and yet this River put a stop to them. God did not give them courage or activity to go over after us; we were not ready for so great a mercy as victory and deliverance; if we had been, God would have found out a way for the *English* to have passed this River, as well as for the *Indians* with their *Squaws* and *Children*, and all their Luggage: *Oh, that my People had hearkened to me, and* Israel *had walked in my ways, I should soon have subdued their Enemies, and turned my hand against their Adversaries*, Psal. 81. 13, 14.

THE SIXTH REMOVE

On Munday *(as I said) they set their* Wigwams *on fire, and went away.* It was a cold morning, and before us there was a great Brook with ice on it; some waded through it, up to the knees & higher, but others went till they came to a Beaver dam, and I amongst them, where through the good providence of God, I did not wet my foot. I went along that day mourning and lamenting, leaving farther my own Country, and travelling into the vast and howling *Wilderness*, and I understood something of *Lot*'s, Wife's Temptation, *when she looked back*:[37] we came that day to a great Swamp, by the side of which we took up our lodging that night. When I came to the brow of the hill, that looked toward the Swamp, I thought we had been come to a great *Indian* Town (though there were none but our own Company). The *Indians* were as thick as the trees: it seemed as if there had been a thousand Hatchets going at once: if one looked before one, there was nothing but *Indians*, and behind one, nothing but *Indians*, and so on either hand, I my self in the midst, and no

[37] See Genesis 19:26.

Christian soul near me, *and yet how hath the Lord preserved me in safety! Oh the experience that I have had of the goodness of God, to me and mine!*

THE SEVENTH REMOVE

After a restless and hungry night there, we had a wearisome time of it the next day. The Swamp by which we lay, was, as it were, a deep Dungeon, and an exceeding high and steep hill before it. Before I got to the top of the hill, I thought my heart and legs, and all would have broken, and failed me. What through faintness, and soreness of body, it was a grievous day of travel to me. As we went along, I saw a place where *English* cattle had been: that was comfort to me, such as it was: quickly after that we came to an *English* Path, which so took with me, that I thought I could have freely lyin down and dyed. That day, a little after noon, we came to *Squakheag*, where the *Indians* quickly spread themselves over the deserted *English* fields, gleaning what they could find; some pickt up ears of Wheat that were crickled down, some found ears of *Indian* Corn, some found Ground-nuts, and others sheaves of Wheat that were frozen together in the shock, and went to threshing of them out. My self got two ears of *Indian* Corn, and whilst I did but turn my back, one of them was stolen from me, which much troubled me. There came an *Indian* to them at that time, with a basket of Horse-liver. I asked him to give me a piece: *What*, sayes he *can you eat Horse-liver*? I told him, I would try, if he would give a piece, which he did, and I laid it on the coals to roast; but before it was half ready they got half of it away from me, so that I was fain to take the rest and eat it as it was, with the blood about my mouth, and yet a savory bit it was to me: *For to the hungry Soul, every bitter thing is sweet.*[38] A solemn sight me thought it was, to see Fields of wheat and *Indian* Corn forsaken and spoiled: and the remainders of them to be food for our merciless Enemies. That night we had a mess of wheat for our Supper.

THE EIGHTH REMOVE

On the morrow morning we must go over the River, *i.e.* Connecticot, to meet with King *Philip*, two *Cannoos* full, they had carried over, the next

---

[38] Proverbs 27:7.

Turn I myself was to go; but as my foot was upon the *Cannoo* to step in, there was a sudden out-cry among them, and I must step back; and instead of going over the River, I must go four or five miles up the River farther Northward. Some of the *Indians* ran one way, and some another. The cause of this rout was, as I thought, their espying some *English Scouts*, who were thereabout. In this travel up the river, about noon the Company made a stop, and sat down; some to eat, and others to rest them. As I sate amongst them, musing of things past, my Son *Joseph* unexpectedly came to me: we asked of each others welfare, bemoaning our dolefull condition, and the change that had come upon us. We had Husband and Father, and Children, and Sisters, and Friends, and Relations, and House, and Home, and many Comforts of this Life: but now we may say, as Job, *Naked came I out of my Mothers Womb, and naked shall I return: The Lord gave, and the Lord hath taken away, Blessed be the Name of the Lord.*[39] I asked him whither he would read; he told me, he earnestly desired it. I gave him my Bible, and he lighted upon that comfortable scripture, Psal. 118. 17, 18. *I shall not dy but live, and declare the works of the Lord: the Lord hath chastened me sore, yet he hath not given me over to death.* Look here, *Mother* (sayes he), did you read this? And here I may take occasion to mention one principall ground of my setting forth these Lines: even as the Psalmist sayes, *To declare the Works of the Lord*, and His wonderfull Power in carrying us along, preserving us in the *Wilderness*, while under the Enemies hand, and returning of us in safety again. And His goodness in bringing to my hand so many comfortable and suitable Scriptures in my distress. But to Return, We travelled on till night; and in the morning, we must go over the River to *Philip's* crew. When I was in the Cannoo, I could not but be amazed at the numerous crew of Pagans that were on the Bank on the other side. When I came ashore, they gathered all about me, I sitting alone in the midst: I observed they asked one another questions, and laughed, and rejoyced over their Gains and Victories. Then my heart began to fail: and I fell a weeping which was the first time to my remembrance, that I wept before them. Although I had met with so much Affliction, and my heart was many times ready to break, yet could I not shed one tear in their sight: but rather had been all this while in a maze, and like one astonished: but now I may say as, Psal. 137. 1. *By the rivers of* Babylon, *there we sat down: yea, we wept when we remembered Zion.* There one of them asked me, why I wept, I could hardly tell what to say: yet I

[39]Job 1:21.

me; yet not one of them offered the least imaginable miscarriage to me. I turned homeward again, and met with my master, he shewed me the way to my Son: When I came to him I found him not well: and withall he had a boyl on his side, which much troubled him: We bemoaned one another a while, as the Lord helped us, and then I returned again. When I was returned, I found myself as unsatisfied as I was before. I went up and down mourning and lamenting: and my spirit was ready to sink, with the thoughts of my poor Children: my Son was ill, and I could not but think of his mournfull looks, and no Christian Friend was near him, to do any office of love for him, either for Soul or Body. And my poor Girl, I knew not where she was, nor whither she was sick, or well, or alive, or dead. I repaired under these thoughts to my Bible (my great comfort in that time) and that Scripture came to my hand, *Cast thy burden upon the Lord, and He shall sustain thee*, Psal. 55. 22.

But I was fain to go and look after something to satisfie my hunger, and going among the *Wigwams*, I went into one, and there found a *Squaw* who shewed herself very kind to me, and gave me a piece of Bear. I put it into my pocket, and came home, but could not find an opportunity to broil it, for fear they would get it from me, and there it lay all that day and night in my stinking pocket. In the morning I went to the same *Squaw*, who had a Kettle of Ground-nuts boyling: I asked her to let me boyle my piece of Bear in her Kettle, which she did, and gave me some Groundnuts to eat with it: and I cannot but think how pleasant it was to me. I have sometimes seen Bear baked very handsomely among the *English*, and some like it, but the thought that it was Bear, made me tremble: but now that was savoury to me that one would think was enough to turn the stomach of a bruit Creature.

One bitter cold day, I could find no room to sit down before the fire: I went out, and could not tell what to do, but I went into another Wigwam, *where they were also sitting round the fire, but the* Squaw *laid a skin for me, and bid me sit down, and gave me some Ground-nuts, and bade me come again: and told me they would buy me, if they were able, and yet these were strangers to me that I never saw before.*

THE TENTH REMOVE

That day a small part of the Company removed about three quarters of a mile, intending further the next day. When they came to the place where they intended to lodge, and had pitched their *Wigwams*, being hungry I went again back to the place we were before at, to get something to eat: being encouraged by the *Squaws* kindness, who bade me come again; when I was there, there came an *Indian* to look after me, who when he had found me, kicked me all along: I went home and found Venison roasting that night, but they would not give me one bit of it. Sometimes I met with favour, and sometimes with nothing but frowns.

THE ELEVENTH REMOVE

The next day in the morning they took their Travel, intending a dayes journey up the River. I took my load at my back, and quickly we came to wade over the River: and passed over tiresome and wearisome hills. One hill was so steep that I was fain to creep up upon my knees, and to hold by the twiggs and bushes to keep myself from falling backward. My head also was so light, that I usually reeled as I went; but I hope all these wearisome steps that I have taken, are but a forewarning to me of the heavenly rest. *I know, O Lord, that thy Judgements are right, and that thou in faithfulness hast afflicted me,* Psal. 119. 71.[42]

THE TWELFTH REMOVE

It was upon a Sabbath-day morning, that they prepared for their Travel. This morning I asked my master whither he would sell me to my husband; he answered me *Nux*,[43] which did much rejoyce my spirit. My mistriss, before we went, was gone to the burial of a *Papoos*, and returning, she found me sitting and reading in my Bible; she snatched it hastily out of my hand, and threw it out of doors; I ran out and catch it up, and put it into my pocket, and never let her see it afterward. Then they packed up their things to be gone, and gave me my load: I complained it was too heavy, whereupon she gave me a slap in the face, and bade me go; I lifted up my heart to God, hoping the Redemption was not far off: and the rather because their insolency grew worse and worse.

But the thoughts of my going homeward (for so we bent our course) much cheared my Spirit, and made my burden seem light, and almost nothing at all. But (to my amazement and great perplexity) the scale was soon turned: for when we had gone a little way, on a sudden my mistress

---

[42] Actually, Psalm 119:75.
[43] Yes.

gives out, she would go no further, but turn back again, and said, I must go back again with her, and she called her *Sannup,* and would have had him gone back also, but he would not, but said, *He would go on, and come to us again in three dayes.* My Spirit was upon this, I confess, very impatient, and almost outragious.[44] I thought I could as well have dyed as went back: I cannot declare the trouble that I was in about it; but yet back again I must go. As soon as I had an opportunity, I took my Bible to read, and that quieting Scripture came to my hand, *Psal.* 46. 10. *Be still, and know that I am God.* Which stilled my spirit for the present: But a sore time of tryal, I concluded, I had to go through. My master being gone, who seemed to me the best friend that I had of an *Indian,* both in cold and hunger, and quickly so it proved. Down I sat, with my heart as full as it could hold, and yet so hungry that I could not sit neither: but going out to see what I could find, and walking among the Trees, I found six *Acorns,* and two *Ches-nuts,* which were some refreshment to me. Towards Night I gathered me some sticks for my own comfort, that I might not lie a-cold: but when we came to ly down they bade me go out, and ly somewhere else, for they had company (they said) come in more than their own: I told them, I could not tell where to go, they bade me go look; I told them, if I went to another *Wigwam* they would be angry, and send me home again. Then one of the Company drew his sword, and told me he would run me through if I did not go presently. Then was I fain to stoop to this rude fellow, and to go out in the night, I knew not whither. *Mine eyes have seen that fellow afterwards walking up and down* Boston, *under the appearance of a* Friend-Indian, *and severall others of the like Cut.* I went to one *Wigwam,* and they told me they had no room. Then I went to another, and they said the same; at last an old *Indian* bade me come to him, and his *Squaw* gave me some Ground-nuts; she gave me also something to lay under my head, and a good fire we had: and through the good providence of God, I had a comfortable lodging that night. In the morning, another *Indian* bade me come at night, and he would give me six Groundnuts, which I did. We were at this place and time about two miles from *Connecticut River.* We went in the morning to gather Ground-nuts, to the River, and went back again that night. I went with a good load at my back (for they when they went, though but a little way, would carry all their trumpery with them) I told them the skin was

---

[44] Meaning that she almost burst out in a rage. Weetamoo was undoubtedly turning back because her own child, who would die shortly (see p. 91), was too sick to travel.

off my back, but I had no other comforting answer from them than this, *That it would be no matter if my head were off too.*

THE THIRTEENTH REMOVE

Instead of going toward the Bay, *which was that I desired, I must go with them five or six miles down the River into a mighty Thicket of Brush: where we abode almost a fortnight.* Here one asked me to make a shirt for her *Papoos* for which she gave me a mess of Broth, which was thickened with meal made of the Bark of a Tree, and to make it the better, she had put into it about a handfull of Pease, and a few roasted Ground-nuts. I had not seen my son a pritty while, and here was an *Indian* of whom I made inquiry after him, and asked him when he saw him: he answered me, that such a time his master roasted him, and that himself did eat a piece of him, as big as his two fingers, and that he was very good meat: *But the Lord upheld my Spirit, under this discouragement; and I considered their horrible addictedness to lying, and that there is not one of them that makes the least conscience of speaking of truth.* In this place, on a cold night, as I lay by the fire, I removed a stick that kept the heat from me, a *Squaw* moved it down again, at which I lookt up, and she threw a handfull of ashes in mine eyes: I thought I should have been quite blinded, and have never seen more: but lying down, the water run out of my eyes, and carried the dirt with it, that by the morning, I recovered my sight again. Yet upon this, and the like occasions, I hope it is not too much to say with Job, *Have pitty upon me, have pitty upon me, O ye my friends, for the Hand of the Lord has touched me.*[45] And here I cannot but remember how many times sitting in their *Wigwams,* and musing on things past, I should suddenly leap up and run out, as if I had been at home, forgetting where I was, and what my condition was: But when I was without, and saw nothing but *Wilderness,* and *Woods,* and a company of barbarous heathens: my mind quickly returned to me, which made me think of that, spoken concerning *Sampson,* who said, *I will go out and shake myself as at other times, but he wist not that the Lord was departed from him.*[46] About this time I began to think that all my hopes of Restoration would come to nothing. I thought of the *English* Army, and hoped for their

[45] Job 19:21.
[46] Judges 16:20.

coming, and being taken by them, but that failed also. I hoped to be carried to *Albany*, as the *Indians* had discoursed before, but that failed also. I thought of being sold to my Husband, as my master spake, but in stead of that, my master himself was gone, and I left behind, so that my Spirit was now quite ready to sink. I asked them to let me go out and pick up some sticks, that I might get alone, *And poure out my heart unto the Lord.* Then also I took my Bible to read, but I found no comfort here neither, which many times I was wont to find: *So easie a thing it is with God to dry up the Streames of Scripture-comfort from us.* Yet I can say, that in all my sorrows and afflictions, God did not leave me to have my impatience work towards himself, as if his wayes were unrighteous. *But I knew that he laid upon me less than I deserved.* Afterward, before this dolefull time ended with me, I was turning the leaves of my Bible, and the Lord brought to me some Scriptures, which did a little revive me, as that Isai. 55.8. *For my thoughts are not your thoughts, neither are your wayes my ways, saith the Lord.* And also that, *Psal.* 37. 5. *Commit thy way unto the Lord, trust also in him, and he shall bring it to pass.* About this time they came yelping from *Hadly*, where they had killed three *English men*, and brought one Captive with them, *viz. Thomas Read.* They all gathered about the poor Man, asking him many Questions. I desired also to go and see him; and when I came, he was crying bitterly, supposing they would quickly kill him. Whereupon I asked one of them, whether they intended to kill him; he answered me, they would not: He being a little cheared with that, I asked him about the wel-fare of my *Husband*, he told me he saw him such a time in the *Bay*, and he was well, but very melancholly. By which I certainly understood (though I suspected it before) that whatsoever the *Indians* told me respecting him was vanity and lies. Some of them told me, he was dead, and they had killed him: some said he was Married again, and that the Governour wished him to marry; and told him he should have his choice, and that all perswaded I was dead. So like were these barbarous creatures to him who was a lyar from the beginning.

As I was sitting once in the *Wigwam* here, *Philips* Maid came in with the Child in her arms, and asked me to give her a piece of my Apron, to make a flap for it, I told her I would not: then my Mistress bade me give it, but still I said no: the maid told me if I would not give her a piece, she would tear a piece off it: I told her I would tear her Coat then, with that my Mistriss rises up, and takes up a stick big enough to have killed me, and struck at me with it, but I stepped out, and she struck the stick into the Mat of the Wigwam. But while she was pulling of it out, I ran to the Maid and gave her all my Apron, and so that storm went over.

that my Son was come to this place, I went to see him, and
...s Father was well, but very melancholly: he told me he was as
much grieved for his Father as for himself; I wondred at his speech, for
I thought I had enough upon my spirit in reference to my self, to make
me mindless of my Husband and every one else: they being safe among
their Friends. He told me also, that a while before, his Master (together
with other *Indians*) were going to the *French* for *Powder*, but by the way
the *Mohawks* met with them, and killed four of their Company which
made the rest turn back again,[47] for which I desired that my self and
he may bless the Lord; for it might have been worse with him, had he
been sold to the *French*, than it proved to be in his remaining with the
Indians.[48]

I went to see an *English* Youth in this place, one *John Gilberd* of
Springfield. I found him lying without dores, upon the ground; I asked
him how he did? He told me he was very sick of a flux,[49] with eating so
much blood: They had turned him out of the *Wigwam*, and with him an
Indian Papoos, almost dead, (whose Parents had been killed) in a bitter
cold day, without fire or clothes: the young man himself had nothing
on, but his shirt and wast-coat. This sight was enough to melt a heart of
flint. There they lay quivering in the Cold, the youth round like a dog,
the *Papoos* stretcht out, with his eyes and nose and mouth full of dirt,
and yet alive, and groaning. I advised John to go and get to some fire:
he told me he cou'd not stand, but I perswaded him still, lest he should
ly there and die: and with much adoe I got him to a fire, and went my
self home. As soon as I was got home, his Masters Daughter came after
me, to know what I had done with the *English man*, I told her I had
got him to a fire in such a place. Now had I need to pray *Pauls* prayer,
2 Thess. 3. 2. *That we may be delivered from unreasonable and wicked
men.* For her satisfaction I went along with her, and brought her to him;
but before I got home again, it was noised about, that I was running away
and getting the *English* youth, along with me; that as soon as I came
in, they began to rant and domineer: asking me where I had been, and
what I had been doing? and saying they would knock him on the head:
I told them, I had been seeing the *English Youth*, and that I would not

---

[47] Having been at war with most New England Algonquians for the preceding decade,
the Mohawks found common cause with the colonists upon the outbreak of King Philip's
War.

[48] Rowlandson fears the French in Canada because they are Catholic. Puritans
regarded the Pope as the Anti-Christ and Catholicism as a form of spiritual slavery.

[49] Dysentery.

run away, they told me I lyed, and taking up a Hatchet, they came to me, and said they would knock me down if I stirred out again; and so confined me to the *Wigwam*. Now may I say with *David*, 2 Sam. 24. 14. *I am in a great strait.* If I keep in, I must dy with hunger, and if I go out, I must be knockt in head. This distressed condition held that day, and half the next; *And then the Lord remembered me, whose mercyes are great.* Then came an *Indian* to me with a pair of stockings that were too big for him, and he would have me ravel them out, and knit them fit for him. I shewed my self willing, and bade him ask my mistriss if I might go along with him a little way; she said yes, I might, but I was not a little refresht with that news, that I had my liberty again. Then I went along with him, and he gave me some roasted Ground-nuts, which did again revive my feeble stomach.

Being got out of her sight, I had time and liberty again to look into my Bible: *Which was my Guid by day, and my Pillow by night.* Now that comfortable Scripture presented itself to me, *Isa.* 54. 7. *For a small moment have I forsaken thee, but with great mercies will I gather thee.* Thus the Lord carried me along from one time to another, and made good to me this precious promise, and many others. Then my Son came to see me, and I asked his master to let him stay a while with me, that I might comb his head, and look over him, for he was almost overcome with lice. He told me, when I had done, that he was very hungry, but I had nothing to relieve him; but bid him go into the Wigwams as he went along, and see if he could get any thing among them. Which he did, and it seems tarried a little too long; for his Master was angry with him, and beat him, and then sold him. Then he came running to tell me he had a new Master, and that he had given him some Ground-nuts already. Then I went along with him to his new Master who told me he loved him: and he should not want. So his master carried him away, & I never saw him afterward, till I saw him at *Pascataqua* in *Portsmouth*.

That night they bade me go out of the *Wigwam* again: my Mistrisses Papoos was sick, and it died that night, and there was one benefit in it, that there was more room. I went to a *Wigwam*, and they bade me come in, and gave me a skin to ly upon, and a mess of Venison and Ground-nuts, which was a choice Dish among them. On the morrow they buried the *Papoos*, and afterward, both morning and evening, there came a company to mourn and howle with her: though I confess, I could not much condole with them. Many sorrowfull dayes I had in this place: often getting alone; *like a Crane, or a Swallow, so did I chatter: I did mourn as a Dove, mine eyes fail with looking upward. Oh, Lord, I am oppressed; undertake for me,* Isa. 38. 14. I could tell the Lord as *Hezekiah*, ver. 3. *Remember now O Lord, I beseech thee, how I have walked before thee in truth.*[50] Now had I time to examine all my wayes: my Conscience did not accuse me, of un-righteousness toward one or other: yet I saw how in my walk with God, I had been a careless creature. As *David* said, *Against thee, thee only have I sinned*: & I might say with the poor Publican, *God be merciful unto me a sinner.*[51] On the Sabbath-dayes, I could look upon the Sun and think how People were going to the house of God, to have their Souls refresht; & then home, and their bodies also: but I was destitute of both; & might say as the poor Prodigal, *he would fain have filled his belly with the husks that the Swine did eat, and no man gave unto him*, Luke 15. 16. For I must say with him, *Father I have sinned against heaven, and in thy sight*, ver. 21.[52] I remembered how on the night before & after the Sabbath, when my Family was about me, and Relations and Neighbours with us, we could pray and sing, and then refresh our bodies with the good creatures of God; and then have a comfortable Bed to ly down on: but in stead of all this, I had only a little Swill for the body, and then like a Swine, must ly down on the ground. I cannot express to man the sorrow that lay upon my Spirit, the Lord knows it. Yet that comfortable Scripture would often come to my mind, *For a small moment have I forsaken thee, but with great mercies will I gather thee.*[53]

THE FOURTEENTH REMOVE

Now must we pack up and be gone from this Thicket, bending our course toward the Bay-towns, I haveing nothing to eat by the way this day, but a few crumbs of Cake, that an *Indian* gave my girle the same day we were taken.[54] She gave it me, and I put it in my pocket; there it lay, till it was so mouldy (for want of good baking) that one could not tell what it was made of; it fell all to crumbs, & grew so dry and hard, that it was like little flints; & this refreshed me many times, when I was ready to faint. It was in my thoughts when I put it into my mouth; that if ever I returned, I would tell the World what a blessing the Lord gave to such mean food.

[50] Hezekiah speaks these words in Isaiah 38:3.
[51] Psalm 51:4 and Luke 18:13, respectively.
[52] Like the quotation immediately preceding, in Luke 15.
[53] Isaiah 54:7.
[54] Rowlandson here contradicts her statement (p. 80) that no one gave her or her daughter any food.

As we went along, they killed a *Deer*, with a young one in her, they gave me a piece of the *Fawn*, and it was so young and tender, that one might eat the bones as well as the flesh, and yet I thought it very good. When night came on we sate down; it rained, but they quickly got up a Bark Wigwam, where I lay dry that night. I looked out in the morning, and many of them had lain in the rain all night, I saw by their Reaking. Thus the Lord dealt mercifully with me many times, and I fared better than many of them. In the morning they took the blood of the *Deer*, and put it into the Paunch, and so boyled it; I could eat nothing of that, though they ate it sweetly. And yet they were so nice[55] in other things, that when I had fetcht Water, and had put the Dish I dipt the water with, into the Kettle of water which I brought, they would say, they would knock me down; for they said, it was a sluttish trick.

THE FIFTEENTH REMOVE

We went on our Travel. I having got one handfull of Ground-nuts, for my support that day, they gave me my load, and I went on cheerfully (with the thoughts of going homeward) haveing my burden more on my back than my spirit: we came to *Baquaug River* again that day, near which we abode a few dayes. Sometimes one of them would give me a Pipe, another a little Tobacco, another a little Salt: which I would change for a little Victuals. I cannot but think what a Wolvish appetite persons have in a starving condition: for many times when they gave me that which was hot, I was so greedy, that I shou'd burn my mouth, that it would trouble me hours after, and yet I should quickly do the same again. And after I was thoroughly hungry, I was never again satisfied. For though sometimes it fell out, that I got enough, and did eat till I could eat no more, yet I was as unsatisfied as I was when I began. And now could I see that Scripture verified (there being many Scriptures which we do not take notice of, or understand till we are afflicted) *Mic.* 6. 14. *Thou shalt eat and not be satisfied.* Now I might see more than ever before, the miseries that sin hath brought upon us: Many times I should be ready to run out against the Heathen, but the Scripture would quiet me again, *Amos*, 3.6, *Shal there be evil in the City, and the Lord hath not done it?* The Lord help me to make a right improvement of His Word, and that I might learn that great lesson, *Mic.* 6. 8, 9. *He hath showed thee (Oh Man)*

[55] Nice, in the archaic sense of fastidious, difficult to please.

what is good, and what doth the Lord require of thee, but to do justly, and love mercy, and walk humbly with thy God? Hear ye the rod, and who hath appointed it.

THE SIXTEENTH REMOVE

We began this Remove with wading over Baquag *River: the water was up to the knees, and the stream very swift, and so cold that I thought it would have cut me in sunder.* I was so weak and feeble, that I reeled as I went along, and thought there I must end my dayes at last, after my bearing and getting through so many difficulties; the *Indians* stood laughing to see me staggering along: but in my distress the Lord gave me experience of the truth, and goodness of that promise, *Isai.* 43. 2. *When thou passest through the Waters, I will be with thee, and through the Rivers, they shall not overflow thee.* Then I sat down to put on my stockins and shoes, with the teares running down mine eyes, and many sorrowfull thoughts in my heart, but I gat up to go along with them. Quickly there came up to us an *Indian*, who informed them, that I must go to *Wachusett* to my master, for there was a Letter come from the Council to the *Sagamores*, about redeeming the Captives, and that there would be another in fourteen dayes, and that I must be there ready.[56] My heart was so heavy before that I could scarce speak or go in the path; and yet now so light, that I could run. My strength seemed to come again, and recruit my feeble knees, and aking heart: yet it pleased them to go but one mile that night, and there we stayed two dayes. In that time came a company of *Indians* to us, near thirty, all on horse-back. My heart skipt within me, thinking they had been *English men* at the first sight of them, for they were dressed in *English* Apparel, with Hats, white Neckcloths, and Sashes about their waists, and Ribbonds upon their shoulders: but when they came near, there was a vast difference between the lovely faces of Christians, and the foul looks of these Heathens, which much damped my spirit again.

THE SEVENTEENTH REMOVE

A comfortable Remove it was to me, because of my hopes. They gave me a pack, and along we went chearfully; but quickly my will proved more

---

[56]This is the letter from Governor John Leverett to the "Indian Sagamores" (Document 8).

than my strength; having little or no refreshing my strength failed me, and my spirit were almost quite gone. Now may I say with *David,* Psalm 119.[57] *22, 23, 24. I am poor and needy, and my heart is wounded within me. I am gone like the shadow when it declineth: I am tossed up and down like the locusts; my knees are weak through fasting, and my flesh faileth of fatness.* At night we came to an *Indian Town,* and the *Indians* sate down by a *Wigwam* discoursing, but I was almost spent, and could scarce speak. I laid down my load, and went into the *Wigwam,* and there sat an *Indian* boyling of *Horses feet* (they being wont to eat the flesh first, and when the feet were old and dried, and they had nothing else, they would cut off the feet and use them). I asked him to give me a little of his Broth, or Water they were boiling in; he took a dish, and gave me one spoonful of Samp,[58] and bid me take as much of the Broth as I would. Then I put some of the hot water to the Samp, and drank it up, and my spirit came

Figure 10: *A Native American House in Seventeenth-Century Massachusetts* Rowlandson's Native American captors quickly put up wigwams with each remove. Most families lived in bark wigwams like this one but those of sachems, such as Weetamoo and Quinnapin, were larger. Compare this house with the kind that Rowlandson had lived in before she was captured (Figure 2). Marilyn Genter/The Image Works.

[57] Actually, Psalm 109.
[58] A corn porridge.

again. He gave me also a piece of the Ruff or Ridding of the small Guts,[59] and I broiled it on the coals; and now may I say with *Jonathan, See, I pray you, how mine eyes have been enlightened, because I tasted a little of this honey,* 1 *Sam.* 14. 29. Now is my Spirit revived again, though means be never so inconsiderable, yet if the Lord bestow his blessing upon them, they shall refresh both Soul and Body.

THE EIGHTEENTH REMOVE

We took up our packs and along we went, but a wearisome day I had of it. As we went along I saw an *English-man* stript naked, and lying dead upon the ground, but knew not who it was. Then we came to another *Indian Town*, where we stayed all night. In this Town there were four *English Children*, Captives; and one of them my own Sisters.[60] I went to see how she did, and she was well, considering her Captive-condition. I would have tarried that night with her, but they that owned her would not suffer it. Then I went into another *Wigwam*, where they were boyling Corn and Beans, which was a lovely sight to see, but I could not get a taste thereof. Then I went to another *Wigwam,* where there were two of the *English Children*; the *Squaw* was boyling *Horses feet*, then she cut me off a little piece, and gave one of the *English Children* a piece also. Being very hungry I had quickly eat up mine, but the Child could not bite it, it was so tough and sinewy, but lay sucking, gnawing, chewing and slobbering of it in the mouth and hand, then I took it of the Child, and ate it myself, and savoury it was to my taste. Then I may say as *Job Chap.* 6. 7. *The things that my soul refused to touch, are as my sorrowful meat.* Thus the Lord made that pleasant refreshing, which another time would have been an abomination. Then I went home to my mistresses *Wigwam*; and they told me I disgraced my master with begging, and if I did so any more, they would knock me in the head: I told them, they had as good knock me in the head as starve me to death.

[59]That is, parts that were rough (difficult or distasteful to eat) or had been gotten rid of because they were considered inedible.

[60]That is, her sister's child.

THE NINETEENTH REMOVE

They said, when we went out, that we must travel to Wachuset *this day.* But a bitter weary day I had of it, travelling now three dayes together, without resting any day between. At last, after many weary steps, I saw *Wachuset* hills, but many miles off. Then we came to a great *Swamp,* through which we travelled, up to the knees, in mud and water, which was heavy going to one tyred before. Being almost spent, I thought I should have sunk down at last, and never gat out; but I may say, as in Psal. 94. 18. *When my foot slipped, thy mercy, O Lord, held me up.* Going along, having indeed my life, but little spirit, *Philip,* who was in the Company, came up and took me by the hand, and said, *Two weeks more and you shal be Mistress again.* I asked him, if he spake true? He answered, Yes, *and quickly you shall come to your master again*; who had been gone from us three weeks. After many weary steps we came to *Wachuset,* where he was: and glad I was to see him. He asked me, *When I washt me?* I told him not this month, then he fetcht me some water himself, and bid me wash, and gave me the Glass to see how I lookt; and bid his *Squaw* give me something to eat: so she gave me a mess of Beans and meat, and a little Ground-nut Cake. I was wonderfully revived with this favour shewed me, *Psal.* 106. 46, *He made them also to be pittied, of all those that carried them Captives.*

My master had three *Squaws,* living sometimes with one, and sometimes with another one, this old Squaw, at whose *Wigwam* I was, and with whom my master had been those three weeks. Another was *Wettimore,* with whom I had lived and served all this while: A severe and proud Dame she was, bestowing every day in dressing herself neat as much time as any of the Gentry of the land: powdering her hair, and painting her face, going with Neck-laces, with Jewels in her ears, and Bracelets upon her hands: When she had dressed her self, her work was to make Girdles of *Wampom* and *Beads.* The third *Squaw* was a younger one, by whom he had two *Papooses.* By that time I was refresht by the old *Squaw,* with whom my master was, *Wettimores* Maid came to call me home, at which I fell a weeping. Then the old *Squaw* told me, to encourage me, that if I wanted victuals, I should come to her, and that I should ly there in her *Wigwam.* Then I went with the maid, and quickly came again and lodged there. The *Squaw* laid a Mat under me, and a good Rugg over me; the first time I had any such kindness shewed me. I understood that *Wettimore* thought, that if she should let me go and serve with the old *Squaw,* she would be in danger to loose, not only my service, but the redemption-pay also. And I was not a little glad to hear this; being by it raised in my hopes, that in Gods due time there would be an end of this sorrowfull hour. Then in came an *Indian*, and asked me to knit him three pair of Stockins, for which I had a Hat, and a silk Handkerchief. Then another asked me to make her a shift, for which she gave me an Apron.

Then came *Tom* and *Peter*, with the second Letter from the Council, about the Captives.[61] Though they were *Indians*, I gat them by the hand, and burst out into tears; my heart was so full that I could not speak to them; but recovering my self, I asked them how my husband did, and all my friends and acquaintance? they said, *They are all very well, but melancholy.* They brought me two Biskets, and a pound of Tobacco. The Tobacco I quickly gave away; when it was all gone, one asked me to give him a pipe of Tobacco, I told him it was all gone; then began he to rant and threaten. I told him when my Husband came I would give him some: *Hang him Rogue (sayes he) I will knock out his brains, if he comes here.* And then again, in the same breath they would say, *That if there should come an hundred without Guns, they would do them no hurt.* So unstable and like mad men they were. So that fearing the worst, I durst not send to my Husband, though there were some thoughts of his coming to Redeem and fetch me, not knowing what might follow; *For there was little more trust to them than to the master they served.* When the Letter was come, the *Saggamores* met to consult about the Captives, and called me to them to enquire how much my husband would give to redeem me, when I came I sate down among them, as I was wont to do, as their manner is: Then they bade me stand up, and said, *they were the General Court.*[62] They bid me speak what I thought he would give. Now knowing that all we had was destroyed by the *Indians*, I was in a great strait: I thought if I should speak of but a little, it would be slighted, and hinder the matter; if of a great sum, I knew not where it would be procured: yet at a venture, I said *Twenty pounds*, yet desired them to take less; but they would not hear of that, but sent that message to *Boston*, that for *Twenty pounds* I should be redeemed.[63] It was a Praying-*Indian*[64] that wrote their Letter for them. There was another Praying *Indian*, who told me, that he had a brother, that would not eat Horse; his conscience was so tender and scrupulous (though as large as hell, for the destruction of poor *Christians*). Then he said, he read

---

[61] No copies of this letter are known to exist.

[62] The General Court was the name of Massachusetts Bay's legislature.

[63] See Document 9. Rowlandson's elaborate explanation of the ransom price she set suggests that she may have been criticized for it by some colonists.

[64] James Printer.

that Scripture to him, 2 Kings, 6. 25. *There was a famine in* Samaria, *and behold they besieged it, until an Asses head was sold for fourscore pieces of silver, and the fourth part of a Kab*[65] *of Doves dung, for five pieces of silver.* He expounded this place to his brother, and shewed him that it was lawfull to eat that in a Famine which is not at another time. And now, says he, he will eat horse with any *Indian* of them all. There was another Praying-*Indian,* who when he had done all the mischief that he could, betrayed his own Father into the *English* hands, thereby to purchase his own life. Another Praying-*Indian* was at *Sudbury-fight,* though, as he deserved, he was afterward hanged for it.[66] There was another Praying *Indian,* so wicked and cruel, as to wear a string about his neck, strung with *Christians* fingers. Another Praying-*Indian,* when they went to *Sudbury-fight,* went with them, and his *Squaw* also with him, with her *Papoos* at her back. Before they went to that fight, they got a company together to *Powaw*; the manner was as followeth. There was one that kneeled upon a *Deer-skin,* with the company round him in a ring who kneeled, and striking upon the ground with their hands, and with sticks, and muttering or humming with their mouths, besides him who kneeled in the ring, there also stood one with a Gun in his hand: Then he on the *Deer-skin* made a speech, and all manifested assent to it: and so they did many times together. Then they bade him with the Gun go out of the ring, which he did, but when he was out, they called him in again; but he seemed to make a stand, then they called the more earnestly, till he returned again: Then they all sang. Then they gave him two Guns, in either hand one: And so he on the *Deer-skin* began again; and at the end of every sentence in his speaking, they all assented, humming or muttering with their mouthes, and striking upon the ground with their hands. Then they bade him with the two Guns go out of the ring again; which he did, a little way. Then they called him in again, but he made a stand; so they called him with greater earnestness; but he stood reeling and wavering as if he knew not whither he should stand or fall, or which way to go. Then they called him with exceeding great vehemency, all of them, one and another: after a little while he turned in, staggering as he went, with his Armes stretched out, in either hand a Gun. As soon as he came in, they all sang and rejoyced exceedingly a while. And then he upon the *Deer-skin,* made another speech unto which they all assented

---

[65] An ancient Hebrew unit of measurement, equivalent to about two liters or 3.5 pints.

[66] The battle of Sudbury, apparently fought while the two Nipmuc messengers were in the Indian camp, was the last major clash engaged in by Rowlandson's captors. As she indicates, it marked a further step in the demoralization of the anti-English forces.

in a rejoicing manner: and so they ended their business, and forthwith went to *Sudbury-fight*.[67] To my thinking they went without any scruple, but that they should prosper, and gain the victory: And they went out not so rejoycing, but they came home with as great a Victory. For they said they had killed two Captains, and almost an hundred men. One *English-man* they brought along with them: and he said, it was too true, for they had made sad work at *Sudbury*, as indeed it proved. Yet they came home without that rejoicing and triumphing over their victory, which they were wont to shew at other times, but rather like Dogs (as they say) which have lost their ears. Yet I could not perceive that it was for their own loss of men: They said, they had not lost above five or six: and I missed none, except in one *Wigwam*. When they went, they acted as if the Devil had told them that they should gain the victory: and now they acted, as if the Devil had told them they should have a fall. Whither it were so or no, I cannot tell, but so it proved, for quickly they began to fall, and so held on that Summer, till they came to utter ruine. They came home on a Sabbath day, and the *Powaw* that kneeled upon the *Deer-skin* came home (I may say, without abuse) as black as the Devil.[68] When my master came home, he came to me and bid me make a shirt for his *Papoos*, of a hollandlaced Pillowbeer.[69] About that time there came an *Indian* to me and bid me come to his *Wigwam*, at night, and he would give me some Pork & Ground-nuts. Which I did, and as I was eating, another *Indian* said to me, he seems to be your good Friend, but he killed two *Englishmen* at *Sudbury*, and there lie their Cloaths behind you: I looked behind me, and there I saw bloody Cloaths, with Bullet holes in them; yet the Lord suffered not this wretch to do me any hurt; Yea, instead of that, he many times refresht me: five or six times did he and his *Squaw* refresh my feeble carcass. If I went to their *Wigwam* at any time, they would alwayes give me something, and yet they were strangers that I never saw before. Another *Squaw* gave me a piece of fresh Pork, and a little Salt with it, and lent me her Pan to Fry it in; and I cannot but remember what a sweet, pleasant and delightfull relish that

---

[67] The powwow Rowlandson has described was a prebattle ceremony of some kind. Although she was ostensibly appalled at the fact that it was organized by a Christian Indian, her detailed description betrays a deeper fascination. Note that the ceremony also modified precolonial Native tradition in its use of guns.

[68] Among New England Algonquians, a powwow referred both to certain kinds of ceremonies and to the spiritual healers who conducted them.

[69] That is, from a pillowcase of a type of linen cloth that originated in the Netherlands.

bit had to me, to this day. So little do we prize common mercies when we have them to the full.

THE TWENTIETH REMOVE

It was their usual manner to remove, when they had done any mischief, lest they should be found out: and so they did at this time. We went about three or four miles, and there they built a great *Wigwam,* big enough to hold an hundred *Indians,* which they did in preparation to a great day of Dancing. They would say now amongst themselves, that the *Governour* would be so angry for his loss at Sudbury, that he would send no more about the Captives, which made me grieve and tremble. My Sister being not far from the place where we now were, and hearing that I was here, desired her master to let her come and see me, and he was willing to it, and would go with her: but she being ready before him, told him she would go before, and was come within a Mile or two of the place; Then he overtook her, and began to rant as if he had been mad; and made her go back again in the Rain; so that I never saw her till I saw her in *Charlestown.* But the Lord requited many of their ill doings, for this *Indian* her master, was hanged afterward at *Boston.* The *Indians* now began to come from all quarters, against their merry dancing day. Among some of them came one *Goodwife Kettle*:[70] I told her my heart was so heavy that it was ready to break: so is mine too, said she, but yet said, I hope we shall hear some good news shortly. I could hear how earnestly my Sister desired to see me, and I as earnestly desired to see her: and yet neither of us could get an opportunity. My Daughter was also now about a mile off, and I had not seen her in nine or ten weeks, as I had not seen my Sister since our first taking. I earnestly desired them to let me go and see them: yea, I intreated, begged, and perswaded them, but to let me see my Daughter; and yet so hard hearted were they, that they would not suffer it. They made use of their tyrannical power whilst they had it: but through the Lord's wonderful mercy, their time was now but short.

On a Sabbath day, the Sun being about an hour high in the afternoon, came Mr. John Hoar[71] *(the Council permitting him, and his own foreward spirit inclining him) together with the two forementioned Indians,* Tom

---

[70] Elizabeth Kettle, also captured at Lancaster.
[71] See Document 11.

and Peter, *with their third Letter from the Council.* When they came near, I was abroad: though I saw them not, they presently called me in, and bade me sit down and not stir. Then they catched up their Guns, and away they ran, as if an Enemy had been at hand; and the Guns went off apace. I manifested some great trouble, and they asked me what was the matter? I told them, I *thought they had killed the* English-man (for they had in the mean time informed me that an *English-man* was come), they said, *No*; They shot over his Horse, and under, and before his Horse; and they pusht him this way and that way, at their pleasure, shewing what they could do: Then they let them come to their *Wigwams*. I begged of them to let me see the *English man*, but they would not. But there was I fain to sit their pleasure. When they had talked their fill with him, they suffered me to go to him. We asked each other of our welfare, and how my Husband did, and all my Friends? He told me they were all well, and would be glad to see me. Amongst other things which my Husband sent me, there came a pound of *Tobacco*: which I sold for nine shillings in Money: for many of the *Indians* for want of *Tobacco*, smoaked *Hemlock*, and *Ground-Ivy*. It was a great mistake in any, who thought I sent for *Tobacco*: for through the favour of God, that desire was overcome. I now asked them, whither I should go home with Mr. *Hoar*? They answered *No*, one and another of them: and it being night, we lay down with that answer; in the morning, Mr. *Hoar* invited the *Saggamores* to Dinner; but when we went to get it ready, we found that they had stollen the great-est part of the Provision Mr. *Hoar* had brought, out of his Bags, in the night: *And we may see the wonderfull power of God, in that one passage, in that when there was such a great number of the* Indians *together, and so greedy of a little good food; and no* English *there, but Mr. Hoar and my self: that there they did not knock us in the head, and take what we had: there being not only some Provision, but also Trading-cloth, a part of the twenty pounds agreed upon: But instead of doing us any mischief, they seemed to be ashamed of the fact, and said, it were some* Matchit[72] Indian *that did it.* Oh, that we could believe that there is nothing too hard for God! God shewed his Power over the Heathen in this, *as he did over the hungry Lyons when* Daniel *was cast into the Den.* Mr. *Hoar* called them betime to Dinner, but they ate very little, they being so busie in dressing themselves, and getting ready for their Dance: which was carried on by eight of them, four *Men* and four *Squaws*; My master and mistriss being two. He was dressed in his Holland shirt, with great Laces sewed at the

[72] Bad.

tail of it, he had his silver Buttons, his white Stockins, his Garters were hung round with Shillings, and he had Girdles of *Wampom upon his head and shoulders*. She had a Kersey[73] Coat, and covered with Girdles of *Wampom* from the Loins upward: her armes from her elbows to her hands were covered with Bracelets; there were handfulls of Neck-laces about her neck, and severall sorts of Jewels in her ears. She had fine red Stockins, and white Shoos, her hair powdered and face painted Red, that was always before Black. And all the Dancers were after the same manner. There were two other singing and knocking on a Kettle for their musick. They keept hopping up and down one after another, with a Kettle of water in the midst, standing warm upon some Embers, to drink of when they were dry. They held on till it was almost night, throwing out *Wampom* to the standers by. At night I asked them again, if I should go home? They all as one said No, except my Husband would come for me. When we were lain down, my Master went out of the *Wigwam,* and by and by sent in an *Indian* called *James the Printer,* who told Mr. *Hoar,* that my Master would let me go home tomorrow, if he would let him have one pint of Liquors. Then Mr. *Hoar* called his own *Indians, Tom* and *Peter,* and bid them go and see whither he would promise before them three: and if he would, he should have it; which he did, and he had it. Then *Philip* smelling the business cal'd me to him, and asked me what I would give him, to tell me some good news, and speak a good word for me. *I told him, I could not tell what to give him, I would anything I had, and asked him what he would have?* He said, two Coats and twenty shillings in Mony, and half a bushel of seed Corn, and some Tobacco. I thanked him for his love: but I knew the good news as well as the crafty *Fox.* My Master after he had had his drink, quickly came ranting into the *Wigwam* again, and called for Mr. *Hoar,* drinking to him, and saying, *He was a good man:* and then again he would say, *Hang him, Rogue*: Being almost drunk, he would drink to him, and yet presently say he should be hanged. Then he called for me, I trembled to hear him, yet I was fain to go to him, and he drank to me, shewing no incivility. He was the first *Indian* I saw drunk all the while that I was amongst them. At last his *Squaw* ran out, and he after her, round the *Wigwam,* with his money jingling at his knees: But she escaped him: But having an old *Squaw* he ran to her: and so through the Lords mercy, we were no more troubled that night. *Yet I had not a comfortable nights rest: for I think I can say, I did not sleep for three nights together.* The night before the Letter came

---

[73] A kind of coarse cloth woven from wool.

from the Council, I could not rest, I was so full of feares and troubles, God many times leaving us most in the dark, when deliverance is nearest: yea, at this time I could not rest, night nor day. The next night I was overjoyed, Mr. *Hoar* being come, and that with such good tidings. The third night I was even swallowed up with all thoughts of things, *viz.* that ever I should go home again; and that I must go, leaving my Children behind me in the *Wilderness*; so that sleep was now almost departed from mine eyes.

On *Tuesday morning* they called their *General Court* (as they call it) to consult and determine, whether I should go home or no: And they all as one man did seemingly consent to it, that I should go home; except *Philip*, who would not come among them.[74]

But before I go any further, I would take leave to mention a few remarkable passages of providence, which I took special notice of in my afflicted time.

1. *Of the fair opportunity lost in the long March, a little after the* Fort-fight,[75] *when our* English Army *was so numerous, and in pursuit of the* Enemy, *and so near as to take several and destroy them: and the* Enemy *in such distress for food, that our men might track them by their rooting in the earth for Ground-nuts whilest they were flying for their lives.* I say, that then our Army should want Provision, and be forced to leave their pursuit and return homeward: and the very next week the *Enemy* came upon our *Town*, like Bears bereft of their whelps, or so many ravenous Wolves, rending us and our Lambs to death. But what shall I say? God seemed to leave His People to themselves, and order all things for His own holy ends. *Shall there be evil in the City and the Lord hath not done it? They are not grieved for the affliction of* Joseph, *therefore shal they go Captive, with the first that go Captive. It is the Lords doing, and it should be marvelous in our eyes.*[76]

2. *I cannot but remember how the* Indians *derided the slowness, and dulness of the* English Army, *in its setting out.* For after the desolations at *Lancaster* and *Medfield*, as I went along with them, they asked me when I thought the *English* Army would come after them? I told them I could not tell: It may be they will come in *May*, said they. Thus did they scoffe at us, as if the *English* would be a quarter of a year getting ready.

---

[74] At this point, Philip opposed the Nipmuc strategy of using the captives' release as a means of opening more general peace negotiations with the English.

[75] Rowlandson refers here to the English attack of the Narragansett Great Swamp Fort in December 1675, and the subsequent Narragansett exodus to Nipmuc country.

[76] Amos 3:6; 6:6–7; Psalm 118:23.

3. *Which also I have hinted before, when the* English *Army with new supplies were sent forth to pursue after the enemy, and they understanding it, fled before them till they came to* Baquaug *River, where they forthwith went over safely: that that River should be impassable to the* English. I can but admire to see the wonderfull providence of God in preserving the heathen for farther affliction to our poor Countrey. They could go in great numbers over, but the *English* must stop: God had an over-ruling hand in all those things.

4. *It was thought, if their corn were cut down, they would starve and dy with hunger: and all their Corn that could be found, was destroyed, and they driven from that little they had in store, into the Woods in the midst of Winter*; and yet how to admiration did the Lord preserve them for his Holy ends, and the destruction of many still amongst the *English*! Strangely did the Lord provide for them; that I did not see (all the time I was among them) one Man, Woman, or Child, die with hunger.[77]

Though many times they would eat that, that a Hog or a Dog would hardly touch; yet by that God strengthened them to be a scourge to His People.

The chief and commonest food was Ground-nuts: They eat also Nuts and Acorns, Harty-choaks,[78] Lilly roots, Ground-beans, and several other weeds and roots, that I know not.

They would pick up old bones, and cut them to pieces at the joynts, and if they were full of wormes and magots, they would scald them over the fire to make the vermine come out, and then boile them, and drink up the Liquor, and then beat the great ends of them in a Morter, and so eat them. They would eat Horses guts, and ears, and all sorts of wild Birds which they could catch: also Bear, Venison, Beaver, Tortois, Frogs, Squirrels, Dogs, Skunks, Rattle-snakes; yea, the very Bark of Trees; besides all sorts of creatures, and provision which they plundered from the *English*. I can but stand in admiration to see the wonderful power of God, in providing for such a vast number of our Enemies in the *Wilderness*, where there was nothing to be seen, but from hand to mouth. Many times in a morning, the generality of them would eat up all they had, and yet have some further supply against what they wanted. It is said, *Psal.* 81. 1 3, 14. *Oh, that my People had hearkened to me, and* Israel *had walked in my wayes, I should soon have subdued their Enemies, and*

---

[77] Rowlandson has described earlier an Indian child on the verge of death from hunger (pp. 89–90) and mentioned the death of Weetamoo's child (p. 91).

[78] Artichokes, undoubtedly Jerusalem artichokes, a plant harvested by Indians throughout eastern North America and the Mississippi Valley.

turned my hand against their Adversaries. But now our perverse and evil carriages in the sight of the Lord, have so offended Him, that instead of turning His hand against them, the Lord feeds and nourishes them up to be a scourge to the whole Land.

5. *Another thing that I would observe is, the strange providence of God, in turning things about when the* Indians *were at the highest, and the* English *at the lowest.* I was with the Enemy eleven weeks and five dayes, and not one Week passed without the fury of the Enemy, and some desolation by fire and sword upon one place or other. They mourned (with their black faces) for their own losses, yet triumphed and rejoyced in their inhumane, and many times devilish cruelty to the *English.* They would boast much of their Victories; saying, that in two hours time they had destroyed such a *Captain,* and his *Company* at such a place; and such a *Captain* and his *Company* in such a place; and such a *Captain* and his *Company* in such a place; and boast how many *Towns* they had destroyed, and then scoffe, and say, *They had done them a good turn, to send them to Heaven so soon.* Again, they would say, *This summer that they would knock all the Rogues in the head, or drive them into the Sea, or make them flie the Countrey:* thinking surely, *Agag*-like, *The bitterness of Death is past.*[79] Now the Heathen begins to think all is their own, and the poor Christians hopes to fail (as to man) and now their eyes are more to God, and their hearts sigh heaven-ward: and to say in good earnest, *Help Lord, or we perish:*[80] When the Lord had brought his people to this, that they saw no help in any thing but himself: then he takes the quarrel into his own hand: and though they had made a pit, in their own imaginations, as deep as hell for the Christians that Summer, yet the Lord hurll'd themselves into it. And the Lord had not so many wayes before to preserve them, but now he hath as many to destroy them.

But to return again to my going home, where we may see a remarkable change of Providence: At first they were all against it, except my Husband would come for me; but afterwards they assented to it, and seemed much to rejoyce in it; some askt me to send them some Bread, others some Tobacco, others shaking me by the hand, offering me a Hood and Scarfe to ride in; not one moving hand or tongue against it. Thus hath the Lord answered my poor desire, and the many earnest requests of others put up unto God for me. In my travels an *Indian* came to me, and told me, if I were willing, he and his *Squaw* would

[79] I Samuel 15:32.
[80] Matthew 8:25.

run away, and go home along with me: I told him *No*: I was not willing to run away, but desired to wait Gods time, that I might go home
quietly, and without fear. And now God hath granted me my desire.
O the wonderfull power of God that I have seen, and the experience
that I have had: *I have been in the midst of those roaring Lyons, and
Salvage Bears, that feared neither God, nor Man, nor the Devil, by night
and day, alone and in company: sleeping all sorts together, and yet not
one of them ever offered me the least abuse of unchastity to me, in word
or action.* Though some are ready to say, I speak it for my own credit;
But I speak it in the presence of God, and to His glory.[81] Gods power is
as great now, and as sufficient to save, as when he preserved *Daniel*
in the Lions den; or the three *Children* in the fiery Furnace. I may well
say as his *Psal.* 107. 1, 2, *Oh give thanks unto the Lord for He is good, for
his mercy endureth for ever.* Let the Redeemed of the Lord say so, whom
He hath redeemed from the hand of the Enemy, especially that I should
come away in the midst of so many hundreds of Enemies quietly and
peacably, and not a Dog moving his tongue. So I took my leave of them,
and in coming along my heart melted into tears, more then all the while
I was with them, and I was almost swallowed up with the thoughts that
ever I should go home again. About the Sun going down, Mr. *Hoar*, and
my self, and the two *Indians* came to *Lancaster*, and a solemn sight it
was to me. There had I lived many comfortable years amongst my Relations and Neighbours, and now not one *Christian* to be seen, nor one
house left standing. We went on to a Farm house that was yet standing,
where we lay all night: and a comfortable lodging we had, though nothing but straw to ly on. The Lord preserved us in safety that night, and
raised us up again in the morning, and carried us along, that before
noon, we came to *Concord*. Now was I full of joy, and yet not without
sorrow: joy to see such a lovely sight, so many *Christians* together,
and some of them my Neighbours: There I met with my Brother, and
my Brother in Law, who asked me, if I knew where his Wife was? Poor
heart! he had helped to bury her, and knew it not; she being shot down
by the house was partly burnt: so that those who were at *Boston* at the
desolation of the *Town*, and came back afterward, and buried the dead,
did not know her. Yet I was not without sorrow, to think how many were
looking and longing, and my own Children amongst the rest, to enjoy
that deliverance that I had now received, and I did not know whither

---

[81] This sentence is another indication that Rowlandson was writing in part to counter
her detractors.

ever I should see them again. Being recruited with food and raiment we went to *Boston* that day, where I met with my dear Husband, but the thoughts of our dear Children, one being dead, and the other we could not tell where, abated our comfort each to other. I was not before so much hem'd in with the merciless and cruel Heathen, but now as much with pittiful, tender-hearted and compassionate Christians. In that poor, and destressed, and beggerly condition I was received in, I was kindly entertained in severall Houses: so much love I received from several (some of whom I knew, and others I knew not) that I am not capable to declare it. But the Lord knows them all by name: *The Lord reward them seven fold into their bosoms of his spirituals, for their temporals!* The *twenty pounds* the price of my redemption was raised by some *Boston* Gentlemen, and Ms.[82] *Usher*, whose bounty and religious charity, I would not forget to make mention of. Then Mr. *Thomas Shepard* of *Charlestown* received us into his House, where we continued eleven weeks; and a Father and Mother they were to us. And many more tender-hearted Friends we met with in that place. We were now in the midst of love, yet not without much and frequent heaviness of heart for our poor Children, and other Relations, who were still in affliction. The week following, after my coming in, the Governour[83] and Council sent forth to the *Indians* again; and that not without success; for they brought in my Sister, and Good-wife Kettle: Their not knowing where our Children were, was a sore tryal to us still, and yet we were not without secret hopes that we should see them again. That which was dead lay heavier upon my spirit, than those which were alive and amongst the Heathen; thinking how it suffered with its wounds, and I was in no way able to relieve it; and how it was buried by the Heathen in the *Wilderness* from among all Christians. We were hurried up and down in our thoughts, sometimes we should hear a report that they were gone this way, and sometimes that; and that they were come in, in this place or that: We kept enquiring and listening to hear concerning them, but no certain news as yet. About this time the Council had ordered a day of publick *Thanks-giving*: though I thought I had still cause of mourning, and being unsettled in our minds, we thought we would ride toward the *Eastward*, to see if we could hear anything concerning our Children. And as we were riding along (God is the wise disposer of all things)

---

[82] This usage was almost certainly unintended, but is here left as printed because it is unclear whether Rowlandson was referring to a *Mr.* or a *Mrs.* Usher. Rowlandson's many editors over the past three centuries have been divided as to Usher's identity and gender.

[83] The governor of Massachusetts Bay, John Leverett.

between *Ipswich* and *Rowley* we met with Mr. *William Hubbard*,[84] who told us that our Son *Joseph* was come in to Major *Waldrens*,[85] and another with him, which was my Sisters Son. I asked him how he knew it? He said, the Major himself told him so. So along we went till we came to *Newbury*; and their Minister being absent, they desired my Husband to preach the *Thanks-giving* for them; but he was not willing to stay there that night, but would go over to *Salisbury*, to hear further, and come again in the morning; which he did, and Preached there that day. At night, when he had done, one came and told him that his Daughter was come in at *Providence*: Here was mercy on both hands: Now hath God fulfilled that precious Scripture which was such a comfort to me in my distressed condition. When my heart was ready to sink into the Earth (my Children being gone I could not tell whither) and my knees trembled under me, *And I was walking through the valley of the shadow of Death*: Then the Lord brought, and now has fulfilled that reviving word unto me: Thus saith the Lord, *Refrain thy voice from weeping, and thine eyes from tears, for thy work shall be rewarded, saith the Lord, and they shall come again from the Land of the Enemy.*[86] Now we were between them, the one on the *East,* and the other on the *West*: Our Son being nearest, we went to him first, to *Portsmouth*, where we met with him, and with the Major also: who told us he had done what he could, but could not redeem him under *seven pounds*; which the good People thereabouts were pleased to pay. The Lord reward the Major, and all the rest, though unknown to me, for their labour of Love. My Sisters Son was redeemed for *four pounds*, which the Council gave order for the payment of. Having now received one of our Children, we hastened toward the other: going back through *Newbury*, my Husband Preached there on the *Sabbath-day*: for which they rewarded him many fold.

On *Munday* we came to Charlestown, where we heard that the Governour of *Road-Island*[87] had sent over for our Daughter, to take care of her, being now within his Jurisdiction: which should not pass without

---

[84] Hubbard was a minister, who became one of the more prominent historians of the war. He had also helped prosecute Joseph Rowlandson for libel a quarter century earlier. See the Introduction.

[85] Major Richard Waldron of Dover, New Hampshire, who became infamous a few months later for luring a large number of Nipmucs and other Native Americans into disarming under the pretext of peace, then capturing them and selling many into slavery. See Evan Haefli and Kevin Sweeney, "Revisiting *The Redeemed Captive*: New Perspectives on the 1704 Attack on Deerfield," *William and Mary Quarterly* 52 (1995): 22–23.

[86] Jeremiah 31:16.

[87] William Coddington.

our acknowledgments. But she being nearer *Rehoboth* than *Road-Island,* Mr. *Newman*[88] went over, and took care of her, and brought her to his own House. And the goodness of God was admirable to us in our low estate, in that he raised up passionate Friends on every side to us, when we had nothing to recompance any for their love. The *Indians* were now gone that way, that it was apprehended dangerous to go to her: But the Carts which carried Provision to the *English* Army, being guarded, brought her with them to *Dorchester,* where we received her safe: blessed be the Lord for it, *For great is his Power, and he can do whatsoever seemeth him good.* Her coming in was after this manner: She was travelling one day with the *Indians,* with her basket at her back; the company of *Indians* were got before her, and gone out of sight, all except one *Squaw;* she followed the *Squaw* till night, and then both of them lay down, having nothing over them but the heavens, and under them but the earth. Thus she travelled three dayes together, not knowing whither she was going: having nothing to eat or drink but water, and green *Hirtle-berries.* At last they came into *Providence,* where she was kindly entertained by several of that *Town.* The *Indians* often said, that I should never have her under *twenty pounds*: But now the Lord hath brought her in upon free-cost, and given her to me the second time. The Lord make us a blessing indeed, each to others. Now have I seen that Scripture also fulfilled, *Deut.* 30. 4, 7. *If any of thine be driven out to the outmost parts of heaven, from thence will the Lord thy God gather thee, and from thence will he fetch thee. And the Lord thy God will put all these curses upon thine enemies, and on them which hate thee, which persecuted thee.* Thus hath the Lord brought me and mine out of that horrible pit, and hath set us in the midst of tender-hearted and compassionate Christians. It is the desire of my soul, that we may walk worthy of the mercies received, and which we are receiving.

Our family being now gathered together (those of us that were living) the South Church *in* Boston *hired an House for us: Then we removed from Mr.* Shepards, *those cordial Friends, and went to* Boston, *where we continued about three quarters of a year: Still the Lord went along with us, and provided graciously for us.* I thought it somewhat strange to set up Housekeeping with bare walls; but as *Solomon* says, *Mony answers all things;*[89] and that we had through the benevolence of Christian-friends, some in this *Town,* and some in that, and others:

---

[88] Noah Newman, a minister of Rehoboth.
[89] Ecclesiastes 10:19.

And some from *England*, that in a little time we might look, and see the House furnished with love. The Lord hath been exceeding good to us in our low estate, in that when we had neither house nor home, nor other necessaries, the Lord so moved the hearts of these and those towards us, that we wanted neither food, nor raiment for our selves or ours, *Prov.* 18. 24. *There is a Friend which sticketh closer than a Brother.* And how many such Friends have we found, and now living amongst? And truly such a Friend have we found him to be unto us, in whose house we lived, *viz.* Mr. *James Whitcomb*,[90] a Friend unto us near hand, and afar off.

I can remember the time, when I used to sleep quietly without workings in my thoughts, whole nights together, but now it is other wayes with me. When all are fast about me, and no eye open, but his who ever waketh, my thoughts are upon things past, upon the awfull dispensation of the Lord towards us; upon his wonderfull power and might, in carrying of us through so many difficulties, in returning us in safety, and suffering none to hurt us. I remember in the night season, how the other day I was in the midst of thousands of enemies, & nothing but death before me: It is then hard work to perswade myself, that ever I should be satisfied with bread again. But now we are fed *with the finest of the Wheat,* and, as I may say, *with honey out of the rock*:[91] In stead of the Husk, we have the fatted Calf:[92] The thoughts of these things in the particulars of them, and of the love and goodness of God towards us, make it true of me, what David said of himself, *Psal.* 6. 6. *I watered my couch with my tears.* Oh! the wonder-full power of God that mine eyes have seen, affording matter enough for my thoughts to run in, that when others are sleeping mine are weeping.

I have seen the extrem vanity of this World: One hour I have been in health, and wealth, wanting nothing: But the next hour in sickness and wounds, and death, having nothing but sorrow and affliction.

Before I knew what affliction meant, I was ready sometimes to wish for it. When I lived in prosperity, having the comforts of the World about me, my relations by me, my Heart chearfull: and taking little care for any thing; and yet seeing many, whom I preferred before my self, under many tryals and afflictions, in sickness, weakness, poverty, losses, crosses, and cares of the World, I should be sometimes jealous least I should have my portion in this life, and that Scripture would come to my

[90] A wealthy Boston resident whose business dealings included buying and selling Indian slaves. See Document 16.

[91] Psalm 81:16.

[92] See Luke 15:11–32.

mind, *Heb.* 12. 6. *For whom the* **Lord** *loveth he chasteneth, and scourgeth every Son whom he receiveth.* But now I see the Lord had his time to scourge and chasten me. The portion of some is to have their afflictions by drops, now one drop and then another; but the dregs of the Cup, the Wine of astonishment: like a sweeping rain that leaveth no food, did the Lord prepare to be my portion. Affliction I wanted, and affliction I had, full measure (I thought) pressed down and running over; yet I see, when God calls a Person to any thing, and through never so many difficulties, yet he is fully able to carry them through and make them see, and say they have been gainers thereby. And I hope I can say in some measure, As *David* did, *It is good for me that I have been afflicted.*[93] The Lord hath shewed me the vanity of these outward things. That they are the *Vanity of vanities, and vexation of spirit;*[94] that they are but a shadow, a blast, a bubble, and things of no continuance. That we must rely on God himself, and our whole dependance must be upon him. If trouble from smaller matters begin to arise in me, I have something at hand to check my self with, and say, why am I troubled? It was but the other day that if I had had the world, I would have given it for my freedom, or to have been a Servant to a Christian. I have learned to look beyond present and smaller troubles, and to be quieted under them, as *Moses* said, *Exod.* 14. 13. *Stand still and see the Salvation of the Lord.*

FINIS.

---

[93] Psalm 119:71.
[94] Ecclesiates 1:2, 14.

The sachems' answers to the colonists' questions about Christianity are more directly revealing. As the Introduction points out, New England Algonquians readily incorporated new sources of manitou (spiritual power) into their own worldview. They were not monotheists, like the Puritans and other Christians, who assumed that there was one "true" religion and that all others were false. In answering the first question, the sachems welcome the Christian God as a source of constructive manitou, without saying that they will worship God exclusively. The sachems are agreeable in their remaining answers, saying either that they already practice what is being asked of them or they see no obstacle to going along with English expectations. It is important to remember that in 1644 there was not yet a missionary program in Massachusetts, so the Indians had no idea of actual missionary practices. In signing, Showanon and the other sachems were forging an alliance that would benefit them by enabling them to survive in a world where the English presence had become dominant.

Ousamequin,[1] Showanon, Cutshamekin,[2] Mascanomet,[3] and Squaw Sachem[4] did voluntarily submit themselves to us, as appears by their covenant subscribed with their own hands, here following, and other articles to which they consented.[5]

We have and by these presents do voluntarily, and without any constraint or persuasion, but of our own free motion, put ourselves, our subjects, lands, and estates under the government and jurisdiction of the Massachusetts, to be governed and protected by them, according to just laws and orders, so far as we shall be made capable of understanding them. And we do promise for ourselves, and all our subjects, and all our posterity, to be true and faithful to the said government, and aiding to the maintenance thereof, to our best ability, and from time to time to give speedy notice of any conspiracy, attempt, or evil intention of any [Indians] which we shall know or hear of against the same. And we do promise to be willing from time to time to be instructed in the

---

[1]Sachem of the Quaboag Nipmucs.

[2]A Massachuset sachem.

[3]Sachem of the Agawam Pawtucket.

[4]A Massachuset saunkskwa (whose own name was never recorded by the English).

[5]The treaty is misleading in stating that the sachems "subscribed with their own hands." None of the sachems were literate in English, and their "signatures" in the original document are in the same handwriting as the rest of the document and are not accompanied by any marks. Massachusetts Archives, CT0/ series 1700X, Proceedings of the Governor and Company of Massachusetts Bay, vol. 2, p. 42. Many later documents produced by New England Native Americans, such as Document 14 below, include their signers' marks.

knowledge and worship of God. In witness whereof we have hereunto put our hands the 8th of the first month, 1643–1644.[6]

CUTSHAMEKIN,
SHOWANON,
OUSAMEQUIN,
MASCANOMET,
SQUAW SACHEM.

Certain Questions propounded to the Indians, and Answers.

First. To worship the only true God, which made heaven and earth, and not to blaspheme him.

An: We do desire to reverence the God of the English, and to speak well of him, because we see he doth better to the English than other gods do to others.

2. Not to swear falsely. An: They say they know not what swearing is among them.

3. Not to do any unnecessary work on the Sabbath day, especially within the gates of the Christian towns. An: It is easy to them; they have not much to do on any day, and they can well take their ease on that day.

4. To honor their parents and all their superiors.

An: It is their custom to do so, for the inferiors to honor their superiors.

5. To kill no man without just cause and just authority.

An: This is good, and they desire to do so.

6. To commit no unclean lust, [such] as fornication, adultery, incest, rape, sodomy, buggery, or bestiality. An: Though sometime some of them do it, yet they count that naught, and do not allow it.

7. Not to steal. An: They say to that as [they said] to the 6th query.

To suffer their children to learn to read God's word, that they may learn to know God aright, and to worship him in his own way.

They say, as opportunity will serve, and English live among them, they desire so to do.

That they shall not be idle.

To these they consented, acknowledging them to be good.

Being received by us, they presented 26 fathoms[7] of wampum, and the Court directed the Treasurer to give them five coats, two yards in a coat, of red cloth, and a potful of wine.

---

[6]April 2, 1644, in today's calendar.
[7]156 feet or 47.5 meters.

2. Philip on the Causes of Anglo-Indian War

2

JOHN EASTON

Excerpt from "A Relacion of the lndyan Warre"
1675

*The following selection is the most fully articulated written rendition we
have of the Native Americans' case against the English in 1675. As the
clouds of war gathered in mid-June, Deputy Governor John Easton and
several other Rhode Islanders met with the Pokanoket Wampanoag sachem,
Metacom, and his councilors in hopes of resolving differences between the
two sides. The Wampanoags had reason to expect that they might receive a
fair hearing of their grievances. Because of its policies of religious toleration
and its alliance with the Narragansetts, Rhode Island had been excluded
from the United Colonies of New England, which consisted of the more mili-
tantly anti-Indian Massachusetts Bay, Connecticut, and Plymouth. Easton's
own family had been expelled from Massachusetts as followers of Antinomian radical Anne Hutchinson when he was a youth, and later the family
converted to Quakerism with its beliefs in nonviolence. In his account of the
meeting, Easton recorded the Wampanoags' many grievances—grievances
that had accumulated, especially within the preceding five years, to the point
where war seemed unavoidable. Although the Wampanoags were clearly
intrigued by Easton's proposals for having the conflict mediated by outsiders,
he could do nothing to address their complaints against the United Colonies.
About one week later, Wampanoags and settlers in the Plymouth town of
Swansea began firing on each other, and the war was on. As Easton had
forewarned Philip during their meeting, Rhode Island sided with the other
English colonies once full-scale war broke out.*

John Easton, "A Relacion of the Indyan Warre" (1675; pub. 1858; reprinted in Charles H.
Lincoln, ed., *Narratives of the Indian Wars, 1675–1699*, New York, 1913), 8–12.

For forty years' time reports and jealousies of war had been very frequent that we did not think that a war was breaking forth, but about a week before it did we had cause to think it would. Then to endeavor to prevent it, we sent a man[1] to Philip that if he would come to the ferry we would come over to speak with him. About four mile we had to come thither. Our messenger come to them, they not aware of it behaved themselves as furious but suddenly appeased when they understood who he was and what he came for. He called his council and agreed to come to us came himself unarmed and about forty of his men armed. Then five of us went over. Three were magistrates. We sat very friendly together. We told him our business was to endeavor that they might not receive or do wrong. They said that was well they had done no wrong, the English wronged them, we said we knew the English said they[2] wronged them and the Indians said the English wronged them but our desire was the quarrel might rightly be decided in the best way, and not as dogs decided their quarrels. The Indians owned that fighting was the worst way then they propounded how right might take place, we said by arbitration. They said all English agreed against them and so by arbitration they had had much wrong, many square miles of land so taken from them for English would have English Arbitrators, and once they were persuaded to give in their arms, that thereby jealousy might be removed and the English having their arms would not deliver them as they had promised, until they consented to pay 100 pounds, and now they had not so much land or money, that they were as good be killed as leave all their livelihood.[3] We said they might choose a Indian king,[4] and the English might choose the governor of New York that neither had cause to say either were parties in the difference.[5] They said they had not heard of that way and said we honestly spoke so we were persuaded if that way had been tendered they would have accepted. We did endeavor not to hear their complaints, said it was not convenient for us now to consider of, but to endeavor to prevent war, said to them when in war against

---

[1]Probably one of those Narragansetts who at the time was still friendly with both parties.
[2]The Indians.
[3]In 1671, Plymouth extracted an agreement from a reluctant Metacom to disarm his followers. But many Wampanoags claimed that the agreement applied only to those present and not, as the colony now claimed, all Wampanoags.
[4]The English often referred to the most powerful sachems and saunkskwas as "kings" and "queens," respectively.
[5]It is unlikely that the United Colonies would have agreed to letting New York governor Edmund Andros mediate the dispute because his colony was then claiming all Connecticut and Massachusetts territory west of the Connecticut River.

English blood was spilled that engaged all Englishmen for we were to be all under one king. We knew what their complaints would be, and in our colony had removed some of them in sending for Indian rulers in what the crime concerned Indian lives which they very lovingly accepted and agreed with us to their execution and said they were able to satisfy their subjects when they knew an Indian suffered duly, but said in what was only between their Indians and not in townships that we had purchased, they would not have us prosecute and that they had a great fear to have any of their Indians should be called or forced to be Christian Indians. They said that such were in everything more mischievous, only dissemblers, and then the English made them not subject to their kings, and by their lying to wrong their kings. We knew it to be true, and we promising them that however in government to Indians all should be alike and that we knew it was our kings will it should be so, that although we were weaker than other colonies, they having submitted to our king to protect them others dared not otherwise to molest them. So they expressed they took that to be well, that we had little cause to doubt but that to us under the king they would have yielded to our determinations in what any should have complained to us against them, but Philip charged it to be dishonesty in us to put off the hearing the complaints; therefore, we consented to hear them. They said they had been the first in doing good to the English, and the English the first in doing wrong, said when the English first came their king's father was as a great man and the English as a little child, he constrained other Indians from wronging the English and gave them corn and showed them how to plant and was free to do them any good and had let them have a 100 times more land, then now the king had for his own people,[6] but their king's brother when he was king came miserably to die by being forced to court as they judged poisoned,[7] and another greivance was if 20 of their honest Indians testified that a Englishman had done them wrong, it was as nothing, and if but one of their worst Indians testified against any Indian or their king when it pleased the English that was sufficient. Another grievance was when their kings sold land the English would say it was more than they agreed to and a writing must be proof against all them, and sum of their kings had done wrong to sell so much. He left his people none

[6]The Wampanoags refer here to their sachem, Massasoit, who maintained friendly relations with Plymouth from its founding in 1621 until he died in 1662.

[7]Massasoit was succeeded by his oldest son, Alexander (or Wamsutta), who died under suspicious circumstances while returning from a conference with Plymouth officials. Upon his death, Philip succeeded to the sachemship.

and some being given to drunkeness the English made them drunk and then cheated them in bargains, but now their kings were forewarned not for to part with land for nothing in comparison to the value thereof. Now whom the English had owned for king or queen they[8] would disinherit, and make another king that would give or sell them their land, that now they had no hopes left to keep any land. Another grievance the English cattle and horses still increased that when they removed 30 miles from where English had anything to do, they could not keep their corn from being spoiled, they never being used to fence, and thought when the English bought land of them that they would have kept their cattle upon their own land. Another grievance the English were so eager to sell the Indians liquors that most of the Indians spent all in drunkeness and then ravened upon[9] the sober Indians and they did believe often did hurt the English cattle, and their kings could not prevent it. We knew before these were their grand complaints, but then we only endeavored to persuade that all complaints might be righted without war, but could have no other answer but that they had not heard of that way for the Governor of York and an Indian king to have the hearing of it. We had cause to think if that had been tendered it would have been accepted. We endeavored that however they should lay down their arms for the English were too strong for them. They said then the English should do to them as they did when they were too strong for the English. So we departed without any discourteousness, and suddenly had letter from Plimouth Governor they intended in arms to conform[10] Philip, but no information what that was they required or what terms he refused to have their quarrel decided, and in a weeks time after we had been with the Indians the war thus begun.

---

[8]The English.
[9]Seized, plundered.
[10]Force into subjection.

3. The Perils of War

3

DANIEL GOOKIN

Excerpt from "An Historical Account of the Doings and Sufferings of the Christian Indians in New England"

1677

The first captives taken during Metacom's War were not English settlers seized by Native Americans but rather were loyal Christian Indians forcibly taken from their homes by Massachusetts and Plymouth authorities to off-shore islands. Most of these Indian captives were taken by Massachusetts to Deer Island. Their experiences were documented by Daniel Gookin, the colony's Superintendent of Indians, as part of his detailed account and defense of Christian Indians during and immediately after the war. In this selection, Gookin recounts the captivity and removal of Christians from Natick, the colony's oldest praying town. He views the removal as part of the larger Indian-hating climate that was engulfing New England. In this context, he asserts that nearby settlers burned down an abandoned English structure and blamed Natick people so that the General Court would remove them from their town. The settlers' strategy was successful. After the Court issued its order, about two hundred Natick residents were taken to Deer Island in the dead of a late autumn night. The Natives' prospects for surviving the coming winter were further diminished by the island's owner, who insisted that the internees cut no firewood nor harm his sheep. Gookin notes that some captives dreaded being "transported out of the country," that is, being sold as slaves into the transatlantic slave trade as had many New England Native Americans during and since the Pequot War.

Daniel Gookin, "An Historical Account of the Doings and Sufferings of the Christian Indians in New England," *Archaeologia Americana, Transactions and Collections of the American Antiquarian Society* 2 (1836): 472–74.

Upon the 26th of October, new clamors and reports were raised and fomented against the Christian Indians of Natick, upon pretence that some of them had fired a house or old barn at Dedham (a poor old house not worth ten shillings, that stood alone far distant from the dwelling-houses). This house, in all probability, was set on fire [on] purpose by some that were back[1] friends to those poor Indians; thereby to take an occasion to procure the removal of all those Indians from Natick. The contrivers whereof well knew that the magistrates generally were very slow to distrust those poor Christians; this artifice was therefore used to provoke them. God (who knows all) will I hope one day awaken and convince the consciences of those persons that have been industriously active to traduce and afflict those poor innocent Christians, without cause; for, as to the body of them, they were always true and faithful to the English, and I never saw or heard any substantial evidence to the contrary. Besides this . . . burning the house, there were other false informations presented at the same time to the General Court, to stir them up to a sharp procedure against those Indians; but the authors of those things being slain, I shall omit to mention them.

This contrivance against the Natick Indians obtained that which it was designed for, viz. the passing of an order in the General Court, forthwith to remove them from their place unto Deer Island, having first obtained the consent of Mr. Samuel Shrimpton, of Boston (in whose possession that Island was) to place them there at present, with this prohibition, that they should not cut down any growing wood, nor do any damage to his sheep kept there. In pursuance of this order, Capt. Thomas Prentiss (who was a person civil and friendly to those Indians) with a party of horse, was commanded to bring them down speedily to a place called the Pines, upon Charles River, about two miles above Cambridge, where boats were appointed to be in readiness to take them on board, and take them to the aforesaid Island. Captain Prentiss accordingly went up to Natick, with a few men and five or six carts, to carry such things as were of greatest necessity; and he declared to them the Court's pleasure for their removal, unto which they quietly and readily submitted, and came down with him at an hour or two warning, about two hundred souls of all sorts. There was one family of them, about twelve in number, the principal man named old Jethro, with his

[1]Former.

sons and relations, who secretly ran away in the night. But this man and his relations were not praying Indians, nor did they live at Natick, only since the wars, but dwelt at a place near Sudbury, Nobscot hill, and never submitted to the Christian profession, but separated from them, being sons of ill fame, and especially the old man, who had the repute to be a powow. Those ran away for fear at this time, and were with the enemy, but were taken afterwards at Cocheco, and hanged at Boston.[2] Good Mr. Elliot,[3] that faithful instructor and teacher of the praying Indians, met them at the place before mentioned, where they were to be embarked, who comforted and encouraged and instructed and prayed with them, and for them; exhorting them to patience in their sufferings, and confirming the hearts of those disciples of Christ; and exhorting them to continue in the faith, for through many tribulations we must enter into the kingdom of heaven. There were some other Englishmen at the place called the Pines with Mr. Elliot, who were much affected in seeing and observing how submissively and Christianly and affectionately those poor souls carried it, seeking encouragement, and encouraging and exhorting one another with prayers and tears at the time of the embarkment, being, as they told some, in fear that they should never return more to their habitations, but be transported out of the country. Of this I was informed by eye and ear witnesses of the English nation that were upon the place at the time. In the night, about midnight, the tide serving, being the 30th of October, 1675, those poor creatures were shipped in three vessels and carried away to Deer Island above mentioned, which was distant from that place about four leagues,[4] where I shall leave them at present.

[2]On Jethro and his sons, see p. 40.
[3]John Eliot, the missionary who had founded Natick.
[4]About twelve miles.

4

The Examination and Relation of James Quanapohit ("Quannapaquait")

January 24, 1676

James Quanapohit was a Christian Indian whom the English released from Deer Island in order to gather intelligence from anti-English Nipmucs about their plans. Quanapohit gave the following report at Daniel Gookin's home after arriving there with news of the planned attack on Lancaster. The account shows how the war sometimes divided indigenous people from the same community and states that the Natives' principal motives for raiding towns like Lancaster was to obtain food and, secondarily, firearms. It is noteworthy that Quanapohit does not mention the seizure of English captives as a goal of the Native Americans. He also offers the most concrete evidence of direct French involvement with anti-English Algonquians during the war. Yet the English ignored his report because they would not trust an indigenous source. The document also shows that those Christian Native Americans who worked on behalf of the colonists acted out of concern for the welfare of their families and friends, whose situations, whether in enemy hands or on Deer Island, were desperate.

An examination of the original manuscript at the Connecticut Archives makes clear that the square brackets were inserted by the original recorder, apparently to distinguish his clarifying additions from Quanapohit's actual words. Ellipses indicate a space where the manuscript is illegible.

The examination & relation of James Quannapaquait, allias James Rumny-Marsh beeing one of the christian Indians belonging to Natick; taken the 24th day of Janry 1675–6, on wch day hee returned from his jorney, [for this man and another called Job of Magungoog[1], a christian man also] were sent forth by order of the councill of Massachusetts upon

[1]Magunaquag, one of the new Nipmuc praying towns that Daniel Gookin had organized in 1674.

J. H. Temple, *History of North Brookfield* (North Brookfield, 1887), 112–18.

the last of December, [as spyes], to discover the enemyes quarters & motions & his state & condition, & to gaine what intelegence they could; for wch end they had particuler instruction. Though when first they were moved to goe this jorny, they saw it would bee a hazardous undertaking, & that they should runne the hazard of their lives in it, yet they were willing to venture upon these & like considerations (1, that they might declare their readines to serve the English). 2^{ly} one of them namly Job had 3 children [even all he had] that were carried away with the Hassanameshe[2] indians &, as he conceived were with the enemy, & he was willing to know their state as wel as the condition of the praying indians of Hassameske & Magunkoog that were hee thought in the power of the enimy. 3^d They hoped to sugest somthing in order to the enemies submission to the English & making peace if they found the enimy in a temper fit for it & if that could bee effected then they hoped the poor christian Indians at the Deer Island & in other places posibly might bee restored to their places againe, & bee freed from much suffering they are now in by this warre, & therby the jelosyes that the English have now of them might bee removed, these & other reasons induced them to runne this adventure for wch also if they returned in safty they had a promise of a reward.

They doubted the indian enimy would mistrust them for spyes, & that they would move them [to] fight for them against the English, unto which doubts they were advised to tell the Indian enemy a lamentable story [& that agreable to truth] of their deepe sufferings by the English; that Job was imprisoned severall daies [as hee was] where hee suffered much, though hee had served the English faithfully as an interprter & in actull armes being with the Mohegins at the fight neare Secunke with Philip,[3] the begining of August last, but imprisonment & suspitions the English had of him was part of his reward for that service to the English. And as for the other, James, he & his brother went out with Captian Prentis with their horses & armes at the first going out against Philipp in June & had done faithfull service for the English as his captains had testified by their certificate & continued in their service many weekes & was in severall fights, & that his bro: Thomas had kild one of Philip's cheefe men & brought in his head to the Governor of Boston, & had also in the service by accident lost the use of his left hand, & that

---

[2]Hassanaamesit, another of the recently established Nipmuc praying towns.
[3]That is, Kattananit had fought alongside Mohegans and English in a battle near Metacom's stronghold at Seekonk.

both James and his brother Thomas had since in November last [beeing called to it] was out with Captain Syll in the Nipmuck contry & [as his captaine had certified] had performed faithfull service; & was instru-mentall to recover an English captive Peter Bentt's servant from the enimey, & his brother savd the lives of two English men at a wigwam at Pakachooge, vizt[4] Mr Mackarty, servant, a surgeon to Captian Hench-man, & one Goodwin, a soldier of Charlestowne, as they both could & would testify. Yet after all these services both they & their wives & children & all their country men that lived at Naticke were mistrusted by the English & thereupon [at a few houres warning] brought away from their place & fort & houses at Naticke & carried down in boats to Deare Island, leaving & loosing much of their substance, catle, swine, horse & corn, & at the Hand were exposed to great sufferings have-ing litle wood for fuell, a bleak place & poore wigwams such as they could make a shift to make themselves with a few matts, & here at the iland had very little provision, many of them, & divers other sorrowes & troubles they were exposed to, & were about 350 soules, men women & children; & that now haveing an oppertuny to get off the iland they came to see how things were with the indians in the woods; & if they preferred them to fight with & for them they were advised to manifest all readines & forwardnes & not shew any aversenes.[5] Things being thus prepared these 2 spyes were sent away without armes excepting hatchetts & with a little parcht meal for provision, & they tooke their jorny from Cambridge the 30th of December, & from Natick they set forth the 31th of December being Friday early in the morning. That day they past through the woods directly to Hassomesed where they lodged that night; on Saterday morn, being the first of Janury they past over Nipmuck River & lodged at Manchage that night. On the 2 Janury they went forward to Maanexit wch is about 10 miles & there they met with seaven Indians of the enimy: some of them had armes; having confered with these indians they were conducted by those indians next day to Quabaage old fort where they met severall other Indians of their com-pany's; & by them the next day were conducted to the enemies quarters which is about twenty miles northward of Quabauge old fort at a place called Menemesseg,[6] which is about 8 miles north of where Captain Hutchison & Captain Wheeler was woonded & several men with them

---

[4]Namely.

[5]That is, if the anti-English Native Americans wanted Quanapohit and Kattananit to fight the English, the two spies should agree to go along.

[6]Menameset, one of the anti-English Indians' major encampments in Nipmuc country.

slayn (in the begining of August last) as these indians informed them. At this place among these Indians they found all the christian Indians belonging to Hassannmiske & Magunhooge wich are about forty men & about 80 women & children. These praying indians were carried away by the enemy somewhat willingly, others of them unwillingly, as they told him. For before they went away they were in a great strait, for if they came to the English they knew they shold be sent to Deere Iland, as others were, & their corne beeing at such a distance about 40 miles from Boston it could not bee caried to susteyne their lives & so they should bee in danger to famish, & others feard they should bee sent away to Barbados, or other places. And to stay at Hassanamesho these indians our enemies[7] would not permit them, but said they must have the corne, but promised them if they would goe with them they should not die but bee preserved; these being in this condition most of them thought it best to go with them though they feared death every way: only Tukuppawillin [the minister] he lamented much & his aged father the deacon & son and som others & would faine have come back to the English after they were gone as far as Manchange but the enimy mockt him, for crying & drew him . . . the rest that were unwilling along with them: These things our spies understood from the p[raying] indians here. The enimys that hee was among & live at the afforesaid places are in . . . small townes about 20 wigwams at a place & they are all within 3 miles com [pass], and to consist of about 300 fighting men besides duble as many women & children . . . they have no fort, but wigwams only, some covred with barks & som with matts. The Indians that are heare are the Nipmuck indians, the Quabaag indians, the Paca-[choog] indians, the Weshakum & Nashaway indians. The cheef sagomeres & captains are Mawtaamp, John with one eye[8] & Sam [of Weshukum or Nashaway] Sagamore John [having one leg bigger than the other] of Pakachooge. Here also is Matoonus & his sons. Of the Hassanamesho & christian Indians, he saw here Captain Tom allias Wattasakomponin & his son Nehimiah. They say that the enimy have solic[it]ed them to take armes & fight against the English but they told James they would not fight against the English, they will rather die. Here he also saw Tukuppawillin their pastor & his aged father their deacon, whome he saith mourn greatly & daily read the bible which is their greatest comfort. Also he there saw James Printer brother to the minister, & Joseph &

[7]That is, the Native American enemies of the English.
[8]Monoco.

Sa . . . two brethern [sons to Robin of Hassameshe deceased]. Hee also saw Pumhamun & Jacob of Magunkoog with divers others that he could have mentioned but those are the principal.

Some of the Indians [our enimies] mistrusted[9] that these two men were spies, especially Matoonus & his sonnes & some others: these solicited James to borrow his hatchet & his knife [when he saw they needed none] which made him cautious of himselfe & suspitious of their evill intention to him, but James [at the second towne] he came to meet with John with one eye, of Weshakum [a stout captaine among them] this man knew James & said thou hast been with me in the warr with the Mauhaks & I know thou art a valiant man & therefore none shall wrong thee nor kill thee here, but they shall first kill me. Therefore abide at my wigwam & I will protect thee. So this man entertained him kindly, & protected him. Job his companion stayd at Pumhams wigwame wher his 3 children were kept: hee and Job aboad with these indians severall daies & sometimes went forth to hunt deere not farr off & returnd againe. Hee laboured to gaine what information hee could of their affayres, & was informed by Capt John [with one eye] his host & others said things, viz. That Philip was quartered this winter within halfe a dayes jorny . . . fort Albany [The same thing is certifyed by a letter from Major Andros Governor of New York sent Mr Leet deputy Governor of Connecticut dated 5th January (75) which letter being sent to Governor Winthrop by Mr Leet was read in our Councill on Thursday last 23 instant. This also may tend to confirme the truth of James his intelegence, as wel as divers other passages both before & aftermentioned]. Moreover they informed our spy that the Hadly Northampton & Spinkfield[10] Indians had their winter quarters between them & Philip & som quartered at Squakeake. They told him also that a cheefe captaine named——of Hadley & Northampton indians, who was a valiant man, had been a chiefe captaine in the Mawhak warre had attempted to kill Philip & intended to do it; alleaging that Philip had begun a warr with the English that had brought great trouble upon them.[11] Hee saieth that these Indians told him that it was som of their number that were in the Nipmuck country to get the corn & that the English came upon them in the wigwam at Hassunnamesuke & there they killed two Englishmen, & that they had got & caried away all the corne at Pakuahooge & in the Nipmuck country

[9]Suspected.
[10]Springfield.
[11]This is the earliest record of antagonism against Philip from within the ranks of the anti-English Indians ranks.

unto their quarters, upon which they had lived this winter, & upon beef & pork they had killed about Quaboage, & venison [of which there is great store in those parts & by reason of the deep snow there beeing mid thigh deep] it is easy to kill deare without gunns. He saieth that ere long, when their beefe & porke & deare is spent & gon, that they wilbe in want of corne, but they intend then to com down upon the English townes, of Lancaster Marlborow Grotaon, & particulely they intend first to cut off Lancaster bridge, & then say they there can be no releef com to them from Boston, the people cannot escape & there they hope to have corne enough. Hee saieth they have store of armes, & have a gun-smith among them, a lame man that is a good workman & keeps their gunns well fixt. They have some armes among them that they tooke in the 2 fights when Captain Beeares & Captain Lothrop was slayne.[12] As for amunition they have some but not great store that he saw: Captian John with one eye shewed him a small kettle full of powder about half a peck & 2 hornes full besides. Hee asked them where they got their ammuntion, hee answered some we had from the English were kild, & som from Fort Albany, but (said he) the Dutch wil not sell us powder; but wee give our bever & wompon to the Mawhakes & they buy it & let us have it of them. They told him that they had sent to the Wompeages & Mawquas to aid them in the spring, that the Wampeages promised them help, but the Maquaws said they were not willing to fight with English, but they would fight with the Mohegins & Pequots that were brethren to the English.[13] Further hee saieth that they told him that the Frenchman that was at Boston this sumer [viz. Monsieur Normanvile] was with Philip & his company as hee went back at their quarter about Pokomtuck, after he returnd from Boston. And that in their sight hee burned certene papers that hee said were letters from Boston to the French, saying what shall I doe with these papers any longer. Hee said to the Indians I would not have you burne the English mill, nor the meeting houses, nor the best houses for we [ie the French] intend to be with you in the spring before planting time & I will bring three hundred of your countrymen that are hunters & have been three years at the

---

[12]A reference to two successful ambushes of English troops in the Connecticut River Valley in September 1675.

[13]Wompeages probably refers to the Algonquian-speaking Wappingers of the Hudson River Valley. Mawquaws, Maquaws, and Maquas were terms used by the English to refer to the Mohawks. This sale of arms and the expression of Mohawk willingness to fight the pro-English Mohegans and Pequots were made prior to January 1676, when the Mohawks actively entered the war on the English side.

French. And we will bring armes & ammunition enough, for wee intend to helpe you against the English & posses our selves of Keneckticut river & other English plantations, and our King [ie the French King] will send shipps to stopp supplyes from coming by sea [from their King] to Boston.[14]

Hee saieth that they told him that the Pennakooge indians were quartered about the head of the Keneticut river, & had not at all ingaged in any fight with the English, & would not, their sagamors Wannalancet & others restrayned the young men (who had an opptunity to have destroyd many of Capt Moselys men when he was at Pennakooge last sumer but their sagamores would not suffer them to shoot a gunne).[15]

Further he saieth that he understood by the cheefe men & old men that they were inclinable to have peace againe with the English, but the young men [who are their principal soldiers] say we wil have no peace wee are all or most of us alive yet & the English have kild very few of us last summer; why shall wee have peace to bee made slaves, & either be kild or sent away to sea to Barbadoes &c. Let us live as long as wee can & die like men, & not live to bee enslaved. Hee saieth there is an English man a young man amongst them alive named Robert Pepper[16] who, being woonded in the legg in the fight when Captain Beares was kild, hid himselfe in the crotch of a great tree that lay on the ground, where an Indian called Sam Sagamore of Nashaway found him alive & tooke him prisoner & hee became his master. Hee lay lame severll weekes but beeing well used by his master & means used hee is now wel recovered. Hee saieth that once since hee was wel his master [carring him abroad with him] left him at Squakeake neare where hee was taken prisoner, his Master wishing him to goe to the English [whither there was a cart way led]. But Robert Pepper told James hee was afrayd his master did it but to try his fidelity to him to intrap him, & that if he should have gon away towards the English they would have intercepted him & so his life

[14]Normanvile apparently refers to Jean de Godefroy de Lintot, a highly placed French-Algonquian interpreter and diplomat who was often confused with his brother, Thomas Godefroy de Normanville. See entries for the two men in *Dictionary of Canadian Biography*, vol. 1 *(www.biographi.ca/en)*. The French did not pursue his plan, undoubtedly concluding that a naval blockade of Boston would have been too risky and expensive.

[15]The Pennacook Indians of the Merrimack River had moved to the upper Connecticut River Valley in order to avoid the war.

[16]Pepper appears briefly in Rowlandson's narrative, during the third remove. See p. 80.

had beene in danger, so he went after his master & enquired after him & at last found him out, he saith Rob Peper would be glad to escape home and hopes hee shall meet with an oppertunity, when the Indians march nearer the English. James said his master told him hee would send him home when hee had convenient opptunety. Also hee was informed that there are two more English men prisoners with Philip & Hadly Indians, one is of Boston servant to a ship carpenter Grenhough, and the other he remembers not his name.

Hee saieth, that before hee & Job came among those indians they told them the Narragants had sent in one or 2 English scalps, but these indians would not receive them, but shot at their messenger & said they were English mens friends all last summer & would not creditt their first messangers.[17] After there came other messengers from Narragansetts & brought more heads [he saw twelve scalpes of English hangd upon trees], that then these Indians beeleved the Narragansset & receved the scalps & paid them [as their manner is], & now they beeleved that the Naragansitts & English are at warre, of which they are glad. The Narragansets told these indians that the English had had fight with them, & killed about forty fighting men & one Sachem, & about 300 old men women & children were kild & burnt in the wigwams, most of which were destroyd. They told him that the Narragansetts said the Mohegins & Pequitts Indians killed & woonded of them, as many as the English had kild. Being questioned by Mr. Danforth whether hee could learne whether the Narragansetts had ayded & assisted Philip & his companey in the summer against the English, hee answered that hee understood by those indians that they had not, but lookt on them as freinds to the English all along til now & their enemies. Hee saieth that hee was informed that the Nargansets said that an Inglish man one Joshua Tift[18] was among them when they had their fight at the English, & that he did them good service & kild & woonded 5 or 6 English in that fight, & that before they wold trust him he had kild a miller an English man at Narragansit, & brought his scalpe to them. Also hee said that the

[17]The Narragansetts had remained formally neutral until the English attacked their Great Swamp Fort in December 1675, hence some Nipmucs' initial distrust.

[18]Joshua Tift, or Tefft, was the only colonist accused of having actively fought against the English. He was also married to a Narragansett woman. After English troops captured him in January 1676, he was convicted of treason and hanged, and his body was drawn and quartered.

Naragansits told these indians that one William that lives in those parts brought them some powder & offered them all his catle for provisions desiring only that his life might bee spared & his children & grandchildren. These Narragansits solicited these indians[19] to send them som help [. . . they knew them to be stout soldiers], they promised to send with them 20 men to goe with them to see how things were, & they determined to begin their jorny last Saturday [ie 22th January] and they also resolved to take Job with them to Narraganset indians; and upon the same day Mawtaamp the sagamor said hee would goe with another company up to Phillip, to informe him & those Indians of the breach betwene the English & Narragansitts & he said that James [our spy] should goe along with him to Philipp to acquaint him of the state of affayres among the English & praying indians. James said to Mataamp I am willing to goe to Philip but not at this present because Philip knowes that I fought against him on the English side at Mount Hope & other places, & hee will not beeleve that I am realy turned to his party, unies I first do some exployt & kill some English men & carry their heads to him. Let me have opportunity to doe somthing of this nature before I goe to Philip. This answer of James seemed to satisfy the sagamore Mawtaump. But James doubting notwithstanding, that he might change his mind and take him with him when hee went, hee was resolved to endevor an escape before the time they intended the jorny, especially considering what Tachupawillin told him in secret that Philip had given order to his men that if they met with these John Hunter, James Speen, this James & Thomas Quannupaquit [brethren & Andrew Pitamee & Peter Ephraim they bring them to him or put them to death].

Accordingly James moved Job [his companion] to contrive a way for an escape. Job concealed his purpose, and upon Wensday the 19th of this instant they 2 early in the morne went out as if they would goe a hunting for deare, as they had don at other times & returnd againe [James having goten about a pint of nokake[20] of Symon Squa one of the praying indians]. They beeing in the woods hunted for deere & killd 4 deare & as they traveld to & fro they percevd that by som footing of indians that some did watch their motions, so towards night they being neare a pond they drew the deer at the pond & tooke up their quarters in thicke swampe & there made a fire & dresd some of the venison, but

---

[19]That is, the Nipmucs with whom Quanapohit was staying.
[20]A dried meal that Native Americans carried when traveling because a portion of any size could be broken off and mixed with water.

no other indians came to them; so about 3 oclock before day, James said to Job now let us escape away if wee can. But Job said I am not willing to goe now, because my children are here and I will stay longer. If God please hee can preserve my life; if not I am willing to die. I will therfore goe backe againe to the indians & goe along with the company to the Naragansitt, & if I returne I will use what policy I can to get away my children. If I live, about . . . weeks hence I will com back & I will com to Naticke & therfore if you can, take 4 or 5 indians to meet me there. I shall if I live by that time get more intelligence of affayres. Then James said to him, I must now goe away for I am not like to have a better opptunity, & if they should carry mee to Philip I shall die. But I am sorry for you Job, lest when I am gon they will kill you for my sake; but you may tel them I runne away from you & was afrayd to goe to Philip before I had don some exployt. So they parted—& James our spy came homeward travilling through the woods night & day untill he came to Naticke to James Spene wigwam, who lives their to looke to som aged & sick folks that were not in capacity to be brought downe to Deare Hand, & on Lord's day came to Serjant Williams at the village & by him was conducted to & so to Boston before the Councel the same day which was the 24th day of this instnt Janury 1675 where his examination & relation was written by 2 scribes: & though this may a little differ from others in some particulars yet for substance it is the same.[21]

Moreover hee said that hee heard that the Narragansit were marched upp into the woods toward Quantesit & they were in company & the first company of above 200 among them were several woonded werre come before the Narragansit come up to these Indians:—being omitted beefore it is put in heare.

---

[21]The other, briefer version was recorded by Daniel Gookin and published as "James Quanapaug's Information" in *Massachusetts Historical Society Collections*, 1st ser., 6 (1799): 205–8.

5

JOB KATTANANIT

Petition to the Governor and Council of Massachusetts

February 14, 1676

Job Kattananit, James Quanapohit's partner in espionage, warned the English on February 9 that anti-English Indians would attack Lancaster that night. Having performed his duty for the English, Kattananit then asked permission to return to their opponents' lands on a more personal mission—to rescue his children and perhaps other Christian Nipmucs who had been captured at their town of Hassanamesit. His petition, dated February 14—just four days after the Lancaster attack—is the document that follows, as transcribed by a nineteenth-century author. The petition was granted, but anti-Indian hysteria among the English remained Kattananit's most serious obstacle. When Massachusetts decided, in March 1676, that its army could resume using friendly Indians, Kattananit joined a contingent of troops with the understanding that he could leave them at an appropriate time to conduct his search. However, Captain Samuel Moseley led a protest movement among the soldiers, who feared that Kattananit would inform the enemy of their movements. The resulting delays caused Kattananit to miss a scheduled rendezvous with a contact behind the lines, so he was unable to locate his children. He and they were safely united by the time the war was over.

The humble petition of Job Kattananit.

Whereas your poor suplyant hath been abroad in your Honours service among the Indian enemies, and have given a true and faithful account of what I could learn among them according to my Instructions; And in my Journey I found my three children with the enemy, together with some of my friends that continue their fidelity to God and to the English, and do greatly mourn for their condition, and long and desire to return to the English if you please, to let them live where or how you will please appoint: And to this end some few of them have agreed

---

Josiah H. Temple, *History of Framingham, Massachusetts* (Framingham, Mass., 1887), 67–68.

with me to meet them at Hassanamesit about the full of the moon, and to endeavor to bring my children with them — My humble request and supplication is that you will please to admit your poor servant: (And if you please to send an Englishman or two with me I shall be glad, but if that cannot be done, then to admit me and James Speen,[1] to go forth to see and meet and bring in my poor children and some few Godly Christians among them; and if they do escape we shall meet them and return within 3 or 4 days, if God please; but if we cannot meet them then I shall conclude they cannot escape, and so shall immediately return; and if your Honours please shall go forth with the army to the enemies' quarters, or to do any other service I can for your Honours and the country and go to the hazard of my life and shall be very thankful to your Honours for this favor.

[1] A Christian Massachuset Indian from the town of Natick.

6

TOWN OF LANCASTER

Petition to the Governor and Council of Massachusetts

March 11, 1676

The consequences of Massachusetts's ignoring James Quanapohit's intelligence were experienced first by the town of Lancaster. Although Job Kattananit's last-minute warning averted an even worse disaster, the attack virtually crippled the town. Moreover, the colony's leaders were unwilling to increase Lancaster's protection afterward, believing that it had to put its resources into pursuing the enemy. This petition, dated March 11 — just one month after the attack in which Mary Rowlandson was captured — details the emotional as well as material condition of the town's remaining residents. The governor and council approved the petition and, by the end of the month, Lancaster was completely abandoned.

Henry S. Nourse, ed., *The Narrative of the Captivity and Restoration of Mrs. Mary Rowlandson* (Lancaster, Mass., 1903), 80–81.

To the Honerd Govrnor and Counseill.

The humble petition of the poor destressed people of Lancaster, humbly sheweth, that since the enemy made such sad & dismall havocke amongst our deare friends & Brethren, & we that are left who have our lives for a[1] pray sadly sensible of Gods Judgment upon us, this with the destresse we are now in does embolden us to present our humble Requests to your Honors, hoping our Conditions may be considered by you and our Requests find acceptance with you, our state is very deplorable, in our Incapacity to subsist, as to Remove away we cannot, the enemy has so Encompassed us, otherwise for want of help our cattle being the most of them carried away by the barbarous heathen, & to stay disenabled for want of food, the Towns people are Generally gone who felt the Judgment but light, & had their catle left them with theyr estats, but we many of us here in this prison, have not bread to last us one month & our other provision spent and gone, for the generality, our Town is drawn into two Garisons wherein are by the Good favours of your Honors eighteen soldiers, which we gladly mayntayn soe long as any thing lasts, & if your Honors should call them off, we are certaynly a bayt for the enemy if God do not wonderfully prevent, therefore we hope as God has made you fathers over us so you will have a fathers pitty to us & extend your care over us who are your poor destressed subjects. We are sorrowful to Leave the place, but hopelesse to keep it unless mayntayned by the Cuntry,[2] it troubles our sperits to give any Incuridgment to the enemy, or leave any thing for them to promote their wicked design, yet better save our Lives than lose Life and Estate both, we are in danger emenent, the enemy lying Above us, nay on both sides of us, as does plainly Apeare. Our womens cries does daily Increase beyond expression which does not only fill our ears but our hearts full of Greefe, which makes us humbly Request your Honors to send a Gard of men & that if you please so command we may have Carts. About fourteen will Remove the whole, eight of which has been present long at Sudbury but never carne for want of a small guard of men, the whole that is, all that are in the one Garison, Kept in Major Willards house, which is all from your Honors most humble servants and suppliants.

Lancaster March 11th. 1675/76

JACOB FARRAR
JOHN HOUGHTON Sen[r]
JOHN MOORE

---

[1]Clearly, some wording is missing here.
[2]The colony.

> JOHN WHITTCOMB
> JOB WHITTCOMB
> JOHNATHAN WHITTCOMB
> JOHN HOUGHTON Jun[r]
> CYPRIAN STEEVENS

The other one Garison are in the like destresse & so humbly desire your like pitty & fatherly care, having widows and many fatherless children. The Number of Carts to Carey away this garrison is twenty Carts.

Your Honors Humble Petitioners.

> JOHN PRESCOTT Sen[r]
> THO. SAWYER Sen[r]
> THO SAWYER Jun[r]
> JONATHAN PRESCOTT
> THO WILLDER
> JOHN WILLDER
> SARAH WHEELER wid
> WIDOW FARBANKS
> JOHN RIGBY
> NATHANIELL WILDER
> JOHN ROOPER
> WIDOW ROOPER

7

Indians' Letter to English Troops at Medfield
February 21, 1676

Shortly after Mary Rowlandson was captured, members of her captor's party attacked and burned the town of Medfield, Massachusetts. When colonial troops arrived, they found a grim message that the raiders had attached to a bridge post. Although it voiced the sentiments of all the Indians, it was written by a Christian Native American who was literate in

Daniel Gookin, "An Historical Account of the Doings and Sufferings of the Christian Indians in New England," *Transactions and Collections of the American Antiquarian Society* 2 (1836): 494.

English. That a "praying Indian" had written the note underscores the fact that learning and using the ways of "civilization" did not invariably lead Native Americans to repudiate their people and their cultural identities.

Know by this paper, that the Indians that thou hast provoked to wrath and anger, will war this twenty one years if you will; there are many Indians yet, we come three hundred at this time. You must consider the Indians lost nothing but their life; you must lose your fair houses and cattle.

4. Mary Rowlandson's Release From Captivity

8

JOHN LEVERETT

Letter to "Indian Sagamores"
March 31, 1676

The process by which Rowlandson and other captives at Mt. Wachusett were ransomed was delicate and protracted. It began when Tom Dublet, a Christian Nipmuc, arrived at Mt. Wachusett with the following letter from Massachusetts' governor John Leverett. The governor's letter makes clear that colonial authorities knew that a Native American who was literate in English would be writing out the anti-English Nipmucs' reply. It is instructive that although Mary Rowlandson acknowledges the roles played by certain Nipmucs in securing her release, she ignores their contributions when sounding her blanket indictments of all Christian Indians.

For the Indian Sagamores & people that are in warre against us. Intelligence is come to us that you have some English, especially women and children in Captivity among you. We have therefore sent the messenger offering to redeem them either for payment in goods or wampum or by exchange of prisoners. We desire your answer by this our messenger what price you demand for every man woman and child, or if you will exchange for Indians. If you have any among you that can write your answer to this our message, we desire it in writing; and to that end have sent, paper pen and incke by the messenger. If you let our messenger have free access to you, freedom of a safe returne, we are willing to do the like by any messenger of yours, provided he come unarmed, and carry a white flag upon a staff, visible to be seen which we take as a

Henry S. Nourse, ed., *The Narrative of the Captivity and Restoration of Mrs. Mary Rowlandson* (Lancaster, Mass., 1903), 96.

flag of truce, and is used by civilized nations in time of warre, when any messengers are sent in a way of treaty, which we have done by our messenger. In testimony whereof I have set my hand & seal.

JOHN LEVERETT *Govr*

Boston 31 March 1676. Passed by the Council

EDWARD RAWSON *Secy*

9

SHOSHANIM ("SAM SACHEM") ET AL.

Letter to John Leverett
April 12, 1676

In replying to Governor Leverett, "Sam" (Shoshanim, the sachem of Nashaway), his colleagues, and their scribe, Peter Jethro, refuse to make any concessions to the colonists. They insist that the English send two messengers, apparently recognizing the risks in placing responsibility for such weighty matters in the hands of a single person. In a passage that echoes the note on the Medfield bridge (Document 7), they also reiterate the heavy losses that the settlers have suffered thus far. They then add an extraordinary postscript in which they directly address Joseph Rowlandson and John Kettle, another Lancaster man who was away during the raid, informing them of the conditions of their captive family members and including, as proof that they lived, the signs of Rowlandson's sister and Kettle's wife. They add a final request, ostensibly from Mary Rowlandson, that Joseph send her three pounds of tobacco. He replied by sending her a pound with each of the two subsequent letters. Mary Rowlandson remarks in her narrative that the request was fraudulent, for she had given up tobacco since being captured. Yet the shipments demonstrated to the Nipmucs that her husband was sincere in pursuing her release.

We now give answer by this one man, but if you like my answer send one more man besides this one Tom Nepanet, and you send with all true heart and with all your mind by two men, because you know and we

Henry S. Nourse, ed., *The Narrative of the Captivity and Restoration of Mrs. Mary Rowlandson* (Lancaster, Mass., 1903), 96–97.

know your heart grew sorrowful with crying for your lost many many hundred men and all your house and all your land, and woman, child, and cattle, as all your thing that you have lost and on your backside stand.

SAM *Sachem*
KUTQUEN and
QUANOHIT *Sagamores*

Peter Jethro
Scribe

Mr Rowlandson, your wife and all your child is well but one dye. Your sister is well and her 3 child. John Kittel, your wife and all your child is all well, and all them prisoners taken at Nashua[3] is all well.

Mr Rowlandson, see your loving sister his[4] hand C Hanah
And old Kettel wif his hand[5] T
Brother Rowlandson, pray send thre pound of Tobacco for me, if you can my loving husband pray send thre pound of tobacco for me.

This writing by your enemies

SAMUEL USKATIUHGUN[6] and GUNRASHIT,
two Indian Sagamores

[3]The sachems here refer to Lancaster by its original name, Nashaway.
[4]Sister's.
[5]Kettle's wife's.
[6]Another name used by Shoshanim.

10

JAMES PRINTER ET AL.

Letter to John Leverett et al.

ca. April 1676

The colony's response to the preceding letter has been lost, but the following reply to it from the Indians shows that the English did add a second messenger, a Nipmuc named Tatiquinea, or Peter Conway. The letter also indicates that the English, in the letter now lost, expressed particular interest in ransoming Mary Rowlandson among the many captives held

Henry S. Nourse, ed., *The Narrative of the Captivity and Restoration of Mrs. Mary Rowlandson* (Lancaster, Mass., 1903), 97–98.

*at Mt. Wachusett. It sets her ransom at twenty pounds, as established
by Rowlandson herself under pressure from her captors. Note that the
sachems' attitude has softened somewhat since their previous letter.
While perhaps in part a response to the tone of the lost English letter, it
also reflects their growing recognition after the battle of Sudbury that
they would be unable to defeat the English. The letter, as the subsequent
English response (Document 11) indicates, was written by James Printer.*

For the Governor and the Council at Boston.

The Indians, Tom Nepennomp and Peter Tatatiqunea hath brought
us letter from you about the English Captives, especially for Mrs Rolanson; the answer is I am sorrow that I have don much to wrong you and
yet I say the falte is lay upon you, for when we began quarrel at first
with Plimouth men I did not think that you should have so much truble
as now is: therefore I am willing to hear your desire about the Captives.
Therefore we desire you to send Mr Rolanson and goodman Kettel: (for
their wives) and these Indians Tom and Peter to redeem their wives,
they shall come and goe very safely: Whereupon we ask Mrs Rolanson,
how much your husband willing to give for you she gave an answer
20 pounds in goodes but John Kittels wife could not tell. and the rest
captives may be spoken of hereafter.

11

MASSACHUSETTS GOVERNOR'S COUNCIL

Letter to "Indian Sachems"

April 28, 1676

*To judge from the tone of the following letter alone, the English were so
dissatisfied with the Indians' previous reply that they were unwilling to
concede anything further. But we know from Rowlandson's narrative
and other sources that in fact they made a major concession when
sending it. For while not dispatching Joseph Rowlandson or John*

Henry S. Nourse, ed., *The Narrative of the Captivity and Restoration of Mrs. Mary Rowlandson* (Lancaster, Mass., 1903), 98.

Kettle, they sent an influential Englishman — John Hoar — with
power to negotiate. On May 2, Hoar returned to Concord with a freed
Mary Rowlandson. Her release opened the way for the return of the
remaining captives.

To the Indian Sachems about Wachusets.

We received your letter by Tom and Peter, which doth not answer ours to you: neither is subscribed by the sachems nor hath it any date, which we know your scribe James Printer doth well understand should be. we have sent the said Tom & Peter againe to you expecting you will speedily give us a plaine & direct answer to our last letter, and if you have anything more to propound to us we desire to have it from you under your hands, by these our messengers, and you shall have a speedy answer. Dated the 28th, April, 1676.

5. English Justice

12

ANDREW PITIMEE ET AL.

Petition to the Governor and Council of Massachusetts

June 1676

As Massachusetts endeavored to punish any and all Native Americans who had fought against them, many Indians voluntarily returned to the colony's jurisdiction while others were captured by English troops and their Christian Indian allies. Colonial authorities then set out to decide which Indians within their grasp deserved punishment. The following two documents center on three Nipmuc families that, along with James Printer, had accompanied the anti-English Natives who attacked Hassanamesit rather than risk being captured by the English. Focusing particularly on Hassanamesit's magistrate, Captain Tom, the documents demonstrate how the authorities went about distinguishing friends from enemies. The petition is especially noteworthy because the accused Indians' loyalty is supported by James Quanapohit (here rendered as Quanahpohkit), Job Kattananit, and three other prominent pro-English natives.

To the Honourable the Govournour and Councill of the Massachusetts Colony, Assembled at Boston this[1] of June 1676:

The humble petition of Andrew Pittimee, Quanahpohkit, alias James Rumney Marsh,[2] John Magus, and James Speen, officers unto the Indian

[1]The date is missing from this document.

[2]James Quanapohit was often referred to by the surname Rumney Marsh.

Daniel Gookin, "An Historical Account of the Doings and Sufferings of the Christian Indians in New England," *Transactions and Collections of the American Antiquarian Society* 2 (1836): 527–28.

soldiers, now in your service, with the consent of the rest of the Indian souldiers being about eighty men;

Humply imploreth your favour and mercies to be extended to some of the prisoners taken by us (most of them) near Lancaster, Marlborough, &c: In whose behalf we are bold to supplicate your Honoures. And wee have three reasons for this our humble supplication; first, because the persons we beg pardon for, as we are informed, are innocent; and have not done any wrong or injury unto the English, all this war time, only were against their wills, taken and kept among the enemy. Secondly, because it pleased your Honours to say to some of us, to encourage us to fidelity and activity in your service, that you would be ready to do anything for us, that was fitt for us to ask and you to grant. Thirdly, that others that are [still] out, and love the English, may be encouraged to come in. More that we humbly intercede for, is the lives and libertyes of those few of our poor friends and kindred, that, in this time of temptation and affliction, have been in the enemy's quarters; we hope it will be no griefe of heart to you to shew mercy, and especially to such who have (as we conceive) done no wrong to the English. If we did think, or had any ground to conceive that they were naught, and were enemies to the English, we would not intercede for them, but rather bear our testimony against them, as we have done. We have (especially some of us) been sundry times in your service to the hazzard of our lives, both as spyes, messengers, scouts, and souldiers, and have through God's favour acquitted ourselves faithfully, and shall do as long as we live endeavour with all fidelitie to fight in the English cause, which we judge is our cause, and also God's cause, to oppose the wicked Indians, enemies to God and all goodness. In granting this our humble request, you will much oblige us who desire to remain

Your Honoures Humble and Faithful Servants,

ANDREW PITTIMEE,
JAMES QUANAPOHKIT,
JOB,[3]
JOHN MAGUS,
JAMES SPEEN.

---

[3]Job Kattananit, whose name was not included with those of the other petitioners at the head of the document.

The persons we supplicate for, are Capt. Tom, his son Nehemiah, his wife and two children, John Uktuck, his wife and children, Maanum and her child.

And if the Council please not to answer our desires in granting the lives and liberties of all these, yet if you shall please to grant the women and children, it will be a favour unto us.

13

Massachusetts Council to James Quanapohit et al.
1676

The Council replied to the Christian Indians' petition by granting mercy to the women and children cited but forcefully rejecting their plea on behalf of Captain Tom. (The disposition of Nehemiah and John Uktuck is not made clear.) In heralding the justice and benevolence of English rule over Native Americans, the Council refers to the experience of the Pequot Indians of Connecticut since their defeat by the English in 1637. Under the Council's declaration in the final paragraph, James Printer and a number of other Nipmucs were cleared of charges of actively supporting the anti-English cause and allowed to return to their people.

In Answer to the Petition of James Quanhpohkit, James Speen, Job, Andrew Pittimee, and Jno. Magus.

Capt. Tom being a lawful prisoner at warr, there needs no further evidence for his conviction; yet hee having had liberty to present his plea before the Councill why he should not be proceeded against accordingly, instead of presenting anything that might alleviate his withdrawing from the government of the English and joining with the enemy, it doth appear by sufficient evidence that he was not only (as is credibly related by some Indians present with him) an instigator to others over whom he was by this government made a Captain, but was also actually present and an

Daniel Gookin, "An Historical Account of the Doings and Sufferings of the Christian Indians in New England," *Transactions and Collections of the American Antiquarian Society* 2 (1836): 528–29.

actor in the devastation of some of our plantations; and therefore it cannot consist with the honour and justice of authority to grant him a pardon.

Whereas the Council do, with reference to the Petitioners, grant them the lives of the women and children by them mentioned. And, further, the Council do hereby declair, that, as they shall be ready to show favour in sparing the lives and liberty of those that have been our enemies, on their comeing in and submission of themselves to the English Government and your disposal, the reality and complacency of the government towards the Indians sufficiently appearing in the provisions they have made, and tranquility that the Pequots have injoyed under them for over forty years; so also it will not be available for any to plead in favour for them that they have been our friends while found and taken among our enemyes.

Further the Council do hereby declare that none may expect privilege bye his declaration, that come not in and submit themselves in 14 days next coming.

By the Council,   EDW. RAWSON, *Clerke*

14

SHOSHANIM ("SAM SACHEM") ET AL.

Letter to John Leverett et al.
July 6, 1676

Through Simon Pottoquam, yet another Nipmuc scribe, Shoshanim ("Sam Sachem") and three other sachems pleaded with the colony's Governor and Council for the release of their wives and children and expressed their continued offer of peace. Note that they address the English as fellow Christians. In a postscript, Shoshanim maintains that he had been searching for other English captives when his family was seized. He also points to the Nipmucs' break with Philip and Quinnapin over the Nipmucs' policy of returning the remaining English captives. The printer who later reproduced the letter attempted to render the signers' marks with conventional typeface.

Henry S. Nourse, ed., *The Narrative of the Captivity and Restoration of Mrs. Mary Rowlandson* (Lancaster, Mass., 1903), 100–101.

To all Englishmen and Indians, all of you hear Mr Waban and Mr Eliott.[1]

July 6 1676. Mr John Leverett, my Lord, Mr Waban, and all the chief men our Brethren Praying to God: We beseech you all to help us: my wife she is but one, but there be more Prisoners, which we pray you keep well: Mattamuck his wife we entreat you for her, and not only that man, but it is the Request of two Sachems, Sam Sachem of Weshakum, and the Pakashoag Sachem. And that further you will consider about the making Peace: We have spoken to the people of Nashobah (viz Tom Dublet and Peter) that we would agree with you and make covenant of Peace with you. We have been destroyed by your soldiers, but still we Remember it now to sit still: do you consider it again: we do earnestly entreat you, that it may be so by Jesus Christ. O let it be so: Amen Amen.

MATTAMUCK his MARK N
SAM SACHEM his MARK X
SIMON POTTOQUAM *Scribe*
UPPANIPPAQUUM his C
PAKASHOKAG his MARK &

My Lord Mr Leverett at Boston, Mr Waban, Mr Eliott, Mr Gookin, and Council, hear ye. I went to Connecticot[2] about the Captives, that I might bring them into your hands, and when we were almost there the English had destroyed those Indians. When I heard it I returned back again: then when I came home, we were also destroyed: After we were destroyed then Philip and Quanipun went away into their own Country again: and I knew they were much afraid, because of our offer to join with the English, and therefore they went back into their own Country and I know they will make no war: therefore because when some English men came to us Philip and Quanipun sent to kill them: but I said if any kill them, I'll kill them.

Sam Sachem

Written by SIMON BOSHOKUM *Scribe*

---

[1]Waban was the Massachuset sachem/magistrate of the praying town of Natick. "Mr. Eliott" refers to the missionary, John Eliot.

[2]Meaning the Connecticut River valley in western Massachusetts.

15

DANIEL GOOKIN

A Memorandum of Indian Children Put Forth into Service to the English

August 10, 1676

The postwar upheavals within Native American communities led not only to large-scale enslavement but also to more "benevolent" forms of subordination to colonists. One such form was a legally formalized extension of the earlier practice of placing Native children in English households as indentured servants who would receive instruction in Christianity and the English language. The following document illustrates the new practice as carried out by Massachusetts. The General Court commissioned Daniel Gookin to head a three-man commission to decide on assignments for fifty Nipmuc and Massachuset children. Gookin itemizes these assignments by numbers of children assigned to each designated master. The masters are not large-scale commercial slave traders but rather a mix of men, including "goodmen" and those titled "Mr.," as well as two widows. Note that Gookin himself and Captain Thomas Prentis, another commissioner, are among those receiving children. Prentis's award of a young boy redresses an alleged seizure of the boy by another colonist. Gookin indicates what he knows about the children's parents and siblings, following the English model of "family" and vows to penalize any family members who encourage or help the children escape from their English masters.

August 10 1676. A memorandum of Indian Children put forth into service to the English Beeing of those indians that came in & submitted with John Sachem of Packachooge, with the names of the persons with whome they were placed & the names and age of the children & the names of their relations & the places they Did belong to, By Mr Daniel Gookin Senr, Thomas Prentis Capt' & Mr Edward Oakes, who were a comittee appointed by the Counsel to mannage that affayr. The termes &

Proceedings of the Colonial Society of Massachusetts, 19 (1916–1917), 25–28.

conditions upon which they are to serve is to be ordered by the General
Court who are to provide that the children bee religiously educated &
taught to read the English tounge

2 Boy A maid	To Samuel Simonds Esq. a boy named John his father named Alwitankus late of quantisit his father & mother p^rent both consenting the boys age about 12 years

To him a girle named Hester her father & mother dead
late of Nashaway her age ten years her onkel named John
woosumpigin of Naticke

1 Boy	To Thomas Danforth esq a boy aged about 13 yeares his name John
1 Boy	To Leift Jonathan Danforth of [Billericay?] a boy aged twelve yeares, son to papamech alius David late of Warwick or Cowesit.
2 Boyes	To Mathew Bridge of CamBridge two Boyes the one named Jabez aged about ten yeares the other named Joseph aged six yeares their father named woompthe late of Packachooge one or both these boyes is away with his father 8 ber 17th 1676
3 A boy & two Girls	To Mr Jerimiah Shepard of Rowley a boy named Absolom his father of the same name late of Manehage aged about ten yeares.

To him a girle sister to the Lad named Sarah aged eleven
yeares. These [*illegible*] of Naticke.

To him another girle aged about 8 yeares her named
Jane her father & mother dead.

1 Mayd	To Mrs Mitchell of Cambridg widdow a maid named Margaret aged about twelve yeares, her father named Suhunnick of quantisit her mother dead.
1 Boy	To Thomas Jacob of Ipswich a boy aged ten yeares, one wennaputanan his guardian & one upacunt of quantisitt his grand mother was present. The Boy [*illegible*].
1 Boy	To on Goodman Read a Tanner of Cambridge a Boy named John aged about thirteen yeares his father Dead.
1 Boy	To Mr Jacob Green of Charel Towne a boy aged about seaven yeares his parrents Dead Late of quantisit but his mother of Narraganset.

1 Boy	To Thomas Woolson of Wattertowne a boy aged about 14 yeares his name John his father dead who was of Cowesit or Warwick, his mother p^rsent.

1 Boy To Ciprian Steuens of Rumny Marsh but late of Lancaster a boy aged about six yeares son to nohanet of Chobnakonkonon. The Boy named Samuel.

1 Mayd To Thomas Eliot of Boston a carpenter a maid aged about ten yeares her name Rebecka.

1 Boy To Jacob Green Junior of Charles towne a Boy named Peter aged nine years his father dead his mother p^rsent named nannantum of quantisit.

1 Boy To on Goodman Greenland a carpenter of Charles towne on misticke side a boy named Tom aged twelue yeares his father named santeshe of Pakachooge.

1 Girle To Mr Edmund Batter of Salem a maid named Abigal aged sixteen her mother a widow named quanshishe late of Shookannet Beyond mendon.

2a Boy A girle To Daniel Gookin Senr A Boy named Joshua aged about eight yeares son to William wunuko late of magunkoog; his father dead.

 To him a girle aged about six yeares daughter to the widdow quinshiske late of Shookanet beyond mendon

1 Girle To Andrew Bordman Tayler of Cambridge a girle named Anne sister to ye Last named.

1 Boy To Thomas Prentis Junior son to Capt Prentis of Cambridge village a boy named John son to William Wunnako late of magnkoy that was executed for Thomas Burney, aged thirteen.

1 Boy To Benjamin Mills of Dedham a boy aged about six years is [named?] Joseph Spoonans late of Marlboro.

1 Boy To Mr Edward Jackson a Boy named Joseph aged about 12 yeares Late of magalygook cosen to Pyambow of Naticke.

1 Mayd To Widdow Jackson of Cambridge village a girle named Hope aged nine yeare her parents dead who wer of Narraganset.

1 Boy	To old Goodman Myles of Dedham a boy of [ ] yeares old. son to Annaweeken Decesed who was late of Hassanamesit his mother p^rsent.

1 Boy   To Capt. Thomas Prentis a Boy named Joseph son to Annaweken decesed Brother to the last named aged about 11 yeares this boy was after taken from Capt Prentice & sent up Mr Stoughton for [ ] Capt Prentis is to bee considered about it for hee has taken more care & paynes about those indians.

1 Boy   To John Smith of Dedham a boy aged about eight yeares his father dead late of Marlborow hee is Brother to James Printers wife

1 Mayd   To Mr John Flint [?] of Concord a mayd aged about [ ] yeares [*illegible*]

1 Boy   To Mr Jonathan Wade of mistick a Boy named Tom Aged about 11 yeares sonne to William Wunakhow of Magunkgog decesed

1 Mayd   To Mr Nathaniel Wade of mistick a maid aged about ten years daughter to Jame Natomet [?] late of Packachooge her father & mother dead

It is humbly proposed to the Honble Generall Court, to set the time these children shall serve; & if not less than till they come to 20 yeares of age. unto which those that had relations seemed willing, and also that the Court lay som penalty upon them if they runne away before the time expire & on their parents or kindred that shall entice or harborr & conceale them if they should runne away

Signed By the Comĩtee   DANIEL GOOKIN SEN^R
Above named   EDWARD OAKES.

Cambridge
8 ber 28 1676

16

JOHN HULL

Excerpts from John Hull's Journal

August 24, September 23, 1676

Whereas Daniel Gookin listed the assignments of Native American children to English households (Document 15), John Hull occasionally performed a comparable service for Massachusetts, overseeing and recording the sales of indigenous captives consigned to enslavement. We have already met Hull as the pious Puritan who took notes on, among other topics, Joseph Rowlandson's sermons in Boston's Old South Church. He was also one of Boston's most prominent merchants in the late seventeenth century, with overseas connections in England and Barbados. In this document, the first list identifies the buyers and provides information on captives' gender, age, and other details that determine their price. The second list indicates only the number of captives being sold. With two exceptions, the first list does not identify any captives by name. Some colonists who bought just a few captives, including Samuel Symons, who also appears on Gookin's list, and Daniel Henchman, a close associate of Gookin's, undoubtedly intended to provide Christian instruction and discipline to the children whose labor they utilized. Other small-scale purchasers probably sought the slaves' labor services only. The purchasers of larger lots of captives—particularly Samuel Shrimpton and Thomas Smith (on both lists)—were, like Hull, transatlantic traders of people and goods. Samuel Moseley was a notorious military officer who, early in the war, was the first to capture, enslave, and sell abroad Christian Indians who sought English protection. James Whitcomb, who owned the house in which the Rowlandson were then living, was another wealthy merchant whose interests included slavery.

George Madison Bodge, *Soldiers in King Philip's War*, 2nd ed. (Leominster, Mass., 1896), 479–80.

Captives Cr. By Sundry Acc'p^ta Viz.

	£.	s.	d.		£.	s.	d.
Isaac Waldron for a Boy					3	00	00
Ephraim Savage for 2 girles					04	10	00
Samuel Shrimpton,							
4 Squawes, 3 girls, 2 infants	30	00	00	⎫			
1 old man, 3 squawes & 2 for one				⎬	41	12	00
returned by order	09	00	00				
1 man	02	12	00	⎭			
Samuel Lynd for 1 maid					03	10	00
Thomas Smith,							
1 girl and 2 men	09	10	00	⎫			
10 Squawes, 8 papooses, & 1 man	25	00	00	⎬	47	02	00
2 Lads, Viz. Pomham & Matoonas	07	00	00				
1 Woman, 4 little children	05	12	00	⎭			
Samuel Symons, Esq.							
For 1 Boy and Girl					05	00	00
George Perkes							
For 2 Boyes					06	00	00
John Mors							
For 1 Girle	02	00	00	⎫			
For 2 Girles	07	00	00	⎬	12	00	00
For 1 Boy	03	00	00	⎭			
John Mann, for 1 Girle					03	00	00
Thomas Davis, for 1 Boy					03	00	00
Daniel Henchman, for 1 squawe & infant					02	10	00
Samuel Mosely,							
1 Boy & Girle	06	00	00	⎫			
13 Squawes & papooses wounded 1 sick	20	00	00	⎭	26	00	00
Timothy Batt, for 1 squawe					02	15	00
——Rawlings, 1 squawe					03	00	00
September 23, 1676.							
Thomas Smith for 41 (captives)					82	00	00
Isaac Waldron for 1					02	00	00
Richard Middlecott for 6					10	00	00
James Meares " 2					03	10	00
Samuel Apleton " 3					04	00	00
John Buttolph " 1					01	15	00
William Gilbert " 1					02	00	00
George Sphere " 1					02	00	00

William Needham	"	1	· · · · · · · · · ·	00	05	00
Thomas Grant	"	5	· · · · · · · · · ·	08	01	00
David Waterhous	"	1	· · · · · · · · · ·	02	00	00
James Whitcomb	"	13	· · · · · · · · · ·	14	15	00
John Turner	"	1	· · · · · · · · · ·	02	00	00
Ann Shepcutt	"	1	· · · · · · · · · ·	01	15	00
Richard Wharton	"	8	· · · · · · · · · ·	08	00	00
—— Rawlins	"	3	· · · · · · · · · ·	04	10	00
John Wait	"	4	· · · · · · · · · ·	04	10	00
Josiah Flynt	"	2	· · · · · · · · · ·	03	15	00
Samuel Leach	"	2	· · · · · · · · · ·	02	00	00
Jarvis Ballard	"	2	· · · · · · · · · ·	02	00	00
James Meares	"	2	· · · · · · · · · ·	02	08	00
John Mason	"	1	· · · · · · · · · ·	02	00	00
Benjamin Gibbs	"	8	· · · · · · · · · ·	05	00	00

17

DANIEL GOOKIN

An Account of the Disposall of the Indians, Our Friends

November 10, 1676

With the war over, the colonies sought to assert control over Native Americans who had not been enslaved or indentured, even though most of these Indians had never fought against the English. Daniel Gookin was commissioned to write a report on Indians in eastern Massachusetts, in which he provides estimated numbers and locations of each Native community and lists those settlers who live near and watch over them. Yet for all the colonists' supposed control over these communities, Gookin can provide only estimates of their numbers, indicating that indigenous residents were still moving about despite the new rules. He does note some Indians who have apparently left the region as well as some who had died or were fighting alongside English troops to the north and east in Abenaki

Daniel Gookin, "An Historical Account of the Doings and Sufferings of the Christian Indians in New England," *Transactions and Collections of the American Antiquarian Society* 2 (1836): 532–33.

country. The figures at the end of each paragraph are Gookin's estimate of the ratio of adult males to women and children. Note that James Quana-pohit, now usually known as James Rumney Marsh, heads a community of Natick Indians at Medfield.

1676, November 10th — An account of the disposall of the Indians, our friends (pro tempore),[1] presented to the Council (at their desire) by Daniel Gookin, sen.

The Punkapog Indians are residing about Milton, Dorchester, and Braintree, among the English, who employ them (as I am informed) to cut cord wood, and do other labors. These are under the inspection of quarter-master Thomas Swift; their number, as I conjecture, may bee about one hundred and seventy-five; whereof 35 men: 140 women and children.

The Naticke Indians are disposed in four companies, as followes, viz., one company, with James Rumny Marsh and his kindrd, live in Medfield, with the approbation and consent of the English; these are in number about twenty-five. 5:20.

Another company live neare Natick, adjoyning to the garrison-house of Andrew Dewin and his sons (who desire their neighbourhood), and are under their inspection; the number of these may be about fifty souls. 10:40.

A third company of them, with Waban, live neare the falls of Charles river, neare to the house of Joseph Miller, and not farr from Capt. Prentce. The number of these may be about sixty souls; whereof are 12:50.

A fourth company dwell at Nonantum-hill, neare Leift. Trowbridge and John Coones, who permitts them to build their wigwams upon his ground. The number of this company, including some that live neare John White's, of Muddy river, and family or two neare Mr. Sparhake, and Daniel Champney, and Mr. Thomas Olivers, which are employed by the said persons to cut wood, and spin, and make stone walls; being but a small distance from the hill of Nonatum, where their meeting is to keepe Sabath. These may be about seventy-five souls. 15:60.

Among the Natick Indians are to bee reckoned such as are left, which came in with John of Pakchoog; which are not many, for sundry of that company are dead (since they came in); above thirty are put out

---

[1] For now, for the time being.

to service to the English; three were executed about Tho. Eames his burning;[2] about twenty rann away; and, generally, such as remaine are of those Indians that formerly (before the war) lived under our government at Hassanamesit, Magunkog, Marlborough, and Wamesitt. The men belonging to these are not above fifteen, and they are abroad with the army at the eastward, under Capt. Hunting.

The Nashobah or Concord Indians live at Concord, with the consent of the English there, and are employed by them; and are under the inspection of the comittee of militia and selectmen of that towne. Their number may be about fifty.   10:40.

The Indians that relate to Wannalancet, are placed neare Mr. Jonathan Ting's, at Dunstable, with Mr. Tyng's consent and under his inspection (when at home); and in Mr. Tyng's absence, the care of them is under one Robert Parris, Mr. Tyng's bayl.[3] The number of these may be about sixty, or more; some of their children are ordered to be put forth to English service, by the selectmen at Chelmsford and committee of militia there.   10:50.

There are about twenty-five live at or about Ipswich, under the government of authority there; som of their children were ordered to be put to service; there are about twenty-five.   8:17.

Besides these, there are some familys of them that live about Watertown and in Cambridge bounds, under English inspection and neare them; as at one Gate's, at Watertown, two families; at Justinias Holden, one family; at or neare Corprall Humand, two familys; at one Wilson, at Shawsin, one family. All these may be about forty souls.   7:33.

117 men, 450 women and children; and in all 567.

It must not be understood, that this computation of the number is exact; they may be a few more or a few less. Also of the men there are above thirty now abroad, under Capt. Hunting, at the eastward.

All these Indians meet together to worship God and keepe the Sabath; and have their teachers at six places, viz.: Meadfield, Andrew Dewins, at Lower Falls, at Nonnanum, at Concord, at Dunstable.

---

[2]That is, for burning the house of Thomas Eames, a settler, during the war.

[3]A bailor was someone who delivers goods in trust or, as in this case, assumes a responsibility in someone's absence.

6. A New England Narrative of Muslim Captivity

18

JOSHUA GEE

Excerpt from "Narrative of Joshua Gee"

1680–1687

*Joshua Gee began writing his narrative in 1680 while still a captive
and before Rowlandson published hers. Like Rowlandson's and most
other English-language captivity narratives of the period, Gee sees
God's providence as having exposed him to repeated suffering, danger,
and redemption. But he departs from other narrators by portraying his
captors as (for better or worse) human rather than uniformly vilifying all
of them on the basis of their religion and culture. He maintains the same
tolerance toward Roman Catholic and Greek Orthodox Christians who
were also captives and suggests that Christian captives in Algiers (though
not in the Turkish capital of Constantinople) were free to worship as they
wished. Also, whereas Rowlandson only slowly and occasionally began
to refer to her captors and fellow captives together as "we," Gee from the
outset uses "we" to refer to whatever group he is part of at that moment.*

*Gee's handwritten narrative remained out of public view for two and a
half centuries during which time it was folded tightly in a box. By the time
it was rediscovered, many of the pages were no longer legible. The legible
portions of the narrative were transcribed and published in 1947. The
following excerpt is based on that edition. Some spelling has been modernized for clarity.*

*Narrative of Joshua Gee of Boston, Mass., while he was captive in Algeria of the Barbary
pirates, 1680–1687*, ed. Albert Carlos Bates (Hartford, Conn.: Wadsworth Atheneum,
1943), 15–24.

Asking my father's advice and liberty to go to sea, I interested myself[1] in a part of a vessel for that end. Before I went I had conceived an opinion that it would be attended with great evil and distress; yet I must proceed. I told some of my friends, one of whom is living, that I had an apprehension that I should be led through fiery trials and carried through them. And telling the same to the master, he said pray that these things come not on us. He said why will you proceed having such apprehensions of the voyage; I answered I must go and cannot avoid it. Yes I do believe that God will carry me through and bring me back to this place to give thanks to his name for his remarkable favors to me through the whole of the voyage.

Our voyage while at Roanoke[2] was attended with great difficulties in which I was eminently delivered from death March 8th. In stress of weather in the night getting ashore on an island, we got fire and with our knives cut bows[3] and made a small shelter from the weather and . . . the same to lie on after giving thanks to God for his mercy in our deliverance. We went to sleep on our green[4] bed. The next day we found a house and relief. Our ship's company, supposing us lost till after two days they seeking of us found us on said island.[5]

On our voyage for England we were short of bread, and in a dream on a day before we were taken I saw a ship that did supply our want of bread but at a dear rate. At the site of an Algerian ship, I apprehended it was the same appearance I had seen in my dream and found it so. We had bread enough at a dear price. We went aboard in the first boat and being asked our loading, I answered tobacco; they said in English you have brought it to a bad market.[6]

[A] remarkable . . . good slave that waited on the boatswain did frequently show me kindness though he could not understand me nor I him. He first gave me tobacco and often after gave me part of what he had to eat though he had but little, a kindness I never saw him show to any other. And as our being put in irons in the hold of the ship, having nothing but stones for our pillows, he gave me his bag in which he had some clothing to lay under my head. After I came ashore I never saw him to repay his kindness. Hence I was led to contemplate divine

---

[1]He interested himself financially, invested.
[2]Roanoke Island, off the coast of what is now North Carolina.
[3]They cut and bent thin tree trunks or branches.
[4]The color of the bows.
[5]Gee and a few other crewmen had set off from their ship in a small boat.
[6]That is, there was little demand for tobacco in Muslim Algiers.

goodness and His sovereign dominion, that can cause the ravens to feed his people if need be. Sometime before I was taken I had minded night and day very frequently that scripture Psalms 37:1-2-3 and on, and now I saw reason to reconsider that my sorrows were many. I lost a considerable interest in vessel and cargo and myself a slave, but the thoughts of the grief it would be to my aged parents did add to my sorrow. Yet with Job I thought I could say, as Job 1:20-21, and that though He kill me I will trust in Him, though afterward with Psalms 30:7, thou hidest thy face. I was troubled I greatly feared being left to distrust God. And did humbly beg that I might be helped to glorify God in the fire although I should be led through the valley of the shadow of death. Psalms 44:19 . . . Lamentations 3:21-27. I did hope I could say the Lord is my portion.

I was sold, Psalms 44:11-12. Coming into my master's house in the room where the slaves kept, on a shelf I saw a bible and with joy took it in my hand and with a sad heart gave thanks to God. Opening the same, the first place came to hand and sight was John 13. Reading the first verse to my great support and surprise, was filled with tears. Considering it was God alone that could give a song in the house of pilgrimage. God turned the heart of my first master to favor me, and Thomas Corbin[7] bought my bible of an English slave for 16 pence and gave it me.

The first voyage I went to sea we had a fight with two English ships, received much damage, and were forced to leave them. The next day we took a ship from New Spain, a rich prize. The second voyage we fought an English ship and received much damage. She escaped, the sea being very high. The third voyage we fought a Genoa[8] ship which got under a castle on Majorca[9] and escaped. After that, war was made with France. We took many ships and did reward ourselves with clothing when we had leave to go on board for prizes, which was a favor shone us.

The last voyage I was in my first master's service. Cruising off the coast of Spain within the straits,[10] which they[11] call Mar Chico, or the Little Sea. With a mighty wind at the west and a great tempest, we stood three days in great distress. Our captain was never seen in that time to lay down his head or at all to sleep, fearing to trust any other to conn[12] the ship night or day. At the end of three days having passed a

---

[7]A fellow Boston seaman who had been captured eighteen years earlier.
[8]A city-state in what is now Italy.
[9]An island in the western Mediterranean.
[10]The Straits of Gibraltar, between the Mediterranean and the Atlantic.
[11]The Spanish.
[12]Steer.

dangerous shoal and passing near a small island called Lampedusa,[13] we were surprised to see three great hollow seas[14] that set the ship almost on end. The moon just rising showed us that we were steering right on the island and very near the wash of the shore. Thus we saw the wonders of God in the depths, Psalms 107:23 and on.

After cruising about Malta, Sicily, and the coast of Morocco in quest of the French, I had opportunity to see and hear of the Greeks' hard living under the Turks. Besides other hard things, the most promising of their children are taken from them and carried to Constantinople[15] and trained in the Mohammedan religion. We put into hovering [at] a maritime port where the Tunis ships of war are kept, . . . and where there are some brass guns to prevent anyone from coming to burn their ships. And also two castles with large guns of brass too big to be mounted on carriages. . . .

Two French ships of war came and did embargo us[16] there. And also six Malta Galleys.... We [slaves] were sent to the masemoars, or prisons underground, about forty steps deep of which there were two. And while we were there, the French appointed[17] us to secure our warden and at midnight they would come with a guard to secure our passage to their boats, which they did and came to our prison doors armed and waited for us near two hours. But our plot was discovered. It was that while we had our warden at playing cards below, we should surprise him stopping[18] his mouth and the same time surprise the doorkeeper above and go forth. But in the very moment, he apprehended his danger, called hastily to the porter to shut the door, and said though you kill me you cannot get out. We were forced to desert the matter and the French lost their labor.[19]

After that we were removed to another of those prisons farther from the sea. In each of the prisons the papists[20] have an altar and place of worship at one end with candle and saints after their manner . . . And sometimes their padres (fathers) or friars come to preach to them on their great holy days at evening. And those papists did not at all interrupt us in our religious exercises when any of us were so inclined. And here it was I had the first religious acquaintance with Captain Crow and here

[13]An island in the central Mediterranean.

[14]Gee appears to mean a cluster of large waves with hollow troughs. Thanks to Andrew Lipman for this suggestion.

[15]The capital of Turkey and its Ottoman Empire, since renamed Istanbul.

[16]Prevent us from leaving.

[17]Communicated to.

[18]Covering.

[19]That is, the labor that Gee and his fellow slaves would have provided them.

[20]A term used by Protestants at the time to refer to Roman Catholics.

had we offered songs in this night of distress, Psalms 137:1. In this time
one of our company, a French man, ran away. Being taken he was beaten
by our captain (who was a renegade[21] Greek) till he ceased to cry, groan,
or stir, and was taken away for dead but recovered.

At our return to Algiers news came of my first master's death in his
voyage to visit his friends in the Black Sea. And then I was put to my second master, Covo Mustafa, the same that took me, being my half master at
[my] first sale in the market. Some small time after my coming to him, one
of our company being absent, he came to the knowledge of it. He caused
us all to be laid down one by one and himself with a great rope (about a
three-inch rope) beat us all very severely, which I took as a hassle. The
slave thus absent was an Englishman and next day beaten so cruelly that
his flesh, especially his buttocks [had] to be dressed by the doctor, his arm
so lame that [he] had not the use of his limbs for some time after.

Soon after this the plague came into the family, and the second year
I had it very dangerous. Mr. Ashly came to visit and pray with me. Most
of the family slaves died. I expected the same but was restored May
20th 1683, and did heartily bless God with the song of Hezekiah, Isaiah
38. The first doctor that dressed my sore, an Englishman, died of the
same distemper. The second doctor a French man taken sick [and] a
third belonging to the bey,[22] both French, were sent off on board *Monsieur Getane* with the rest of the French slaves. My fourth doctor was a
Hollander[23] and my fellow slave with my first master. God blessed his
end ever for my recovery, Psalms 107:21-22.

[On] another voyage, we took a Portugal flyboat soon after she came
out of Portugal. She was bound for Brazil. I had leave to go on board her.
I tarried all night and threw away my old clothes and put on new and as
many as I could well carry. . . . [Back on the ship later,] none on board
were above deck, only two slaves in the foretop. I went over the side to
drive in[24] a porthole but the rope I had to hold by gave way. I fell in the
sea. . . . I called for help. Those in the top called to those below deck,
my master and others, who could afford me no relief, no boat being
aboard and the other ship much to windward out of call, and [its] boat
on the windward side of her. . . . My master looking till he could see me
no more said my little carpenter is lost. . . . As the boat came near me,
the sea uncovered me. I laid hold on a boat hook they put [toward me.]

---

[21]Someone who had abandoned his Christian religion for that of his captors.
[22]Ottoman official.
[23]Dutch.
[24]Clear.

After war was made with France we chased a French ship and came not up with her till [before] we boarded her, the ship blew up. There I was in the hold to be ready to stop any leak that might happen underwater. The blow so listed our ship that all our guns seemed to lift from the deck, that it seemed as if the deck would fall considering the age and weakness of our ship. Our master esteemed our deliverance miraculous and said surely God hath some peculiar love for someone in this ship for whose sake we are all saved. Of the French ship's company only three were saved by our boat, which was then out near the ship that blew up. Sometime after their being sold in Algiers, they were ransomed. And after that it was known that it was Master Marchand and [the] boatswain and that they blew up their ship on purpose that we with them might perish rather then they would be slaves. The captain of our ship said, had he known it before they were sold he would have hung them at the yardarm and shot them to death.

7. The Captivity of Hannah Dustin

19

COTTON MATHER

Excerpt from Decennium Luctousum

1699

Prompted by Mary Rowlandson's literary success, New England ministers expanded their use of Indian captivity as means of demonstrating the vulnerability of human beings before God. Among the most successful was Cotton Mather, son of Increase, who, like his father, widely published his sermons and other works. Mather's best-known use of captivity is his account of the next truly prominent captive after Rowlandson, Hannah Dustin. Mather reiterates many of the familiar themes found in Rowlandson's narrative, but with even more sensationalism and melodrama. He also uses Dustin's experience to expand on the significance of captivity for New England. Besides being Native Americans, her captors are also devout Catholics. As such, they demonstrate how the Catholic "anti-Christ" in nearby Canada has become entwined with Indian "savagery." Most strikingly, Dustin actively engineers not only the captives' escape but also the murder and scalping of their captors. Mather draws on the biblical story of Jael to show that, under extreme circumstances, women could legitimately assume male roles—even to the point of murdering and dismembering enemies. By comparison, Rowlandson conformed more closely to the deferential behavior prescribed for women in Europe and its colonies. Of course, with no servants in her household, Dustin probably used an axe regularly to slaughter domestic animals and was generally more accustomed to hard physical labor. In her quick recovery from childbirth, she more closely resembles indigenous women than most female settlers. Also, the small number of Dustin's male captors made retaliation possible, which would not have been the case among Rowlandson's captors.

Charles H. Lincoln, ed., *Narratives of the Indian Wars*, 1675–1689 (New York, 1913), 263–66.

Mather notes Dustin's triumphant arrival in Boston and the scalp bounty that was awarded to her and her accomplices. He adds that Dustin's admirers included Francis Nicholson, the Anglican royal governor of Maryland, who added a reward of his own.

Mather first told Dustin's story in a sermon and later worked it into an article (chapter) in Decennium Luctousum *(Sorrowful Decade), his account of the New England colonies' experience with Indian warfare during the Nine Years War. In 1702, Mather incorporated* Decennium Luctousum *into a still larger work,* Magnalia Christi Americana, *his sprawling, multivolume history of the Puritan church in New England.*

ARTICLE XXV

A Notable Exploit; wherein Dux Foemina Facti.[1]

On March 15, 1697, the Salvages made a descent upon the Skirts of Haverhill, Murdering and Captivating about Thirty-Nine Persons, Burning about Half a Dozen Houses. In this Broil, one Hannah Dustan, having lain in about a Week, attended with[2] her Nurse, Mary Neff, a Widow, a Body of Terrible Indians drew near unto the House, where she lay, with Designs to carry on their Bloody Devastations. Her Husband hastened from his Employments abroad, unto the Relief of his Distressed Family; and first bidding Seven of his Eight children (which were from Two to Seventeen years of Age) to get away as fast as they could, unto some Garrison in the Town, he went in, to inform his Wife of the horrible Distress come upon them. E'er she could get up, the fierce Indians were got so near, that utterly despairing to do her any Service, he ran out after his Children; Resolving that on the Horse which he had with him, he would Ride away with That which he should in this Extremity find his Affections to pitch most upon, and leave the Rest unto the care of the Divine Providence. He overtook his Children about Forty Rod from his Door; but then, such was the Agony of his Parental Affections, that he found it impossible for him to Distinguish any one of them from the rest; wherefore he took up a Courageous

---

[1]The Latin phrase translates as "a woman the leader in the achievement."
[2]By.

Resolution to Live and dy with them all. A party of Indians came up with him; and now, though they Fired at him, and he Fired at them, yet he manfully kept at the Reer of his Little Army of Unarmed Children, while they Marched off, with the pace of a Child of Five years old; until, by the Singular Providence of God, he arrived safe with them all, unto a place of Safety, about a Mile or two from his House. But his House must the mean Time have more dismal Tragedies acted at it. The Nurse trying to Escape, with the New-born Infant, fell into the Hands of the Formidable Salvages; and those furious Tawnies coming into the House, bid poor Dustan to Rise Immediately. Full of Astonishment, she did so; and sitting down in the Chimney with an Heart full of most fearful Expectation, she saw the Raging Dragons rifle all that they could carry away, and set the House on Fire. About Nineteen or Twenty Indians now led these away, with about Half a Score other English Captives; but e'er they had gone many Steps, they dash'd out the Brains of the Infant against a Tree; and several of the other Captives, as they began to Tire in the sad Journey, were soon sent unto their Long Home; the Salvages would presently bury their Hatchets in their Brains, and leave their Carcases on the Ground for Birds and Beasts to feed upon. However, Dustan (with her Nurse), notwithstanding her present Condition, Travelled that Night, about a Dozen Miles, and then kept up with their New Masters in a long Travel of an Hundred and Fifty Miles, more or less, within a few Days Ensuing, without any sensible Damage, in their Health, from the Hardships of their Travel, their lodging, their Diet, and their many other Difficulties.

These Two poor Women were now in the Hands of those, whose Tender Mercies are Cruelties; but in the Good God, who hath all Hearts in His own Hands, heard the Sighs of these Prisoners, and gave them to find unexpected Favour from the Master, who laid claim unto them. That Indian Family consisted of Twelve Persons; Two Stout men, Three Women, and Seven Children; and for the Shame of many an English Family, that has the Character of Prayerless upon it, I must now Publish what these poor Women assure me: 'Tis this; In Obedience to the Instructions which the French have given them, they would have Prayers in their Family, no less than Thrice Every Day; in the Morning, at Noon, and in the Evening; nor would they ordinarily let their Children Eat or Sleep, without first saying their Prayers. Indeed these Idolaters were like the rest of their whiter Brethren, Persecutors; and would not endure, that these poor Women should Retire to their English Prayers, if they could hinder them. Nevertheless, the poor Women had nothing but fervent Prayers, to make their Lives Comfortable, or Tolerable; and by being daily sent out, upon Business, they had Opportunities together and asunder, to do like another Hannah, in Pouring out their Souls before the Lord: Nor did their praying Friends among ourselves, forbear to Pour out Supplications for them. Now, they could not observe it without some wonder, that their Indian Master, sometimes when he saw them Dejected, would say unto them, "What need you Trouble your self? If your God will have you delivered, you shall be so!" And it seems, that our God would have it so to be. This Indian Family was now travelling with these Two Captive Women (and an English Youth, taken from Worcester, a year and a half before) unto a Rendezvous of Salvages, which they call, a Town, some where beyond Penacook; and they still told these poor Women, that when they came to this Town, they must be Stript, and Scourg'd and run the Gantlet through the whole Army of Indians. They said, this was the Fashion, when the Captives first came to a Town; and they derided some of the Fainthearted English, which they said, fainted and swoon'd away under the Torments of this Discipline. But on April 30, While they were yet, it may be about an Hundred and Fifty Miles from the Indian Town, a little before Break of Day, when the whole Crew was in a Dead Sleep; (Reader, see if it prove not So!) one of these Women took up a Resolution, to imitate the Action of Jael upon Sisera;[3] and being where she had not her own Life secured by any Law unto her, she thought she was not Forbidden by any Law to take away the Life of the Murderers, by whom her Child had been butchered. She heartened the Nurse, and the Youth, to assist her in this Enterprize; and all furnishing themselves with Hatchets for the purpose, they struck such Home Blows, upon the Heads of their Sleeping Oppressors, that e'er they could any of them Struggle into any Effectual Resistance, *at the Feet* of these poor Prisoners, *they bow'd, they fell, they lay down: at their feet they bowed, they fell; where they bowed, there they fell down Dead.*[4] Only one Squaw escaped sorely wounded from them, in the Dark; and one Boy, whom they Reserved Asleep, intending to bring him away with them, suddenly wak'd, and skuttled away from this Desolation. But cutting off the Scalps of the Ten Wretches, they came off, and Received Fifty Pounds from the General Assembly of the Province, as a Recompence of their Action; besides which they Received many presents of Congratulation from their more private Friends; but none gave 'em a greater Tast of Bounty than Colonel Nicholson, the Governor of Maryland, who hearing of their Action, sent 'em a very generous Token of his Favor.

[3]Judges 4.
[4]Judges 5:27.

8. Revolutionary Remembering

20

Image of Mary Rowlandson
1770

Mary Rowlandson gained a new kind of fame as white colonists resisted British imperial officials and Native Americans during the 1760s and 1770s. This engraving was inserted immediately after the title page in a 1770 edition of her narrative and depicts Rowlandson as a female patriot. She stands with one hand holding up her rifle while the other grasps a powder horn. In this respect, she represents a gendered extension of the convention in which both European and Native American men are portrayed standing alongside their weapons (see Figure 1 and Document 21). She wears a militiaman's hat along with her woman's dress and apron. Behind her is a British fort, a symbol of the barrier imposed by the empire to contain settlers' expansion.

The engraving did not originally depict Rowlandson. It first appeared in a children's adventure story, "The Life and Adventures of a Female Soldier," in 1762. When the printer decided to publish an edition of Rowlandson's narrative, he reused the earlier image.

A Narrative of the Captivity, Sufferings and Removes of Mrs. Mary Rowlandson. Boston: Nathaniel Coverly, 1770.

Courtesy of the American Antiquarian Society, Worcester, Massachusetts.

21

PAUL REVERE

Philip. King of Mount Hope
1772

The publisher of Benjamin Church's Entertaining History of King Philip's War *commissioned the militant anti-British artisan, Paul Revere, to engrave portraits of Church and Philip for the volume. Revere was already popular because of his dramatic print depicting the Boston Massacre, published two years earlier. Like Rowlandson in the preceding document, Philip stands with a gun at his side and wears a costume that suggests "savage" royalty. As befits a "king," his "subjects" gather behind and below him. Yet nothing in the image originated with Revere or has anything to do with the historical Metacom. Revere's Philip is based primarily on an image of a Mohawk sachem in a famous print, "Four Kings of Canada," that depicted four Native Americans who traveled to London on a diplomatic visit in 1710. Revere replaced the sachem's bow with the gun that Philip holds. The rest of the imagery originated in other, widely circulated prints.*[1]

---

[1]Bradford F. Swan, *An Indian's an Indian or, the Several Sources of Paul Revere's Engraved Portrait of King Philip* (Providence, R.I.: Roger Williams Press, 1959).

PHILIP. *KING* of Mount Hope.

Courtesy of the American Antiquarian Society, Worcester, Massachusetts.

A Rowlandson Chronology (1524–1773)

1524	Earliest recorded Native–European encounters in the future New England.
1553	Puritan movement begins in England under Queen Mary I.
1616–1618	Epidemic disease devastates coastal Algonquians from Cape Cod northward.
1620	First permanent New England settlement established at Plymouth.
1629–1642	"Great Migration" of fourteen thousand English to southern New England.
1633–1634	Smallpox sweeps through indigenous communities in New England.
ca. 1637	Mary White born in Somerset county, England.
1637	English colonies and their Indian allies defeat Pequots in Pequot War. Antinomian Anne Hutchinson and followers challenge Massachusetts leaders; exiled from Massachusetts.
1639	White family emigrates from England to Salem, Massachusetts.
1643	United Colonies of New England established. English settlement begins at Nashaway.
1644	Massachusetts treaty with Nashaway and five other Indian communities; communities agree to allow Christian preaching; Nashaway sachem Showanon identifies as Christian.
1653	English town of Nashaway renamed Lancaster. White and Rowlandson families move to Lancaster.
1654	Matthew succeeds Showanon as principal sachem at Nashaway.
ca. 1656	Mary White marries Joseph Rowlandson.

1660s   Fur trade declines in southern New England; English demand for land escalates.

1662   Wampanoag sachem Alexander (Wamsutta) dies; Wampanoags accuse the English of poisoning him. Succeeded by Philip (Metacom).

1673   Massachusetts government grants full autonomy to Lancaster.

ca. 1673   Christian Nashaway sachem Matthew dies; succeeded by anti-Christian Shoshanim.

1674   Nashaway rejects Daniel Gookin's effort to organize it as a praying town.

1675   *March*   John Sassamon found dead.

June   Plymouth executes three Wampanoags for murdering Sassamon. King Philip's War begins with fighting between Wampanoags and Plymouth; Massachusetts troops aid Plymouth.

July   Nipmucs and other tribes divide into anti-English, pro-English, and neutral groupings. Anti-English Wampanoags elude English forces; some join anti-English Nipmucs; others move to Narragansett country.

August   Nashaway Nipmucs stage first attack on Lancaster.

September   Indians in western Massachusetts attack nearby English towns.

October   Massachusetts moves Christian Indians to Deer Island.

December   English troops attack and burn Great Swamp Fort, inhabited by several hundred Narragansetts and some Wampanoags. Survivors elude English troops and join anti-English Nipmucs and Wampanoags encamped in central Massachusetts.

1676   *January*   Metacom travels to Schaghticoke, New York, to seek broader Algonquian support; Algonquians routed by Mohawks. James Quanapohit informs Massachusetts of planned attack on Lancaster.

February   Four hundred Nipmucs, Narragansetts, and Wampanoags attack and burn Lancaster; take Mary Rowlandson and twenty-two other captives to Menimeset; Lancaster evacuated.

March   Rowlandson's captors carry her north of Baquag River; rendezvous with Philip.

April   Rowlandson returns to central Massachusetts. Battle of Sudbury. Nipmucs and colonial officials begin negotiating for peace, including release of captives.

May   Rowlandson released from captivity. Anti-English Indians disperse, some surrendering to English.

June   Rowlandson children reunited with parents in Boston.

July   Most remaining anti-English Indians captured or surrender; many executed or enslaved.

August   Philip executed. Ongoing war ends in southern colonies; Nipmucs and other Native Americans attack outlying English towns from Abenaki country. Massachusetts supervises remaining Christian Indians.

1677   Rowlandsons move to Wethersfield, Connecticut.

1678   Joseph Rowlandson dies.

1679   Mary Rowlandson marries Samuel Talcott.

1680   First settlers return to Lancaster.

1682   Four editions of Mary Rowlandson's narrative published.

1689–1697   Nine Years War. Lancaster attacked by Native Americans allied with France (1692, 1697).

1691   Samuel Talcott dies.

1702–1713   War of the Spanish Succession. Lancaster attacked by Native Americans allied with France (1704, 1705, 1711).

1711   Mary Talcott (Rowlandson) dies at about the age of 73.

1720   Fifth edition of Rowlandson's narrative published.

1770–1773   Four new editions of Rowlandson's narrative published.

Questions for Consideration

1. What were Rowlandson's reasons for writing a narrative of her captivity? Were some of these reasons more important than others?

2. How did Rowlandson's life before her capture affect her experience as a captive? How did it affect her relations with her captors?

3. What does Rowlandson say was most important in enabling her to survive captivity? What do you think was most helpful to her?

4. How does Rowlandson view her own society during and after her experience as a captive?

5. Who besides Rowlandson shaped her published narrative? In what ways? For what reasons?

6. For what audience was Rowlandson writing? How do you think her narrative affected their religious beliefs? Their attitudes toward Native Americans and toward their own society?

7. What are the similarities and differences between Rowlandson's narrative and Joshua Gee's narrative of Muslim captivity? How does this comparison affect your understanding of New England Puritanism in the late seventeenth century?

8. What does Rowlandson's experience as a captive and author tell us about women in seventeenth-century New England? How does Rowlandson's gender shape her narrative?

9. Why does Rowlandson place so much emphasis on Christian Indians in her account?

10. How does your understanding of Native American history during the seventeenth century affect your reading of Rowlandson's narrative?

11. How did the prior relationship between the Nipmucs of Nashaway and the English of Nashaway/Lancaster shape their relations during King Philip's War?

12. In what ways does Rowlandson's narrative provide evidence about Native Americans' experiences and viewpoints during King Philip's War? In what ways does Rowlandson seek to obscure indigenous perspectives in her narrative?

13. How might one of Rowlandson's captors have answered her narrative?
14. How would a narrative of their own captivities by James Quanapohit or James Printer compare with Rowlandson's?
15. Why have the experiences of white American captives drawn so much more attention than those of indigenous and other non-white captives?

Selected Bibliography

NATIVE AMERICANS AND EUROPEAN COLONIZATION

Anderson, Virginia DeJohn. *Creatures of Empire: How Domestic Animals Transformed Early America.* New York: Oxford University Press, 2004.

Brooks, Lisa. *The Common Pot: The Recovery of Native Space in the Northeast.* Minneapolis: University of Minnesota Press, 2008.

———. *Our Beloved Kin: A New History of "King Philip's War."* New Haven, Conn.: Yale University Press, 2018.

Bragdon, Kathleen J. *Native People of Southern New England, 1500–1650.* Norman: University of Oklahoma Press, 1996.

———. *Native People of Southern New England, 1650–1775.* Norman: University of Oklahoma Press, 2009.

Bross, Kristina. *Dry Bones and Indian Sermons: Praying Indians in Colonial America.* Ithaca, N.Y.: Cornell University Press, 2004.

Calloway, Colin G. *The Western Abenakis of Vermont, 1600–1800: War, Migration, and the Survival of an Indian People.* Norman: University of Oklahoma Press, 1990.

———. *New Worlds for All: Indians, Europeans, and the Remaking of Early America.* 2nd ed. Baltimore, Md.: Johns Hopkins University Press, 2013.

Cronon, William. *Changes in the Land: Indians, Colonists, and the Ecology of New England.* New York: Hill and Wang, 1983.

DeLucia, Christine M. *The Memory Lands: King Philip's War and the Place of Violence in the Northeast.* New Haven, Conn.: Yale University Press, 2018.

Drake, James D. *King Philip's War: Civil War in New England, 1675–1676.* Amherst: University of Massachusetts Press, 1999.

Greer, Allan. *Property and Dispossession: Natives, Settlers, and Land in North America, 1500–1800.* Cambridge and New York: Cambridge University Press, forthcoming, 2018.

Lepore, Jill. *The Name of War: King Philip's War and the Origins of American Identity.* New York: Alfred A. Knopf, 1998.

Lipman, Andrew. *The Saltwater Frontier: Indians and the Contest for the American Coast.* New Haven, Conn.: Yale University Press, 2015.

Lopenzina, Drew. *Red Ink: Native Americans Picking Up the Pen in the Colonial Period.* Albany: State University of New York Press, 2012.

Newell, Margaret Ellen. *Brethren by Nature: New England Indians, Colonists, and the Origins of American Slavery.* Ithaca, N.Y.: Cornell University Press, 2015.

O'Brien, Jean M. *Dispossession by Degrees: Indian Land and Identity in Natick, Massachusetts, 1650–1790.* Lincoln: University of Nebraska Press, 2003.

Plane, Ann Marie. *Colonial Intimacies: Indian Marriage in Early New England.* Ithaca, N.Y.: Cornell University Press, 2000.

Pulsipher, Jenny Hale. *Subjects unto the Same King: Indians, English, and the Contest for Authority in Colonial New England.* Philadelphia: University of Pennsylvania Press, 2005.

Richter, Daniel K. *Facing East from Indian Country: A Native History of Early America.* Cambridge, Mass.: Harvard University Press, 2001.

Salisbury, Neal. *Manitou and Providence: Indians, Europeans, and the Making of New England, 1500–1643.* New York: Oxford University Press, 1982.

Senier, Siobahn et al., eds. *Dawnland Voices: An Anthology of Indigenous Writing from New England.* Lincoln: University of Nebraska Press, 2014.

Warren, Wendy. *New England Bound: Slavery and Colonization in Early America.* New York: Liveright, 2016.

Wyss, Hilary E. *Writing Indians: Literacy, Christianity, and Native Community in Early America.* Amherst: University of Massachusetts Press, 2000.

ENGLAND: COLONIES AND EMPIRE

Anderson, Virginia DeJohn. *New England's Generation: The Great Migration and the Formation of Society and Culture in the Seventeenth Century.* Cambridge: Cambridge University Press, 1991.

Conforti, Joseph A. *Saints and Strangers: New England in British North America.* Baltimore: Johns Hopkins University Press, 2006.

Grandjean, Katherine. *American Passage: The Communications Frontier in Early New England.* Cambridge, Mass.: Harvard University Press, 2014.

Gura, Philip F. *A Glimpse of Sion's Glory: Puritan Radicalism in New England, 1620–1660.* Middletown, Conn.: Wesleyan University Press, 1984.

Hall, David D. *Worlds of Wonder, Days of Judgment: Popular Religious Belief in Early New England.* New York: Alfred A. Knopf, 1989.

Jaffe, David. *People of the Wachusett: Greater New England in History and Memory, 1630–1860.* Ithaca, N.Y.: Cornell University Press, 1999.

Norton, Mary Beth. *Founding Mothers and Fathers: Gendered Power and the Forming of American Society.* New York: Alfred A. Knopf, 1996.

Pestana, Carla Gardina. *Protestant Empire: Religion and the Making of the British Atlantic World.* Philadelphia: University of Pennsylvania Press, 2009.

————. *The English Atlantic in an Age of Revolution, 1640–1661.* Cambridge, Mass.: Harvard University Press, 2004.

Ulrich, Laurel Thatcher. *Good Wives: Image and Reality in the Lives of Women in Northern New England, 1650–1750.* New York: Alfred A. Knopf, 1980.

CAPTIVITY: HISTORICAL AND LITERARY STUDIES

Baepler, Paul. "The Barbary Captivity Narrative in Early America." *Early American Literature* 30 (1995): 95–120.

Bauer, Ralph. "Creole Identities in Colonial Space: The Narratives of Mary White Rowlandson and Francisco Núñez de Pineda y Bascuñán." *American Literature* 69 (1997): 665–95.

Burnham, Michelle. *Captivity and Sentiment: Cultural Exchange in American Literature, 1682–1861.* Hanover, N.H.: University Press of New England, 1997.

Cameron, Catherine M. *Captives: How Stolen People Changed the World.* Lincoln: University of Nebraska Press, 2016.

Chaplin, Joyce E. "Enslavement of Indians in Early America: Captivity without the Narrative." In *The Creation of the British Atlantic World,* edited by Elizabeth Mancke and Carole Shammas, 45–70. Baltimore: Johns Hopkins University Press, 2005.

Colley, Linda. *Captives: Britain, Empire and the World, 1600–1850.* New York: Pantheon, 2003.

Derounian-Stodola, Kathryn Zabelle, and James A. Levernier. *The Indian Captivity Narrative, 1550–1900.* New York: Twayne, 1993.

Faery, Rebecca Blevins. *Cartographies of Desire: Captivity, Race, and Sex in the Shaping of an American Nation.* Norman: University of Oklahoma Press, 1999.

Haefli, Evan, and Sweeney, Kevin. *Captors and Captives:The 1704 French and Indian Raid on Deerfield.* Amherst: University of Massachusetts Press, 2003.

Namias, June. *White Captives: Gender and Ethnicity on the American Frontier.* Chapel Hill: University of North Carolina Press, 1993.

Pearce, Roy Harvey. "The Significances of the Captivity Narrative." *American Literature* 19 (1947): 1–20.

Slotkin, Richard. *Regeneration through Violence: The Mythology of the American Frontier, 1600–1800.* Middletown, Conn.: Wesleyan University Press, 1973.

Strong, Pauline Turner. *Captive Selves, Captivating Others: The Politics and Poetics of Colonial American Captivity Narratives.* Boulder, Colo.: Westview Press, 1999.

————. "Transforming Outsiders: Captivity, Adoption, and Slavery Reconsidered." In *A Companion to American Indian History,* edited by Philip J. Deloria and Neal Salisbury, 339–56. Malden, Mass.: Blackwell, 2002.

Stratton, Billy J. *Buried in Shades of Night: Contested Voices, Indian Captivity, and the Legacy of King Philip's War.* Tucson, Az.: University of Arizona Press, 2013.

Toulouse, Teresa A. *The Captive's Position: Female Narrative, Male Identity, and Royal Authority in Colonial New England.* Philadelphia: University of Pennsylvania Press, 2007.

Voigt, Lisa. *Writing Captivity in the Early Modern Atlantic: Circulations of Knowledge and Authority in the Iberian and English Imperial Worlds.* Chapel Hill: University of North Carolina Press, 2009.

Index